Unwelcome Americans

Early American Studies

DANIEL K. RICHTER
Director, McNeil Center for Early American Studies,
Series Editor

Exploring neglected aspects of our colonial, revolutionary, and early national history and culture, Early American Studies reinterprets familiar themes and events in fresh ways. Interdisciplinary in character, and with a special emphasis on the period from about 1600 to 1850, the series is published in partnership with the McNeil Center for Early American Studies.

A complete list of books in the series is available from the publisher.

Unwelcome Americans

Living on the Margin in Early New England

RUTH WALLIS HERNDON

PENN

UNIVERSITY OF PENNSYLVANIA PRESS

Philadelphia

10 9 8 7 6 5 4 3 2 1

Published by
University of Pennsylvania Press
Philadelphia, Pennsylvania 19104-4011

Library of Congress Cataloging-in-Publication Data

Herndon, Ruth Wallis
Unwelcome Americans: living on the margin in early New England / Ruth Wallis
Herndon
       p. cm. — Early American studies
    Includes bibliographical references and index
    ISBN 0-8122-3592-4 (alk. paper). —ISBN 0-8122-1765-9 (pbk. : alk paper)
    1. Marginality, Social—New England—History—18th century. 2. Poor—New
England—Biography. 3. Poor laws—New England—History—18th century. 4. New
England—Social conditions—18th century. I. Title. II. Series
HN79.A11 H47 2001
305.5′6′0974—2

                         00-047975

To the Memory of

KAREN SCHMIDT WAGNER

Contents

Preface

PHEBE PERKINS is responsible for this book. The testimony she gave to Hopkinton, Rhode Island, officials in 1785 came to light in 1991 under such unusual circumstances that it forced me to pay attention to her, and it set me on a detective hunt through historical documents to discover everything I could about her. By the time I had pieced together fragments of information and had seen the shape of her life, I was fiercely determined that her poignant story—and others like it—should be published.

In 1991, I was in the midst of researching twelve Rhode Island towns in the revolutionary era, a project that required that I essentially camp out in one town hall after another for weeks at a stretch, reading through historic documents that enabled me to see in my mind's eye the town of two hundred years ago. Hopkinton—Phebe Perkins's town—had served as my prototype, and I had spent a solid six months in 1990 working through every eighteenth-century document housed at the town hall. Town clerk Jenarita Aldrich shared my passion for her town records, and she scouted for old documents in odd places during rare free moments. In April 1991, she made a startling discovery: a cache of eighteenth-century papers housed in old boxes in the town hall attic. The local news media were most interested in a 1776 manuscript copy of the Declaration of Independence found among the papers, but what set my heart racing was the rough draft notes of the council meeting at which Phebe Perkins had given her testimony some two hundred years before.

Until then, I had paid little attention to Phebe Perkins. She was mentioned only briefly in the town council minutes of that meeting in January 1785, for town clerk Abel Tanner had not considered her testimony worth including when he copied his notes into the official town books. As I read her compelling testimony, I found myself mentally berating Tanner for obscuring this story. By excluding her testimony from the final record, he had veiled the splash her story made in Hopkinton in 1784 and 1785. When I went back to the official council minutes for another look, I found a trail

of references to her, and I discovered that the town councilmen had convened a special meeting at the house where she was staying in order to question her. Phebe's situation had prompted the most powerful men in the
community to journey through the January cold to interrogate her about
her life. Here was a story that should be told.

Galvanized by Phebe Perkins's case, I began to trace the stories of other
poor and unwelcome people, my interest sparked originally by some particularly intriguing piece of evidence such as a transient examination or warning-out order. I began to collect methodically all the information I could
about individuals like Phebe Perkins. As the collection grew, I realized there
was a whole population of unwelcome people whose existence I had never
realized. This volume grew out of my desire that these people have their stories told, to reverse the process by which their stories were obscured two
centuries ago. By extracting relevant information from eighteenth-century
records and constructing whole narratives of their lives, I hope to put these
people back on the landscape of the New England town.

At every stage of this project, I benefited from the support and expertise of others. Years ago, my adviser at American University, Roger H.
Brown, taught me by word and example that the best research is the kind
you do for yourself, and he gave me a thirst for uncovering hidden lives in
the archives. Once in the archives, I received practical and intelligent
encouragement from the curators of the records. I am especially grateful to
Hopkinton town clerk Jenarita Aldrich, Jamestown town clerk Teresa Dono-
van, and Providence city archivist Carole Pace for giving me unencumbered
access to their documents. Rick Stattler at the Rhode Island Historical Society Library and Gwenn Stearn and Ken Carlson at the Rhode Island State
Archives accommodated my frequent searches for corroborating evidence
—sometimes long-distance—with generous and cheerful efficiency. Mandy
Marvin tracked down settlement examinations and removal orders in a
number of English county records offices to verify the English origins of
New England practice.

Many colleagues gave their time and thought to this project. Thomas
Barden, Joanna B. Gillespie, James Herndon, John E. Murray, Kunal Parker,
Alden V. Rollins, Bernard Rosenthal, Nikki Taylor, Stephanie G. Wolf, and
Karin A. Wulf read and critiqued entire drafts of the introduction and sever-
al narratives. Fred Anderson, Mary S. Bilder, Colin G. Calloway, Cornelia
Hughes Dayton, Russell G. Handsman, Ann M. Keppel, Gloria Main, Bruce
Mann, Joanne P. Melish, Alice Nash, Jean M. O'Brien, Ann Marie Plane,

Paul B. Robinson, Patricia Rubertone, Sharon V. Salinger, Ella Wilcox Sekatau, and Holly Snyder read and advised on particular narratives. Billy G. Smith and an anonymous reader with University of Pennsylvania Press read several drafts of the entire manuscript with great care and made valuable suggestions that helped bring the book to its present shape. Billy Smith's eleventh-hour assistance in the last stages of writing was a model of collegial generosity.

This book would never have happened without the valiant friendship of Monique Bourque and Susan E. Klepp, who midwived the project from its inception. They read all the original testimonies and then labored with me to select the "best" 300, then 150, then 40. With each permutation of the manuscript, they suggested effective ways to organize and present the narratives. Having seen the book on its way to birthing, Susan Klepp then gave it its title, "Unwelcome Americans."

I also thank Richard Dunn who, as director of the McNeil Center for Early American Studies, saw the potential in the warning-out records and gave this project its first public hearing at the McNeil Center seminar in September 1995. He continued to nurture the manuscript through several gawky phases until it grew to its present form, gave it its subtitle, and championed its publication with University of Pennsylvania Press.

Capable colleagues smoothed the mechanics of book production. Edward J. Keen used his cartography skills to produce the Rhode Island map outline. Jennifer Bond, assistant graphics curator at the Rhode Island Historical Society, organized the bulk of the document illustrations. Robert E. Lockhart skillfully coordinated the publication team at University of Pennsylvania Press.

Family members and friends made a critical difference at key moments in the research and writing of this book. They know who they are and I thank them all. Wilber and Marie Wallis especially will be gratified to see it in print. I dedicate this book to Karen Schmidt Wagner, who loved a good story and lived a great one herself before her last chapter drew to a close much too soon.

Abbreviations

Acts and Laws (1767)	*Acts and Laws of the English Colony of Rhode Island and Providence Plantations.* Newport, R.I.: Samuel Hall, 1767.
Bartlett	*Records of the Colony/State of Rhode Island and Providence Plantations in New England,* 10 volumes covering the years 1636–1792, plus unnumbered volumes covering the years 1792–1805, ed. John Russell Bartlett. Providence: various printers, 1856–1865.
Petitions	*Petitions to the Rhode Island General Assembly,* Rhode Island State Archives
PTP	Providence Town Papers, Rhode Island Historical Society
Public Laws (1798)	The Public Laws of the State of Rhode-Island and Providence Plantations. Providence: Carter and Wilkinson, 1798.
Rhode Island 1790 Census	*Heads of Families at the First Census of the United States Taken in the Year 1790: Rhode Island.* Washington, D.C.: U.S. Government Printing Office, 1908.
RICR	Rhode Island Colony Records [unedited original mss], multi-volume, Rhode Island State Archives
RISR	Rhode Island State Records [unedited original mss], multi-volume, Rhode Island State Archives
TC	town council
TCM	town council meeting
TCR	town council records
TM	town meeting
TMR	town meeting records

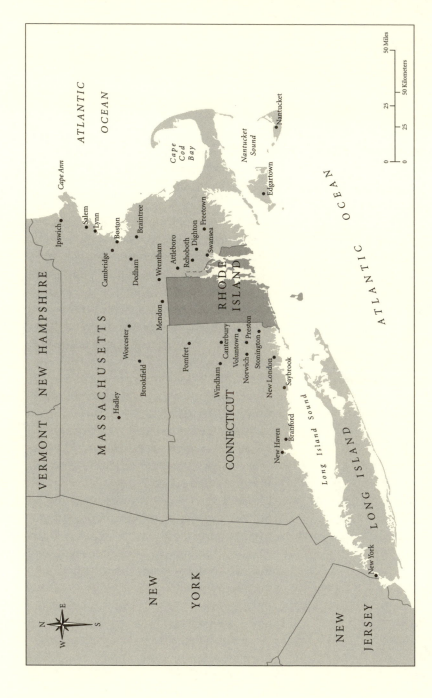

Map 1. New England in the eighteenth century.

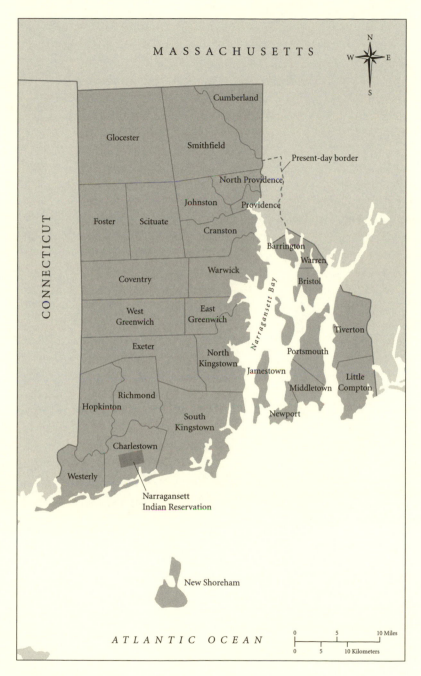

Map 2. Rhode Island in the eighteenth century.

Introduction:
The World of People on the Margin

I N THE AUTUMN of 1784, a poor, unmarried woman named Phebe Perkins gave birth to a baby in the home of the Cary Clarke family in Hopkinton, Rhode Island. Perkins was not a relative, neighbor, or friend of the Clarkes; rather, the Clarkes had agreed to be her caretakers during this difficult period of her life. They sent someone to fetch the doctor when the delivery went awry; they nursed Perkins and her baby through the first weeks after childbirth; they provided food and drink for Perkins; they provided linens for the baby; they mended and washed the new mother's clothing; they burned extra firewood to keep them warm. For providing these necessities, the Clarkes were reimbursed directly out of the Hopkinton town treasury and indirectly out of the pockets of every taxpayer in the town.[1]

In eighteenth-century America, no centralized system of welfare existed to rescue people like Phebe Perkins: no Social Security or Medicaid or unemployment insurance or old age pensions in any form. No colony or state created and maintained a safety net for those unable to support themselves; instead, each local government administered "poor relief" to its own inhabitants. In rural communities, the caretaker system—sometimes termed "outdoor relief"—predominated; in more populous commercial centers such as Boston, Newport, Philadelphia, and Charleston, almshouses and poorhouses were constructed so that needy people could be grouped together in an institutional setting under the management of an overseer.

Whatever the form of poor relief, its funding originated with local taxpayers. In New England, freeholders met regularly in town meeting to levy taxes on themselves in order to resupply the "exhausted" town treasury. More often than not, the cause of the treasury's exhaustion was the high cost of poor relief, and voters frequently shied away from raising taxes, preferring to charge town leaders with cutting expenses. This was particularly true in the latter part of the eighteenth century, when Rhode Islanders paid the price of waging the Revolutionary War in the form of extra taxes levied by town, state, and Continental Congress. At a time when many of the middling sort could visualize themselves falling into ruin from three thick layers of taxation, they were not inclined to be generous with those already in poverty.

New England town leaders, annually elected by their fellow townsmen to govern the affairs of the town, were thus simultaneously administrators of poor relief and guardians of the town treasury. They exercised a dual responsibility: to care for the poor and to answer for the amount spent on them. Officials sought to resolve this tension by carefully distinguishing between those legally entitled to poor relief and those not legally entitled, and by sending away the latter. Settlement laws in every colony provided that all those needing poor relief would receive it—but *only* in their towns of legal settlement. If poor people moved elsewhere in search of work or a more congenial community, they would have to return to their hometowns for help. Phebe Perkins, for example, had been living in Richmond, Rhode Island, when she became pregnant; before her baby was born, Richmond officials sent her to Hopkinton, which they judged to be her hometown and therefore responsible for her care.

This was the "warning-out" system, by which town authorities sent away from their towns those people who had no legal claim on the town treasury. Town officials spent considerable time and money identifying and sending away such people, but the results were considered worth the effort. Through warning out, towns avoided the greater costs of supporting frail, ill, or injured people over the long term; they also avoided setting a precedent of providing care for those not entitled to it. Consequently, New England authorities vigorously employed warning out in the eighteenth century.[2]

Between 1750 and 1800, Rhode Island officials interrogated thousands of people who were likely candidates for warning out, and over nine hundred of these legal examinations were written down in town records. After a careful scrutiny of each examination, I selected forty to present in this book as narratives that flesh out the bare-bones stories preserved in the record. Each narrative represents the whole body of testimonies in some way, and was chosen because its detail allows twenty-first-century readers to enter the world of the eighteenth-century unwelcome poor.

Although these testimonies were recorded in Rhode Island town books, they are representative of a process that occurred throughout

Anglo-America in the eighteenth century. Authorities interrogated and removed "paupers" everywhere in England and in the English colonies, but most especially in New England, where some system of warning out was in place in every locality. The Rhode Island records, however, are unique in their illuminating detail, and they provide much more information than names of transients, which often is the extent of warning-out records elsewhere.[3] In the Rhode Island examinations, warned-out people left a small history of their lives: where they had been born; where they had lived; what work they had done; the names of parents, masters, spouses; the number and ages of children. The life stories thus revealed are widely representative of the circumstances of poor people throughout southern New England. About half of the transients questioned in Rhode Island actually came from hometowns in Massachusetts, Connecticut, and a few more distant regions; they had migrated to Rhode Island, sometimes quite deliberately, in search of jobs, land, family, or community. The difficulties that galvanized people into leaving their hometowns were not Rhode Island problems but regional problems; the economic and social upheaval that transients describe was common to much of New England and in fact to much of Anglo-America in the eighteenth century.[4]

There is much we can learn from these brief histories of unfortunate people caught up in the system of warning out. At the most immediate and literal level, the examinations tell us how the poor lived in eighteenth-century New England and throughout early America. The rarity of such short biographies lends great significance to this collection, for seldom do we hear the voices of the poor and the unwelcome so clearly and directly over the span of intervening centuries. The great majority of studies of poor people in early America have focused on statistical data, lacking the necessary personal documentation that allows human faces to emerge.[5] The warning-out testimonies give us just such human faces, make the poor our informants, and counterbalance the narratives of the elite and privileged who have been the dominant voices from this crucial period in American history. The warning-out testimonies are not rags-to-riches success stories, like the well-known life of Benjamin Franklin, who started his career as a runaway apprentice but ended up an internationally known scientist, diplomat, and author. The very necessity for official interrogation meant that these people had failed to prosper in their adopted homes. Thus their tales of trouble prompt us to redraw the picture of New England and by implication all the colonies and states in their founding years, this time including the less fortunate, the despised, and the unwelcome.

At a deeper and more contextual level, these testimonies also illuminate the conflict between the poor and the prosperous. Warned-out people were ordered to appear before town leaders because they had chosen to live where others—property owners—now (suddenly) did not want them. Their appearance before local magistrates was permeated with tension and frustration. On one side of the council table sat people who, in the eye of the law, truly belonged to the community: well-to-do leaders charged with maintaining order, trying to keep track of the many poor and troublesome people living under their jurisdiction, protecting the peace and property of the taxpaying inhabitants who elected them to office. On the other side of the table stood people who, in the eye of the law, did not belong, however deep their attachments in the community: unpropertied people with few advocates, few advantages, and few prospects, struggling to maintain a place in the towns where they lived. The examinations disclose these antagonistic purposes and expose the gulf that separated unwelcome Americans from those of power and status in their communities.

The Warning-Out System

New England town officials did not invent warning out. The English colonies inherited it, along with the rest of English law. Various pieces of seventeenth- and eighteenth-century parliamentary legislation, referred to collectively as the Poor Law, codified and regularized the various means of poor relief that had sprung up in the sixteenth century after the dissolution of the manors, monasteries, and guilds that formerly had given aid to the needy. The Poor Law placed the responsibility for poor relief directly on local governments, and one particular provision, the 1662 Settlement Law, stipulated how local officials should determine who came under their jurisdiction and how they should remove poor people to their home parishes. Such legislation grew naturally from the official ideal of a static society rooted in the land: where community ties overlapped with kinship ties, and where everyone *had* a place and *knew* that place. By sending needy people back to their hometowns, the law put the poor "in their place" and prevented any one locality from becoming a magnet for those seeking relief.[6]

Rhode Island magistrates adapted English poor law to their own particular case, concentrating on the distinctions between "inhabitants" and "transients." "Transient" conveyed very different meanings in the eighteenth century than it does today. Then, it referred neither to travelers nor to homeless vagrants. Instead, it specifically identified persons who had been living in a town but had not become legal "inhabitants" in that town. In the eighteenth century, there were four principal ways to acquire an official settlement in a Rhode Island town: by being born there; by serving out an apprenticeship or other servitude to a master who lived there; by purchasing a freehold; or (for women) by marrying a man who belonged there. A default provision, granting legal settlement to persons who lived continuously in a town for one year without being ordered out, created an alternative way for poor people to become inhabitants, but local officials blocked this pathway by issuing yearly citations that kept transients "under warning" without actually forcing them out, thus effectively preventing long-term residents from ever claiming the rights and privileges associated with belonging to a town.7

Transients remained in residence only by the permission of town leaders, and they were perpetually at risk of being sent away. Many of them would have ended their transient status, if only they could. But these people were of the poorer sort; their labor brought them little beyond the necessities of life. Many had moved in search of work, rather than resort to receiving poor relief in their home communities. To purchase enough real estate to become legally settled inhabitants was beyond their means. Thus, those warned out might have worked and worshiped peaceably in a town for months, years, or even decades; they might have raised children and buried spouses there; they might have made fast friends among their neighbors and become a familiar sight to all. To no avail. None of this could change their status as legal transients, and so in every year, in every season, warned-out men, women, and children packed up their belongings, however meager, and left behind the place they had tried to make their home.

Town officials had to have plausible reasons for picking out certain people from the general population of transients who lived in every town. In most cases, officials were responding to reports made by "respectable" (land-owning) inhabitants who were neighbors or employers of transients. These "complaints" often referred to apparent suffering and need in the transient family. When the Tiverton councilmen learned that Nathaniel Manchester and his wife were "in a suffering condition" and "in great need," they ordered the couple removed "directly out of this town."

When sailor Primus Thompson (Chapter 4) slipped on an icy wharf and broke his thigh, rendering himself unable to work, Jamestown officials had him removed to Westerly. Twenty-four-year-old Nancy Newport, who had moved to Glocester to work as a spinner, was returned to Scituate when she was "visited with sickness" and could no longer labor enough to pay for her own upkeep.[8]

Other times the complaint referred to the transients' behavior, which "respectable" people found objectionable. It might have been something as minor as trespassing on someone else's property or keeping a dog that irritated the neighbors. It might have been something as serious as operating an illegal tavern or a bawdy house. Mary Worsley was ordered out of Glocester because of her "unruly tongue" and "no good behavior." Olive Goddard and her two children were removed from Providence to Newport when officials received a credible report that she was "a lewd woman." Benjamin Austin and his family were ordered removed from East Greenwich to Warwick because they kept "such a disorderly house that they are general disturbers of the neighbors." Jonathan Bliven and Pardon Green were warned out of Hopkinton because several inhabitants had complained that the pair were "unwholesome persons and of bad character, being apt to break the peace." Samuel Eldred, his wife, and his four children were considered "unwholesome" and "people of bad morals" who were known to "make great disturbance in the neighbourhood where they live." Thus, even if transients had jobs and every prospect of maintaining themselves economically, they might still be vulnerable to complaints about their behavior—complaints that could easily escalate into a warning out.[9]

When a poor family came to official attention by means of a complaint, town leaders summoned the household head and questioned him or her during a council meeting. The interrogation had two purposes: to determine *whether* a transient family should be warned out and to determine *where* the family should be sent. After hearing and discussing the information provided by the transient person, the six councilmen made a judgment: the family might be permitted to remain for a limited time or might be warned out of the community.

This sorting and sending away of transients served as the first step in the administration of poor relief, a culling out of those not entitled to town support, so as to limit the expense to taxpayers. Those who were entitled found poor relief a severe charity, and it is not surprising that many of the poorer sort preferred to move away in search of work and run the risk of being warned out of another place, rather than "throw themselves upon the town." Poor-relief recipients lost their privacy and family coherence and came under the close supervision of town officials. Councilmen and overseers of the poor directed where and how the poor would live: in an individual household under a town-approved caretaker, or in a poorhouse or workhouse (if the town had constructed one), where they would live cheek by jowl with other down-and-outs under the dictatorial rule of an overseer whose main objective was to minimize the public cost of poor relief. Wherever they lived, their labor was coopted by officials who determined where, when, and how much they would work toward their own and their family's support. Their children were, in most cases, taken from them and bound out until adulthood in indentured servitude under circumstances dictated by town officials, not by the children's parents. This was not an enviable life, and transient status might well be preferable. Thomas Strait, for example, explained to his hometown councilmen that he had moved away in search of work; moving back home would constitute a "great disadvantage," as he was now in "good employ and in a fair way to live" as a transient in West Greenwich.[10]

Local and colony/state laws required new residents like Thomas Strait to register with town authorities, but just as often officials learned of a transient's presence through an overseer's report or some other complaint. Sometimes this information concerned people who were genuine newcomers to the community, as in the case of Nathan Pierce, a "delerious" transient man whom the West Greenwich officials described as "unknown of to us." But other times, the transient had actually lived for many years in the community, and officials were galvanized to action only when need became desperate or when neighbor trouble developed. Sometimes officials were unaware or had forgotten that a long-time resident was in fact legally a transient; in these cases, in a flurry of activity, councilmen scrambled to examine the transient, discover the responsible town, and remove the person or family. Elderly widow Abigail Carr (Chapter 5) had lived and worked in Providence for thirty years before town officials thought to question her settlement status; when she became needy, they gave her one month to leave Providence for her "hometown" of South Kingstown, where her former master had freed her from slavery some forty years before. Seventy-year-old Ezra Aldrich had lived in Cumberland so long that he could remember when the town was first incorporated more than fifty years earlier, but the Cumberland councilmen claimed he had never actually obtained a legal settlement in their town; they removed him to Smithfield when he fell into need, sending him to a place where his long-dead father had once owned real estate. Transients caught unprepared in situations like this lost their homes and connections in addition to falling into poverty, and the councilmen's actions revealed the particularly pernicious aspects of the warning-out system.[11]

Transients sometimes complicated the process further by failing to leave when ordered out. Some genuinely needed assistance in moving because of illness or accident, like seaman Dan Jack, who fell sick while in Providence and was unable to get himself back to North Carolina, where his wife and children lived; the overseer of the poor arranged for Jack to be taken on board a ship and paid for his voyage to North Carolina. Others dallied because they were reluctant to leave a job or community, or because they wanted to spite town officials. In every locality, the town sergeant and his constables were sent from time to time to transport ailing or foot-dragging transients to their towns of legal settlement, where they were delivered into the care of local officials. If that hometown was far distant, the town sergeant took the family only as far as the adjoining town, beginning a relay system whereby the transients were passed from one town to another in a straight line back to their town of legal settlement. The journey could take weeks. In July 1785, John Skyrme, a blind man, was transported from Eastchester, New York, back to his hometown of Providence. On his twenty-one-day journey he was transferred twenty-four times from one pair of official hands to another, as each constable delivered him to the door of the constable in the adjoining town.[12]

The actual removal of a transient was accomplished by the town sergeant or one of his constables, whose sustained contact with those being warned out gave him a very personal view of the whole process. The sergeant or constable physically confronted the unwelcome transients with a written document, signed and sealed by local authorities. If necessary, he prodded the transients into action by threat of force, as did Tiverton town sergeant Benjamin Sawdy, who was paid for "driving Amos Lewis out of the town." The sergeant or constable made arrangements for transportation and lodging along the way in those cases where the transients could not manage for themselves. Cumberland constable Asa Carpenter presented the councilmen with an account for "aide, horse, carriage and removing" Mehitable Burt Dedeo and her children to North Providence; his charges included "keeping said woman and children one night at Isaac Arnold's." Providence sergeant Gideon Young had the task of removing the four young Townsend children (Chapter 1) to Newport after their parents abandoned them; his charges included £1 10s. for "my trouble & expences with the nurse and children." When Exeter sergeant Isaac Wilcox removed Hannah Townsend and her child to Newport, his costs included paying an assistant for "carrying the child," paying the ferryman "for carrying us over" the water to Newport, and paying a hosteler in Newport "for horsekeeping"; upon his return to Exeter, he immediately undertook the task of removing William Reese and family to South Kingstown, using "oxen and cart & horse & myself & hand." These were clearly laborious, slow, and tedious journeys for all concerned.[13]

The journey ended at the door of the overseer of the poor in the transient's hometown. Overseers of the poor were obligated to take in transients who arrived in the care of a town sergeant or constable armed with an official warrant, and they boarded and lodged the transients until other arrangements were made.

Arriving back in their hometown was not always the end of the warning-out process for either transients or town authorities. Transients sometimes thwarted officials by returning to the towns from which they had been warned out, prompting exasperated councilmen to send them away again after fining them or having them whipped by the town sergeant. Jonathan Hayden, removed from Cumberland in 1764, "made his escape" from official hands in Wrentham, Massachusetts, en route to his hometown of Braintree, and returned to Cumberland, where he continued to live in such a way that he appeared likely to "bring himself to ruin and others also with whom he keeps company." Cumberland officials ordered him removed once again, promising "corporal punishment" if he persisted in returning. Nathaniel Bowdish (Chapter 3) similarly aggravated the Charlestown councilmen by returning repeatedly, even after several public whippings, and he further defied their authority when he "did damn this council & say that he would stay in this town if they whipt him again." While the councilmen wanted to see the last of this man who had "frighted & abused some of the inhabitants of this town, by behaving himself in a disorderly manner," they had no recourse beyond another whipping and removal. When Bowdish was spotted "lurking about this town" two weeks later, stymied officials could do nothing more than order the sergeant (once again) to find and whip him. Warning out could become a complicated and vexatious process both for town leaders and for warned-out people.[14]

The system of warning out described here had its own peculiar language and conventions, which varied from colony to colony. Studies of the Vermont and Massachusetts records, for example, suggest that actual removals of transients occurred much less frequently there than in Rhode Island. In Vermont and Massachusetts, "warning out" did not mean actual removal, but only a simple notification of the transient that he or she was not eligible for poor relief within the community. Rhode Island officials employed different language for those preliminary steps. A "citation" summoned a transient to appear at town council meeting to be questioned about his or her legal settlement; then officials formally "rejected" the transient as a legal inhabitant, divesting the town of responsibility for his or her welfare. When a "warning-out order" was issued, it followed those two first steps, and it meant serious action, not simply a bureaucratic procedure. First came the preparation of an official warrant, then a town constable at the door, and then a forced departure. It is this Rhode Island meaning of the term "warning out" as *removal* that is employed in this book.[15]

Patterns of Warning Out

Officials warned out people in every season, but they were slightly more likely to send away transients in the coldest months (see Appendix Figure A1, p. 203). In the winter, when jobs and health were at hazard for the poorer sort, transients were more apt to come to official notice. Authorities tried to get transients out of town before deep winter set in and their need for support became urgent. Consequently, the favorite month for warn-outs was December, when the agricultural cycle was complete and field laborers, desired in every other season, were no longer needed. When John Hall of West Greenwich brought a transient woman into town in June, "to work for him this season," he asked authorities for permission to keep her there "until the 25th day of December" and promised that he would then "see that she departs the town." In another December, when "the season of the year is now fast approaching when the necessaries of life will be and are now in great demand and difficult to be obtained," several Providence inhabitants asked their councilmen to identify transients who were likely to "be a tax on the good and industrious citizens" and remove them from the town "without delay."[16]

This seasonal variation is most marked for male household heads warned out of agrarian towns (Appendix Figure A2, p. 204). There, winter weather brought a cessation of agricultural activity, along with higher food prices and the need for increased shelter, clothing, and heat. In addition, pulmonary diseases flared up in small, smoky cabins, while dietary deficiencies led to a variety of health problems; men who supported their families by hiring themselves out to farmers were unable to secure a living from the end of the harvest to the beginning of the spring planting. Seasonal variations were much less distinct for transients warned out of commercial towns and for women warned out everywhere, but overall, midsummer was the time of fewest removals. Transient families were less likely to be in need in the summer, when jobs were plentiful and food cheapest, when firewood and heavy clothing were least needed, and when resourceful people could live off the land. Then, transient parents could more easily feed and clothe their children and thus avoid the sharp eyes of watchful neighbors.

Just as warning out fluctuated over the seasons, so it also fluctuated over the fifty-year period from 1750 to 1800 (Appendix Figure A3, p. 204). The number of warn-out orders fell sharply at the outbreak of the Seven Years' War (1756) and the Revolutionary War (1776). Officials, distracted by more urgent problems, temporarily ignored the needy and troublesome transients within their borders; at the same time, employment opportunities increased and some of those needy people disappeared. Some poor men found a temporary livelihood as soldiers and sailors; others, both men and women, found work by following the army and supporting the troops; still others found work in farms and shops that needed extra hands as their owners took advantage of increased demand for food and clothing. They left the towns where they had been living on the edge of destitution to pursue wartime opportunities.

Warning out resumed rapidly after the outbreak of war and peaked during the mid-1780s, evidence of the economic depression that settled on New England in the wake of the Revolutionary War. But numbers alone do not tell the whole story. In most Rhode Island towns, the population grew rapidly after the war, and if transient removals are measured as a percentage of the population, a different pattern emerges. The percentage of warn-outs remained reasonably steady through 1775, fell to an all-time low during the war, jumped to an unprecedented high in 1784, and then rapidly diminished to its lowest peacetime levels in the late 1790s (Appendix Figure A4, p. 205). Thus after 1784 a decreasing proportion of people were actually being sent out of town.

There are several ways to interpret this decline in the 1780s and 1790s. First, town officials may have changed the subjective criteria for warning out transients after 1784. As the population of Rhode Island towns boomed and more absolute numbers of people came under their jurisdiction, councilmen and overseers of the poor may have developed a greater tolerance for "troublesome" behavior. They may also have redefined the physical condition they termed "likely to become chargeable," with the result that some transients were less likely to be targeted for removal.

If, on the other hand, town officials' criteria for warning out remained steady over the period, then a declining percentage of transient people was actually prompting complaints about need or trouble. This may have been in part because poor people were able to find work more easily as the postwar economy improved or because they eluded official gaze by mingling in with the growing population of the town. It may also signify that some poor people were leaving Rhode Island, heading elsewhere in search of better land or more reliable work.

While the pattern of warning out may not prove a straightforward indicator of changing economic conditions throughout the revolutionary era, its undeniable peak (by any measure) in the mid-1780s underscores the deleterious effect of the postwar depression on poor people, as it plunged an extraordinary number into such dire circumstances that authorities were prompted to order them back to their hometowns. The many difficulties laboring people faced in eking out a living were magnified in those years.

Many workers were left jobless or reduced to hopelessly meager wages by cycles in the economy. In the downturn of the mid-1780s, merchants and ship captains scrambled to reestablish credit and overseas trade connections; artisans who had supplied the army with munitions, equipment, and clothing searched for new customers; former privateers, seamen, soldiers, and their families were set adrift on land; farmers struggled to find markets for their products. High taxes, rapid inflation of paper money, and a scarcity of hard money pinched inhabitants of farm and shop alike, leading to numerous personal tax delinquencies as well as entire towns defaulting on their share of taxes levied by the state legislature. A steady western migration began, taking potential employers of the poor from Rhode Island to central New York and other places, where men and women put their money and energy into more extensive or productive tracts of land.[17]

Other laboring people struggled with long-standing structural problems in a society based on racism and sexism. Many Native Americans, African Americans, and white women were consistently disadvantaged in the job market because they entered it with fewer marketable skills, fewer patronage and credit connections, and less capital to establish themselves. Setting an independent course after years of dependency proved an enormous challenge for those trained only for work that carried little market value. Such laborers had few possibilities of supporting themselves, much less advancing their economic position. All too often, former servants and slaves, widows, and wives of long-absent mariners found their meager wages would not stretch to cover the necessities of rent, food, clothing, and firewood. Women were also made vulnerable by childbearing, which temporarily halted a woman's ability to work and simultaneously created a greater need for her wages; young children figured prominently in the testimonies of transient women, and unmarried women in particular were often cast into poverty by the birth of a baby.

Struggling transient laborers were often children of poor people, born into families trapped in poverty and all too likely to carry forward this legacy of privation. Unlike some born into wealthy families, they did not prosper in the pre-industrial market economy; instead, they were kept at the bottom by the social and economic structure of eighteenth-century New England society. Others became poor through misfortune—disease, accident, natural disaster, or destructive behavior. While Providence's catastrophic epidemics of yellow fever were still a decade off in the mid-1780s, periodic outbreaks of smallpox and other "fevers" took their toll, depriving families of economically productive members. So did bitter weather, which left laborers with frozen fingers and toes, broken bones from falls, and respiratory ailments from exposure. Fires and floods destroyed what little property some poor people had, while others were victims of theft or of a family member who drank and gambled away the household's meager earnings.

This concentration of miseries had little to do with immigration, before the Revolutionary War or after. Over the entire period, only a tiny fraction (3.4%) of warned-out transients were foreign-born; the vast majority were native-born New Englanders, not new arrivals from the British Isles or elsewhere. This evidence indicates that by the latter part of the eighteenth century, transience and poverty were homegrown—not imported—problems. New England was not a place of opportunity for all; many born and raised there struggled to survive.

Faced with the upsurge in the number of the poor in the mid-1780s, town officials began to experiment with institutions as a way of caring for the needy within their jurisdictions, both inhabitants and transients. The decline in warning out in the 1780s and 1790s probably in part reflected this new strategy, since almshouses and workhouses sprang up in most Rhode Island towns during this period. Poor farms, asylums, and reformatories followed in the early nineteenth century.[18] Town officials began to send needy and troublesome transient people to these institutions rather than remove them to their places of legal settlement. Later in the nineteenth century, many "paupers" and "lunaticks" were placed under the care of a central state welfare authority, reducing even further the numbers of transient people over whom town officials had jurisdiction. While the settlement laws stayed in place until 1942 and unsettled people could, technically, be removed by officials from one place to another during that time, the actual practice of warning out trailed off in the nineteenth century. Never again were town leaders swamped, as they were in the 1780s and 1790s, by the business of interviewing and removing transient people in need.[19]

Nowhere did officials work harder to control transiency in the 1780s than in Providence. The great majority of surviving examinations come from Providence town records, reflecting not only the meticulous record-keeping habits of the town clerks but also the wave of people moving to the area during the latter part of the eighteenth century. Between 1750 and 1800, Providence officials warned out 682 people, five times the number for any other Rhode Island town; thus Providence's six councilmen were five times as busy at this task as any of the other six-man councils throughout the state. In fact, the influx of people overwhelmed the system in the 1780s and 1790s. Unable to collect information about transients in an orderly fashion *before* trouble arose, officials scrambled to keep abreast of the complaints against transients. The determined councilmen convened special meetings just to examine groups of ten, fifteen, or more transients—a lengthy process that could fill most of the day. While transients were a presence in every town, they were an administrative problem in Providence.

Providence was Rhode Island's great attraction in the late eighteenth century. It boasted an expanding mercantile economy, a rising upper class, and a promising market for crafts and trades. It rapidly outstripped Newport, formerly Rhode Island's largest town, in the years following the Revolutionary War. At the beginning of the conflict, British bombardment of Newport damaged wharves and warehouses and drove away many residents (including merchants), bringing about a cessation of normal business. Then, for three years, occupying British troops imposed martial law, choked off trade, stripped incoming ships, and plundered surrounding farms. After the war, it was to Providence—not Newport—that job seekers flocked, and they came from a considerable distance to try their fortune. Well over half (57.5%) of the transients warned out of Providence originated in towns at least twenty miles away. Some had walked the roads, some had begged rides from amiable carters, and some had worked their way on ships. They had come from New London, southern Rhode Island, western Massachusetts, Boston, Cape Cod, and many more distant locations, including Europe. No other Rhode Island town drew people over that kind of distance in this era of slow and deliberate travel; in towns outside Providence, the majority of transients (64.2%) were from neighboring towns and had come less than ten miles.[20]

The People Warned Out

Some of those who moved in search of better opportunities prospered; others did not. In late eighteenth-century New England, the latter had no legal claim to relief in their new communities.[21] Town leaders went to considerable trouble and expense to ascertain the unfortunate person's hometown and to send him or her back to it. When these officials issued a warning-out order, they directed the warrant to one individual: the person they examined. But that individual usually represented an entire family or household, and that family also suffered the judgment of the town council. Warned-out people lived in families or households; they were seldom unattached individuals living on their own. While the warning-out documents focused on heads of households, in reality those households included children, wives, sisters, mothers, other kin, and occasionally even servants. The most conservative estimate adds two or three people to each individual named in the record. Local officials may have talked with only one individual, but their decisions redirected the lives of entire families.[22]

Some of these transient families looked very much like the most respectable of their legally settled neighbors. Mothers and fathers laboring for a subsistence, raising well-behaved children, living for years in the same neighborhood—this seemed to fit the ideal Euro-American pattern of independent, nuclear families. And indeed families headed by white males constituted the largest group of transients, 42.1 percent of the whole. But if transients proportionally represented the dominantly white and patriarchally organized society in which they lived, the figure should be much higher. In fact, women and people of color figured in the transient population far out of proportion to their numbers in the general population.

The prevalence of women was perhaps the most striking characteristic of transient families. Fully two-thirds of the adult transients were female. Many of these women were wives who are hidden in the official record because only their husbands were questioned by officials following the usual patriarchal order of things. But men headed only half the households (50.4%). Women without husbands headed the other half (49.6%): to conduct those interviews, officials had to treat these widowed, separated, abandoned, and never-married women as heads of their own families. Both as household heads and as wives, women dominated the ranks of adult transients.[23]

The women in the transient population were considerably younger than the men (see Appendix Table A1, p. 206). The male heads of household presented a more typical family pattern: men in their thirties and forties, with wives and children. But the female heads of household were more often in their twenties, with small children in tow. One-third of the women were quite young—between sixteen and twenty-one—but they answered for themselves before town leaders, who apparently regarded them as fully adult, at least for the purposes of examination and warning out.

Because of this strong female presence, fewer than half (46%) of the warned-out households conformed to English patriarchal structure; instead, in the majority of cases, separated spouses, single mothers, widows, and unmarried couples managed their own households and attempted to support their dependents with their own labor. From the official perspective, these transient wives, daughters, sisters, and mothers were not in their proper place, detached as they were from settled, patriarchal households. While these women constitute a skewed sample of the female population at large, their dominance in the transient population is a logical consequence of English settlement law. Only unpropertied people could be warned out—people who had not purchased a freehold in the community—and both law and custom discouraged the ownership of real estate by women in the New England colonies. Thus, the great majority of women were dependent on men for their settlement status. By virtue of birth, they claimed their father's settlement; by virtue of labor, they claimed their master's settlement; by virtue of marriage, they claimed their husband's settlement. Certainly some women made themselves transient by leaving their home communities, but more had transient status foisted upon them by fathers, masters, and husbands who did not maintain a livelihood for their households, who abandoned their families in places far from home, or who released their servants to fend for themselves. Separated from their home communities, women became transients. Separated from their husbands, fathers, and masters, they could seldom gain settlement anywhere else.

In addition, women were particularly vulnerable to being warned out because of their childbearing potential. The impending birth of a baby frequently galvanized officials to send away a poor woman who was unaccompanied by a man. Every town council wanted to avoid the immediate costs of caring for a birthing and recovering mother and her infant and also the long-term costs of raising an illegitimate child born within their jurisdiction. As soon as observant neighbors passed along information that a transient woman was "big with a bastard child," councilmen acted quickly to remove her to her place of legal settlement. In 1771, for example, the Providence councilmen ordered Sarah Arnold to be removed to Smithfield because she "is like to be chargeable if not timely removed, she the said Sarah being pregnant." When the Middletown councilmen learned that a pregnant woman had recently arrived in town in 1785, they tasked one of their own number to go question the newcomer directly, "and if he finds that she doth not belong to the town that he immediately grant an order to remove her out of the town." When the pregnant woman was the daughter of a transient, the councilmen often warned out the entire family, as happened with William Greenman, whose daughter Martha's pregnancy precipitated the removal of the whole household from Jamestown, Rhode Island, to Swansea, Massachusetts. Because leaders often learned of a woman's pregnancy belatedly, these removals sometimes occurred on the very eve of childbirth, and occasionally a removal was abruptly halted when a woman went into labor. One Cumberland town constable, for example, "attempted" to remove Mary Johnston, but his efforts were "prevented by her lying-in."[24]

Transient women often formed communities of support, bound together in some measure by their vulnerability to official interference. In 1757, three transient seafaring wives—Mrs. Tower, Mrs. Meachins, and Mrs. Manning—were examined together by the Providence councilmen; in their husbands' absence, they had formed their own household with their eleven children. In 1782 transient Margaret Bowler was renting "the old gaol house" in Providence and had as tenants a number of other transient women. In 1799 transient Jenny Rose was supporting herself and her two children, while her husband was at sea, by domestic service and by taking in boarders. Such living arrangements stand out against the backdrop of the "official" representation of New England as a region of families organized along patriarchal lines.[25]

As might be expected, given the heavy proportion of women in the transient population, transient households often included children. Nearly half of the women and well over half of the men questioned by officials in the fourteen study towns had minor children with them, at least 900 children living in about 340 households. The very presence of these many children often spurred town leaders to action. Children who were ill, hungry, or lacked adequate clothing often prompted neighbors to report the family to town officials, thus launching the warning-out process. This was particularly true when a woman appeared to be supporting children without assistance from a man. When Hannah Staples of Cumberland reported to the town council that she had taken into her house a widowed mother with three children, whom she described as in "low and indigent circumstances," the councilmen ordered Staples to post bond or the family would be removed to their legal home in New York.[26]

People of color were also a significant presence among transients (Appendix Figure A5, p. 205). Over the entire fifty years, about one-fifth (21.9%) of transient heads of household were identified as "Indian," "mustee," "mulatto," "Negro," "black," or "of color." This was not a steady percentage over the period. People of color constituted about 10 percent of transients until the mid-1780s, when an increase in manumissions resulted in a growing population of free blacks faced with very limited job opportunities. From the mid-1780s on, people of color made up a much larger percentage of the transient population, peaking at 40 percent and more during the 1790s. These percentages do not mesh with contemporary counts of black and Indian people in the general population, which find people of color to be a declining presence in Rhode Island's population, falling from around 12 percent of the population in 1755 to about 5 percent in 1800.[27]

The much higher percentage of people of color suggests that poverty and transience were increasingly their fate, and that, at a time when the overall percentage of transients being warned out was declining (Appendix Figure A4), people of color were especially unwelcome. It also suggests that record keepers were increasingly careful to identify transient people by race in the 1780s and 1790s, when growing numbers of newly freed people were drifting loose from their moorings on the farms and in the households of the elites. The above-mentioned communities of transient women in Providence—the three sea wives, Bowler, and Rose—illustrate this heightened race sensitivity. In 1757, the three sea wives were not identified by race, though they were almost certainly white women, as indicated by the clerk's use of "Mrs." before their names. In 1757 few transients—white, black, or Indian—were identified by race. But in 1782 Margaret Fairchild was identified as a "Negro woman" and various of her tenants were identified as "Negro," "black," and "mulatto" women. Jenny Rose and her boarders were identified as "black" in 1800.

The majority of these nonwhite transients, like Bowler and Rose, ended up in Providence, part of the emerging community of color there. In the wake of the Revolution, newly freed slaves (and some runaways) throughout the northern states migrated purposefully from their places of servitude to the seaboard cities where men could find work on the docks and on the ships, where women could find jobs in the households of the well-to-do, and where people of color could live in relative peace. A shadow lay over this community, however: the complicated settlement status of people who had once been chattel property. The one sure place they "belonged" was in the towns of their former masters—the one sure place most of them did not want to be. They lived as free people, but also as transients vulnerable to warning out.[28]

"Vulnerable" is very much the operative word here, since white officials began to target people of color for removal in the 1780s and 1790s. While the statistical profile of warned-out people tells this story indirectly, some towns expressed their race anxiety directly by authorizing group "roundups" of people of color. In 1780, for example, the councilmen of

East Greenwich ordered "all the Indians, mulattoes & Negros that does not belong to this Town to depart the same immediately," and in 1786 the Tiverton councilmen ruled that all transient "black people" leave within one month or face being put into the workhouse and forced to labor. Providence councilmen implied that a similar group warn-out was in the works when they ordered that a "list" be compiled of "all transient white people in poor circumstances, as also of the blacks of all descriptions whatever dwelling in this Town." In these cases, officials apparently did not follow the usual procedure of individually questioning transients and then personally ordering them out. Instead, the constable or sergeant confronted and ordered out one transient after another, using a blank warrant on which he could add names as he saw people who fit the general description in the council's warrant. Thus, warning out proved a useful way to control the presence and movement of people of color; it enabled officials to draw a circle around those who "belonged" to the community in such a way that people of color fell outside.[29]

Transients were people accustomed to hard work. Between one-third and one-half of the household heads had been either slaves or indentured servants in the past (Appendix Table A1). As free people, transients worked at jobs not far removed from bound service—the most grueling and least well-paying jobs. In Providence, nearly one-quarter (23.9%) of warned-out families named seafaring as their occupation, another 8 percent named general unskilled labor, which Mark Noble (Chapter 3) described as "chopping wood, butchering, etc." The two trades best represented by transient families in Providence were shoemaking (11.4%) and blacksmithing (8.0%). In agrarian communities outside Providence, the occupation of transients is rarely mentioned, though most probably participated in such unskilled agricultural jobs as mowing hay and cleaning flax.

When transients arrived in a town where they found work, they stayed. These family units were not usually vagrant or homeless in the present-day meaning of those terms, although a small fraction of truly footloose people counted in the transient population. Instead, most transient families showed a certain determination to settle; on average, they had lived in the town at least four years before being warned out (Appendix Table A1). Women of color were particularly rooted, having been in place an average of more than seven years. In most cases, then, when councilmen warned out a family, they displaced persons who had a great deal to lose by removal: jobs, neighbors, connections, a sense of place.

The majority of these poor working people were illiterate, unable to sign the written transcriptions of the information they had provided orally to the town councilmen in the course of the transient examination. Not equally so, however: women were considerably less literate than men and people of color less literate than whites. Fewer than one-third of white women and only 6 percent of women of color could sign their names; but two-thirds of white men and 21 percent of men of color could sign. While the concept of republican motherhood expanded educational opportunities for the middling and wealthy sorts, diminishing the differences between women's and men's access to the written word, poor women still lived in a world of sharply gendered difference. For the most part, transients were people who lived by the spoken, not the written, word. They told their stories fluently and easily, from all appearances, and could remember details of their early lives some decades later. To have their histories put down in writing—and to put their names or their marks on the paper—was something out of the ordinary.[30]

Taken collectively, the records of warning out provide the above profile of the transient poor, highlighting their hard labor both in raising children and in making a livelihood, their lack of literacy and opportunity, their acquaintance with bondage and oppression, their economic and social vulnerability, their gendered and racialized differences in opportunity. Taken individually, the transient examinations allow us to see the lives and life courses of unprivileged people. They provide a sense of the range of options available to poor, unpropertied people in a society that valued fixity of place and ownership of real estate. The realities of most of these lives are both grim and compelling.

Most immediately evident in the transient examinations is the conditional and discriminatory nature of poor relief, despite the apparently nondiscriminatory poor laws that recognized every inhabitant's right to be "relieved and supported" at the direction of local officials.[31] In fact, town leaders were reluctant to dispense poor relief, and they were insistent in their demands that potential recipients demonstrate conclusively that they "belonged" to the community in a legal sense. In practice, some people were more likely to be cared for than others. I have argued elsewhere that women, and women of color in particular, were less likely than men to receive training in marketable skills as children and thus less likely as adults to support themselves and their sons and daughters and more likely to fall into need; conversely, women, and women of color in particular, were less likely than men to receive direct assistance from the community. Since poor relief was not a sure safety net (and meager charity in any case), economically vulnerable women and men resorted to transiency in order to find jobs to maintain their households.[32]

The voices in these histories reveal the personal consequences of a transient life. Husbands lived separately from wives and children separately from parents in order that each might secure the necessities of life. Many transient parents put their children "to service" with more prosperous householders while they themselves worked in another location. Sometimes these service arrangements were regularized by indentures, sometimes not. Phillis Merritt Wanton (Chapter 3) spoke for many transient women and men when she told the Providence town council that her ten-year-old son and seven-year-old daughter were "both bound out in the town of Foster"; she had her four-year-old daughter with her while she labored in domestic service in Providence. Inevitably, in such situations, allegiances shifted and family members lost track of each other. Hannah Clements told a familiar tale when she reported that "it is six years last March since she hath lived with her husband, and that she hath had nothing from him in that time towards her subsistence." These records take us inside the lives of the eighteenth-century poor and show us the effects of transience in human relationships as well as in the material circumstances of those who lived on the margin.[33]

The Narratives

The forty narratives in the heart of this book put a human face on poverty. They reveal how individual poor people grew up, formed families, supported themselves, suffered misfortune, grew old, and died. These are stories permeated with disappointment, grief, desperation, and real tragedy, but also with courage, loyalty, determination, resourcefulness, and wit. The lives of these unwelcome Americans arouse both pity and admiration.

The best method to present these narratives is a classic historian's dilemma. What language should we use to tell the story of people who left us no words of their own? Neither the original town documents nor these present-day reconstructions capture exact words. But even a complete transcript of the dialogue between a transient and town officials could not reveal the social context of such a conversation—the tones and volume of voices, the interruptions and silences, the glances and facial expressions, the gestures and postures. Try as we might, we can never truly hear these transients tell their own tales. We are inevitably left with someone else's version of their stories.

There are compelling reasons for not presenting transient examinations in their "raw" state. First, in no sense were the examinations intentional, voluntary autobiographies produced by the transients. The information contained in them was coerced, extracted from people who had little control over the interrogation. They are the result of people being forced to remember (or invent) their lives when confronted by the power of the state, when the "wrong" answer might result in disaster for themselves and their families. In another setting, these people doubtless would have told very different stories.

Second, the examinations recorded in the town books are wreathed in cumbersome legal phraseology that apparently satisfied officials' need to abide by procedure and obtain a document that could be used in court of law. This formulaic language, in some cases, constitutes more than half of the recorded examination, thus overwhelming and obscuring the very human story that had been told to the councilmen during that interrogation.

Third—and perhaps most important—the examinations were heavily mediated by the clerks who selected which spoken words to write down in ink on paper; no transient wrote down her or his own story independently. The amount of detail in the examinations reflects not the richness or thinness of transients' lives but rather the editorial decisions of the gate-keeping clerks, quintessential local leaders whose wealth, education, social connections, and continuous reelection to office for decades put them in a position of great power in their communities. Their marginal notations, their cross-outs and additions, and their general editing of the record shaped the testimonies of transients in significant ways. Phebe Perkins's testimony, for example, never was written into the official record of the Hopkinton town council meeting at which she was questioned; her story remains only in the clerk's draft notes of the meeting, which—fortunately—have been preserved.

To counteract these problems, I have fleshed out each transient examination with other information and rendered the whole narrative in present-day language, using direct quotations from the eighteenth-century documents where particular words and phrases are especially illuminating. My goal has been to reconstruct these transient people's lives as fully as possible and to make their tales as accessible as possible to twenty-first-century readers. Those interested in reading examinations and supporting documentary evidence in the original format and language will find this material for six narratives reproduced in the Appendix.

Selecting which people's stories to include and which to exclude was one of the most challenging aspects of this study. The amount of documentary evidence was a key criterion, and I winnowed the field to fewer than one hundred narratives by excluding those transients for whom I had no substantial data beyond the examination. Then I had to choose between similar stories. For example, I hesitated for a time over whether to include Briton Saltonstall or Bristol Rhodes, both black disabled Revolutionary War veterans about whom I had good information. But when I discovered Bristol Rhodes's obituaries and found myself deeply moved by the impression he made on those around him, my decision was made. In the end, my judgments rested intuitively on which stories seemed the most compelling, and it may be that my choices reflect the combined storytelling gifts of transient and clerk two centuries ago. Some of them told a very good story, and they have inspired me to do likewise.

To construct each narrative, I corroborated and extended the information in the examination with other archival material. Few transients appear in vital records (which note the births, marriages, and deaths of white, settled, propertied, and "respectable" inhabitants), and few appear in eighteenth-century census records (which counted households clearly recognized as such by town officials). The paper trail for transients leads instead into town council and town meeting minutes and into the Providence Town Papers, which contain letters, petitions, tax records, and receipts related to eighteenth-century town business. Petitions to the Rhode Island General Assembly and official state correspondence provided more details about some transients, and Revolutionary War archives proved a fruitful source of information about some dozen transients who were veterans or widows of veterans. Finally, a few transients turned up in newspaper advertisements, either because they had run away and were "wanted" or because they had placed an ad for their own purposes.

Despite extensive detective work, the stories presented here often lack a beginning and an ending. We do not know in every case what trouble led to the examination or what happened to the warned-out family after removal. The existing records provide only bits and pieces of information that do not always add up to a satisfying whole. Still, these narratives bring us closer than ever before to the lived experience of poor and unwelcome people who left no records for themselves and who had no opportunity to tell us their stories in their own way.

The following forty stories represent, as much as possible, the transient poor as profiled in this introduction. The majority were warned out after 1780, reflecting the upsurge in numbers in the last two decades of the century. About half of these transients came from outside Rhode Island. About half were women, half were men. Sixteen of the forty examinants were described as nonwhite. Most of the men were living with spouses; most of the women were not. About half the households included young children. Most told of working as unskilled laborers, with about a third reporting a history of slavery or bound servitude. Most could not sign their names. In one way, the narratives diverge from the typical profile: Providence-based stories dominate the narratives. This is because the Providence records are considerably richer than those of outlying towns, and more corroborating details could be discovered for the transients questioned there. But however many appeared in Providence, none of them *came* from Providence, and their stories reveal the hardships of life in communities throughout New England.

The narratives are organized to carry the reader through the life course of poor, transient people. Each story spotlights a key moment in an individual's life, and these moments are arranged so as to unfold the human experience from birth to death. Phebe Perkins leads off the narratives because her story tells more than any other about the circumstances into which many poor people were born. Similarly, Bristol Rhodes closes the narratives because his story tells more than any other about the physical frailties that ended many poor people's lives. In between are stories that illuminate moments of childhood, family life, and work life, and also stories that highlight crisis moments, when misfortune of one kind or another redirected the course of transients' lives.

These transient examinations provide much insight into issues of race and gender, and I considered organizing the narratives accordingly. With so many people of color represented among the transient poor, for example, why not shape whole chapters around the distinctive experiences of Indian, white, and black people? But eighteenth-century racial labels were the judgments of white officials, not self-designations by transients, and I did not want to carry forward the town fathers' racial classifications. Further, to cluster stories on the basis of race or sex would ultimately obscure the common ground of life experiences shared by all transients. In the end, I chose the birth-to-death organization because it best illuminated that common ground and because it allowed me, within each individual narrative, to emphasize relevant issues of race, class, and gender.

Chapter 1 shows how the impending birth of a child often prompted a warning out and describes how infants and children were affected by transiency. Chapter 2 opens up the world of personal relations among transients, showing how people living on the margin grouped themselves in families and households and related to each other as mates, kin, friends and neighbors. Chapter 3 shows the range of labor skills possessed by transient people and illuminates the economic situations that underlay transiency. Chapter 4 focuses on the personal misfortunes, community problems, and deliberate choices that brought transient people to a point of crisis and warning out. Chapter 5 gathers together stories that illuminate the end of life for poor transient people and shows how families, households, and communities viewed their responsibilities to the elderly. In a concluding chapter, I draw together elements of these forty transients' lives into one whole, sketching out the "typical" life course of poor, unwelcome people.

The stories presented in this volume tell of a world of hardship and conflict that contrasts dramatically with the harmonious, prosperous vision of early New England that is often lodged in our historic imaginations. By hearing these very real and agonized tales from an otherwise idealized place and time, we can better understand the complexity and severity of eighteenth-century American life. It is easy to overlook and marginalize the poor and the unwelcome in our reconstructions of the past, because their voices are so often muted in existing documents. Here they are not, and these narratives enable us to restore unwelcome Americans more fully to their place in early New England and all early America.

1. Birth, Infancy, and Childhood

*T*HE NARRATIVES in this chapter focus on the experience of children caught up in the warning-out process at any time between childbirth and adulthood, defined legally in Rhode Island as eighteen for girls and twenty-one for boys. A majority of warned-out adults had such underage children with them; other removals involved unmarried transient women about to give birth to a child; still others involved children on their own, separated from their parents. Children figure prominently in the warning-out records.

The large number of children is not surprising, since sexually active women of childbearing age had babies quite regularly—about every two years—in an era before reliable birth control. Typically, married women bore six or eight live children, so that childbirth was a regular and expected part of the female life course in the 1700s. Many children did not live to adulthood, however, because of inadequate nutrition, illness, and accidents; infants were particularly vulnerable to "overlaying"—being smothered or squashed during sleep when rolled upon by the mother or another family member. Somewhere between 20 and 35 percent of children died before age ten, the rates varying with race and class.

The average transient household, which had one or two adults and between two and three children, was somewhat smaller than the mean household size of 6.2 persons in the general Rhode Island population, as measured by the 1782 census. This smaller family size does not necessarily signify a lower fertility rate. Rather, it reflects the young age (averaging 28) of transient women, many of whom would bear more children. And it reflects the poverty of these transient families, which put children at even greater risk through exposure and starvation, the result of inadequate clothing, inferior housing, and insufficient food. Poverty also frequently necessitated a separation of parents and children, so that the family size reported by transients did not always represent the real number of children born to the parents. Hometown officials customarily intervened in families in obvious financial distress, removing the children and binding them out as indentured servants in more prosperous households; many poor parents avoided this action by voluntarily "placing" their children with better-off kin or neighbors, while they pursued employment elsewhere. Phillis Wanton (Chapter 3) had only her four-year-old daughter with her when she was warned out of Providence in 1800; her ten-year-old son and seven-year-old daughter were bound out elsewhere.

Officials rarely gave special consideration to transient families with children. Pregnant women were sent away on the eve of childbirth; parents were removed with newborn babies in their arms; and sometimes children were sent in one direction and parents in another. Such actions were prompted in part by Rhode Island settlement law, which until 1798 left ambiguous the status of transient children. For most of the eighteenth century, a person's primary settlement was "the place of his birth" until some other circumstance—purchase of land, completion of indentured servitude, marriage—created a new settlement. Until 1798, the law presumed that children would be born in the same place their parents had been, and there were no special provisions for children born away from their parents' hometowns. In 1798, however, the bureaucratic problems created by babies being born to transient women finally nudged legislators into revising the law so that legitimate children took their fathers' settlement, illegitimate children took their mothers' settlement, and no children could claim settlement in their place of birth unless one parent already had a settlement there.[1]

Since removing pregnant women was necessary to keep their children from gaining settlement by birth, officials must have kept a sharp eye on the profiles presented by transient women of childbearing age. This vigilance sometimes thwarted unmarried women who had left their hometowns in order to have "bastard" children elsewhere among relatives or friends. "Bastard" indicated that the child had no legal rights to the name or property of the father, who refused to provide either present support or future inheritance. Rhode Island law required town officials to make stringent efforts to discover the father and to hold that man responsible for the costs of raising his child.[2] While officials often relied on the midwife to discover the name of the father while the mother was in labor, they themselves sometimes investigated by questioning her during an official council meeting. They posed such questions as "Who is the father of the child you are now pregnant with?" and "At what time was it when [he] had the carnal knowledge of your body?" and "Hath any other person except [him] had the carnal knowledge of your body?" When the woman named a man who could offer no satisfactory "proof to the contrary," the council—and subsequently the community—judged him to be the "putative" or "reputed" father.

If an unmarried, pregnant, transient woman did not produce a settlement certificate whereby her hometown took full financial responsibility for her and her unborn child, or if relatives did not post bond or otherwise promise to keep the town "indemnified" from all costs of maintenance and later removal (if necessary) of the mother and child, such a woman was very likely to be forcibly returned to her hometown just weeks before childbirth. This was the fate of Phebe Perkins (this chapter). Officials sometimes did not realize a woman's condition in time; Coventry officials' removal of Lydia Aylworth, for example, was stymied because "before there could be an officer had to remove the said Lydia, she was brought to bed with a bastard child."[3] In such cases, officials proceeded to remove the mother and new baby soon after birth, hoping to limit public expenses and belatedly establish the town's rejection of the woman as a legal inhabitant. In such a manner, Martha Hathaway and her newborn (this chapter) were sent away from East Greenwich.

Long after their mother's pregnancy and childbirth, children drew official eyes to transient families. Sometimes youngsters' boisterous or "disorderly" behavior irritated neighbors and provoked complaints of juvenile mischief. In Providence, for example, fourteen-year-old Rufus Potter caused such a disturbance at one point that the councilmen gave the boy's transient parents a choice of binding out their son as an indentured servant or leaving town under a warning-out order.[4] But more often illness, hunger, and lack of clothing—which could rarely be concealed in the crowded lodgings most transients could afford—prompted neighbors to complain to officials. In such manner, attention was drawn to six-year-old Susannah Guinea (this chapter), prompting officials to remove her, thus separating her from her parents.

Perhaps the most poignant stories are those involving children who lacked the protection and support of parents. Recently born Jerusha Townsend and her three older sisters (this chapter) were abandoned by their parents, and six-year-old Kate Jones (this chapter) was left an orphan when her parents died. Town records provide glimpses of many other sad tales in such brief entries as "three black children found in distress on Poppesquash [Creek] in December last." Some older children appeared to be wandering about on their own, such as Hannah Hall, "a girl of about or not far from ten years of age," who showed up at a house in Westerly one day, prompting the family to ask the council for "directions" on what to do with her. Perhaps she had run away from her parents or her master; perhaps she had been abandoned and was seeking aid.[5]

Ultimately, the task of removing these abandoned, orphaned, or runaway children fell to the town sergeant or his constables. When young children were involved, officials usually hired a nurse or an extra hand, testimony to the difficulties of transporting children. The business of warning out seems particularly harsh when it involved parentless children, who were thus completely in the hands of strangers on an unwelcome journey. Once back in their hometowns, these children would almost certainly be bound out as indentured servants, which at least ended their trauma of being passed from hand to hand until someone made them a permanent part of a household.

Indentured servitude was the most common strategy authorities used to ensure that poverty-stricken, orphaned, and abandoned children received the "necessities of life" and practical training for adulthood. Such training was the essence of education in the eighteenth-century meaning of the term—before public schools were mandatory and when only the privileged few received formal training in anything beyond basic reading, writing, and arithmetic. A master who would stand in the role of parents and see that a child learned essential husbandry or housewifery skills and the three Rs was a valuable man to the town officials.

In return, the master received the benefit of the child's labor until he or she became an adult, an important consideration for households in need of an extra pair of hands. Most children were not protected from hard work in the eighteenth century; on the contrary, they were considered important contributors to the economic well-being of their households. Childhood was a time when young humans learned the skills by which they would gain a living in the world. By the time they were five or six, most boys and girls assisted adults in gender-segregated tasks they would later undertake as serious labor. By the time they reached adolescence (twelve or fourteen years of age), children were "apprentice adults," expected to labor nearly as hard as adults, although they were not considered capable of full adult work until they were in their later teens. Thus taking on a young child as a bound servant was often a sound investment, for with proper training and good maintenance, the dependent child might well develop into one who contributed fully to the household. When John and Isabel Brown (this chapter) were bound out, their master had to pay the town $10, because he was gaining a considerable advantage by having rights to years of the children's labor.

The narratives in this section should be read with an understanding that transient children suffered not only fragile health and poverty in their birth families, but also the rigors and griefs of physical relocation and incorporation into new households. Both physically and psychologically, children were the most vulnerable of transients, and their removals illustrate the harshest aspects of warning out.

Phebe Perkins

Phebe Perkins's story illustrates particularly well the vulnerability of pregnant transient women. As long as she was able to work, town officials let her be; there is no evidence that she was ever questioned as a transient in any Rhode Island town before 1784. But when she became pregnant she was no longer welcome in the place where she had been living for two years. When she was most in need of support, she was sent away to her supposed home, and her removal ignited a lawsuit between two towns because neither wanted to shoulder financial responsibility for her.

Phebe Perkins was born in Newport in 1760, and when she was very young, she was "bound an apprentice" to Westerly householder Abraham Burden. While the contract was still in force, Burden "carried her" to the home of Stephen Perry in neighboring Charlestown. Perkins later said she knew of "no contract between said Burden and said Perry concerning her living with said Perry," but she clearly "saw her indentures at Perry's," so it seems likely that Burden transferred her contract to Perry in some fashion. Burden's circumstances may have changed so that he no longer needed a servant, or perhaps he or someone in his family took a dislike to Phebe Perkins and wanted her out of the household.

While Perkins was part of his household, Stephen Perry moved from Charlestown to Hopkinton, so that when his servant completed her indenture on her birthday in 1778, she became an inhabitant of Hopkinton. She was now free to make her own living, such as it would be in the precarious wartime and postwar economy. Apparently trained as an agricultural

laborer, she began to migrate from farm to farm in the border region of
Rhode Island and Connecticut, going where work was available and staying for as long as it lasted. She picked produce such as greens and strawberries and probably also performed general farm and household labor,
helping with the grain harvest, butchering hogs and salting meat, spinning
thread, making candles, washing clothes. Among her stints of work were
three weeks at "one Avery's in Connecticut," two weeks at Thomas Sweet's
farm in Hopkinton, and an autumn and winter at Amos Collins's place in
Stonington, Connecticut.

If Phebe Perkins could write, she did not show it by signing her examination. Whatever her literacy skills, they did not figure prominently in her
work. She calculated time in agricultural terms rather than by calendar
months, recalling that she stayed at Benjamin Wilbur's house "till the
spring following when people began to pick greens for sauce," and that she
lived at Thomas Sweet's house "till strawberries began to be ripe." Her
economic security lay in the strength of her back and hands; she had no
family connections or social influence to carry her through hard times.

In 1782 she finally found long-term employment in Richmond, in the
household of Edward Perry, who was probably related to her former master, Stephen Perry. Edward Perry was one of the richest men in Richmond,
and he served in the most important town offices during the revolutionary era, as town councilman, treasurer, tax assessor, and deputy to the
General Assembly. During the years that Phebe Perkins labored in his
household, Perry was repeatedly elected town council president and was
arguably the most powerful and influential man in the town. Perkins
seemed to have found an excellent position, with as much security as an
unskilled transient laborer could expect to find in that region and in that
time.

In 1784, after more than two years of working in Perry's household,
Phebe Perkins became pregnant. The father of her child is not identified,
either in her examination or in other town records pertaining to her.
Perhaps she refused to name the man when she was questioned by authorities; she may have been shielding a person of means and status who
refused to take responsibility for his child. Perhaps she did name him, but
he was dead or long disappeared into the anonymity of seasonal transience. That he was not mentioned suggests that the council concluded
there was no way to hold the father responsible for the maintenance of the
child.

The complaint about Perkins's pregnancy very likely originated in the household of Edward Perry, who now dealt with her both as her employer and as the chief official of the town where she lived. Although he was a man of substantial wealth and position, he did not shield her from the consequences of an out-of-wedlock pregnancy; the councilmen, led by Perry, ordered her to be removed from the town. Perhaps Perry felt betrayed by Perkins's sexual activity; perhaps he wanted to distance himself from her as much as possible, to prevent or quiet any rumor that he might be the father of her child. Apparently her pregnancy and removal did not affect his status, for he continued to be elected president of the town council for five years afterward. But for Phebe Perkins the withdrawal of Perry's protection resulted in her dislocation from a place of steady employment within an elite household to exile among strangers and meager support as "the poor of the town" elsewhere.

The Richmond council first sent Perkins to Newport, her birthplace, but when officials there rejected her and sent her back, Richmond focused on Hopkinton, where she had been a bound servant. In October 1784 the Richmond sergeant delivered her to the door of Edward Wells, Hopkinton overseer of the poor, who had to work fast, for Perkins was nearing the time of delivery. Wells arranged for her to be boarded at the home of Cary Clarke, whose spouse may have been a midwife. There Perkins gave birth. Some kind of "sickness" associated with childbirth—complicated delivery or postpartum infection—necessitated a visit from townsman Ross Coon in his capacity as doctor (he was also tax collector) to bleed her and give her "strong drops." She was ill for considerably longer than the usual two-week "lying-in" period, and there is no mention of the child, which suggests that she or he did not survive, a not uncommon fate in eighteenth-century America.

In January, after twelve weeks of being tended in Cary Clarke's household, Perkins was well enough to be moved to yet another household, where she was expected to labor toward her own support. There, on 19 January 1785, the Hopkinton council convened to decide what to do with this impoverished and dislocated new mother who had cost Hopkinton a good deal of money. She had arrived in town in a nearly destitute state, and the necessities of life involved paying the cobbler to repair her shoes as well as paying caretakers to feed, warm, and doctor her and her baby, if it survived. In three months' time, the Hopkinton treasury dispensed more than £8 on her care, a staggering sum for a town whose entire poor-relief expenses for 1784—as revealed in the town council and town meeting records—had totaled £22.[6]

The Hopkinton councilmen decided to sue Richmond for sending away Perkins. They questioned whether Perkins had any claim to poor relief in Hopkinton, since her former master had moved away some years before and Perkins herself had not lived in Hopkinton for some time. A judge might conclude that Richmond was responsible for her, since she had been living in that town for more than two years prior to the birth of her baby.

Phebe Perkins disappears from the Hopkinton town records at this point, and other documents that might reveal the rest of her story have been destroyed by theft (Richmond town records) and flood (county court records). But the existing pieces of information illuminate the extreme vulnerability of pregnant women who were poor and transient. Without the security and support of a familiar home at one of the most dangerous moments of their lives, mother and child were thrown among strangers by the warning-out and removal process. Both Phebe Perkins and her baby were "unwelcome Americans."

Anthony Hathaway

Anthony Hathaway's mother, Martha Hathaway, was an unmarried woman who gave birth to at least four or five illegitimate children, of whom he was one. His first rocky years read like a soap opera or a bad fairy tale: born a "bastard"; as a newborn, transported to another town; as a toddler, abandoned by his mother and taken in by poor-relief caretakers; as a three-year-old, bound out as an indentured servant. This was poverty and transience showing their harshest aspects.

Martha Hathaway was born in 1763 in Warwick, Rhode Island, where her father owned real estate and had a legal settlement, but he sold his property and moved his family to Coventry when Martha was "fifteen years of age or thereabouts." When she was twenty years old, she left Coventry, apparently in order to have a baby—one of Anthony's older siblings—who was born in Providence in June 1783.

Following this birth, Hathaway had "a severe fit of sickness with the fever," probably an infection following the trauma of childbirth. Her illness was so great that when the Providence officials learned of her presence they arranged for her to be tended in their town for the time being rather than moved back to her hometown right away. The family of Nathaniel Jenckes provided room, board, and general nursing care for her from mid-June to early August; two additional persons were paid "to watch with her" each night from 22 June to 13 July, when she was most seriously ill; and her sister Mary was brought from East Greenwich by horse and chaise, at the expense of the town, to tend Martha personally. Finally, on 6 August, Hathaway was well enough to attend council meeting and be questioned by the Providence authorities, who ordered her removed to Warwick, her hometown. She did not wait around for the town sergeant to remove her; she "went away" voluntarily three days later.

The next summer, Hathaway turned up in East Greenwich, probably to be near her sister; there she was questioned by the councilmen in June 1784. She represented herself as a "widow" and she had not one but two little girls with her whom she claimed as "daughters." Perhaps she already had one child before she went to Providence in 1783. At any rate, she was sent away from East Greenwich and back to Warwick, along with the two little girls. From later events, it seems likely that East Greenwich wanted her out because she was pregnant once again.

By January 1786, Martha Hathaway had returned to East Greenwich and was once again questioned by authorities. The first two daughters were no longer with her; perhaps they were being raised by relatives or masters elsewhere. This time she had a one-year-old daughter, born in 1784 after she had been removed from East Greenwich, and a new baby boy, Anthony, "a male bastard child born of the body of Martha Hathaway," whose birth in East Greenwich had focused council attention on Martha. Once again, the East Greenwich town council ordered her removed to Warwick. Legally, only Martha belonged to Warwick, where she was born and where her father had once owned land. Her son Anthony belonged to East Greenwich, where he had been born, but Warwick officials agreed to receive the baby along with his mother, because he was still "a nurse child," whom they considered "a natural appendage upon the said Martha." It was exactly this sort of situation that prompted lawmakers to change the settlement law in 1798; had Anthony Hathaway been born in 1799, he would have been an inhabitant of Warwick, because his mother belonged there.

For nearly two years, Martha and Anthony Hathaway lived together in Warwick. Then, in April 1788, Martha Hathaway "did voluntarily depart from the said Anthony." Abandoned by his mother, the two-year-old was cared for by townspeople who would later be repaid out of the town's poor-relief budget. Five months later, when the little boy was nearing the age of three, the Warwick town council resolved to send him to East Greenwich, his legal home; from the official perspective, there was no reason to keep the boy in Warwick after his mother left. Anthony Hathaway was transported to East Greenwich and put into the care of one of the overseers of the poor there.

A month after arriving in East Greenwich, three-year-old Anthony Hathaway was bound out as an indentured servant to Capt. Sylvester Sweet, a wealthy, influential, and multiskilled man whose expertise extended to "bonesetting" surgery. He and his family also made something of a business out of providing room and board for people, and such a household undoubtedly could care for a toddler, train him to useful service, and put him profitably to work in due time. Fifteen years earlier, Sweet had taken an indenture of a small "Negro" child, Simon Talbury, who by 1788 must have been nearing the end of his servitude. It may have been Talbury's imminent departure that prompted Sweet to take on another youngster to be trained to take up Talbury's tasks.

Martha Hathaway produced at least one more "bastard child"—her fifth—in the summer of 1790. Daughter Mahala's birth prompted voters, mindful of high taxes that paid for the maintenance of such children, to complain that officials had done little to track down "the putative father" in order to extract some "support and maintenance," and these irritated taxpayers directed the overseer of the poor to take whatever "legal measures" were necessary to obtain "a bond or securities" from the putative father. There is no indication that the man responsible was ever identified or persuaded to support his daughter, and Mahala Hathaway was bound out as an indentured servant when she was twenty months old. Her master, Thomas Arnold of Warwick, received a special "premium" of £7 10s. for taking on so young a child, who would not be able to labor productively for some while yet. Siblings Anthony and Mahala Hathaway barely knew their mother, apparently never knew their father(s), and probably did not know each other. They were raised in different households and claimed by different towns. Transience, poverty, and bastardy made a grim combination for children.

Kate Jones

When town councilmen wanted to discover the circumstances of a transient child without parents, they rarely asked the youngster directly. Instead, they gathered information from family members and neighbors such as those who cared for young Kate Jones after her parents died. Officials also consulted their counterparts in other towns, if there was any question about the child's legal settlement, so that the correct hometown took financial responsibility. Such an exchange of information created a discernible paper trail about Kate.

Kate Jones was the second child of Nathaniel Jones, "a free Negro man" of Johnston, and Eunice Phenix, "with whom he lived," at times in Providence and at other times in Johnston. Nabby, Kate's older sister, was born in Providence in 1779; Kate was born in Johnston in 1780. Their parents never married according to Anglo-American legal convention, but white officials recognized them as mates and so recognized Nabby and Kate as orphans when Jones and Phenix died.

On 4 January 1781 Nathaniel Jones had enlisted in the Rhode Island Regiment for the town of Johnston, tempted by the lucrative bounty the voters offered: one hundred silver dollars, almost a year's wages for an unskilled laboring man. In 1781, such payments were the only way reluctant men could be persuaded to join the Continental Army, for popular enthusiasm had waned as soldiers returned from their tours of duty and reported the deprivations and inconveniences they had experienced in this war that dragged on past all expectations. When Jones went off to join the army, he left his $100 bounty money with Benjamin Waterman of Johnston, "in case he should not return." The money was to be used "for this child," his baby daughter Kate.

"Nat" Jones did not return to Johnston. He died almost exactly a year after he enlisted, on 9 January 1782. Eunice Phenix subsequently moved from Johnston to Providence, where she raised her two daughters with the help of her sister, Margaret Abbee, and other friends. Prime Brown's household became the place that Kate knew as home. If Phenix knew about the bounty money that Jones had left for Kate, there is no evidence that she obtained access to it or used it in any way to support her daughter.

Then, early in 1786, Eunice Phenix died, leaving both girls as full orphans at the ages of five (Kate) and six (Nabby). The children continued to be cared for by members of Prime Brown's family, but someone advised the Providence council of the children's "destitute" state and their father's earlier provision of money for Kate. Nabby, born in Providence, came under the jurisdiction of the Providence officials, but Kate had been born in Johnston and was thus an inhabitant of that town. When Providence officials first learned of the situation, they assumed both girls "belonged" to Johnston, and they ordered the clerk to write to the Johnston council, "requesting" them "to provide for the children as inhabitants of said town of Johnston."

Apparently, the Johnston officials set them straight and advised them that only Kate had a hometown in Johnston. Official procedure moved slowly, and it was not until the spring of 1787 that Providence officials wrote once again to the Johnston officials, proposing that both Kate and Nabby remain in Providence and that "Mr. Waterman" send the money "in his hands" (Kate's inheritance) to support her there. The Providence councilmen had "procured" a "place" for Nabby, probably by placing her with a master, but they could not do the same for Kate, who was not under their jurisdiction. Still, they wanted Kate to be cared for "in the best and cheapest manner" in Providence.

The Johnston officials did not agree to this arrangement, so in June 1787 the Providence councilmen prepared to remove Kate to Johnston. They first verified her hometown by questioning her aunt, Margaret Abbee, who testified that Eunice Phenix had "left a young child by the name of Kate Jones, now about seven years old," that Kate had been "born in the town of Johnston," and that Phenix herself "was never married." Two months later, the council issued a warrant to remove Kate, but for some reason the warrant was not put into effect for another eighteen months. Finally, on 11 February 1789, sergeant Henry Bowen delivered Kate to one of the Johnston overseers of the poor. Kate would have been close to nine years old when she was actually moved from the place that had been her home. In Johnston, very likely, she was bound out as an indentured servant.

There is no evidence of what Benjamin Waterman did with Nathaniel Jones's $100 legacy for his daughter Kate or what Job Waterman (perhaps a kinsman of Benjamin) did with the 24 shillings (about $4) in back pay he had collected posthumously on Jones's behalf. The money may have been held by town officials until Kate came of age and then given to her; it may have been spent by town officials to cover costs associated with her care while a transient in Providence or to secure an apprenticeship contract in Johnston so that there was little left for her later; or it may have been fraudulently appropriated by other parties, so that Kate herself never benefited from it. Her story highlights the legal vulnerability of poor parents and their children, who had to trust those with greater wealth, influence, and knowledge of the law to protect their interests. Such a substantial inheritance could have enabled Kate to purchase a piece of property or otherwise secure a modicum of independence—if, and only if, the Watermans and town authorities had made sure she received it.

Susannah Guinea

Present-day readers are often startled by the seemingly unregretful way in which authorities sometimes separated children and parents during the warning-out process. Such separations were the result of the vagaries of settlement law, which until 1798 mandated that a child born in a Rhode Island town was an inhabitant of that town by the "birthplace" rule, regardless of the parents' legal settlement(s) elsewhere. This penalized poor parents who moved around and had children in places other than their own birthplaces; when each member of the family was sent "home," separation was the result. This was the case with Susannah Guinea, who at age four was separated from her mother and her father when the family was sent out of Providence. Susannah's parents, Titus Guinea and Binah Pearce, appeared to be longtime mates, but they never married according to Anglo-American law, and so Pearce had never acquired Guinea's settlement by virtue of marriage. Each member of this little family had a different hometown: Titus Guinea in Ipswich, Massachusetts, Binah Pearce in Providence, and Susannah Guinea in North Providence.

Titus Guinea, "a Negro man" who had been "born in Guinea" about the year 1728, was enslaved there as a young man of twenty-one or twenty-two; he was "brought as a slave to this country," first to Newport and then to Boston in 1751. He "was sold to Abijah Wheeler of Ipswich," a master with whom he lived "about 3 years." His next master was "one Daniel Giddings" of Boston, "with whom he lived about 4 or 5 months." Then he "was sold to Ebenezer Hoskin of Cape Ann" and lived with him "about 2 years & an half." Finally he "was sold to Theophilus Pickering of Ipswich," for whom he labored "about 11 years." During this time Guinea "bought his time of his said master," purchasing his freedom through labor. But before the deal was completed, Pickering died, leaving Guinea to his brother Thomas Pickering of Salem. In what seems to have been a deliberate strategy to honor the bargain between slave and former master, Thomas Pickering "sold" Guinea—or perhaps sold whatever of Guinea's time remained under the agreement—to Joseph Russ, who released him ("let me go at large"). Russ also "gave bond to indemnify the town of said Ipswich from any charge they may be at on my account." In 1769, when he was about forty years old, Titus Guinea became a free man.

Guinea moved to Providence, an international port where a healthy man of color might find employment in the warehouses or on the wharves. He became a significant member of the community of free people of color there, establishing an independent household and meriting an entry in the 1782 census as "Titus, A Negro," with three other "Negroes" in his household.

While in Providence, Guinea formed a relationship with Binah Pearce, who was apparently a white or part-white woman. He also learned how to write, and very likely to read as well, for he signed his 1770 examination in a spidery and perfectly legible hand: "Titus Guinea." In 1784, the two had a little girl, Susannah, whom officials described as "Negro or mulatto," suggesting Pearce was not full "Negro," unlike the African-born Guinea.

In 1788, these three people came to the attention of Providence officials. Perhaps Titus Guinea, who had been in Providence "about nineteen years" and was now "about 60 years of age," was no longer able to earn enough to keep himself and his family sheltered, warm, and well fed. But since council attention was focused on Susannah, it may have been she who roused their concern. In mid-March, after questioning both her father and her mother, the Providence officials ruled that Susannah "belonged" to North Providence, where she was born and where she should be sent "immediately." Indeed, the very same day, a warrant was prepared for the removal of this "Negro or mulatto bastard child in the fifth year of her age" (meaning four years old). Two weeks later, in late March 1788, town sergeant Henry Bowen "delivered" Susannah into the hands of Eleazar Jencks, an overseer of the poor for North Providence. Soon after that, she would almost certainly have been bound out as an indentured servant.

For nineteen months after Susannah was taken away, Titus Guinea

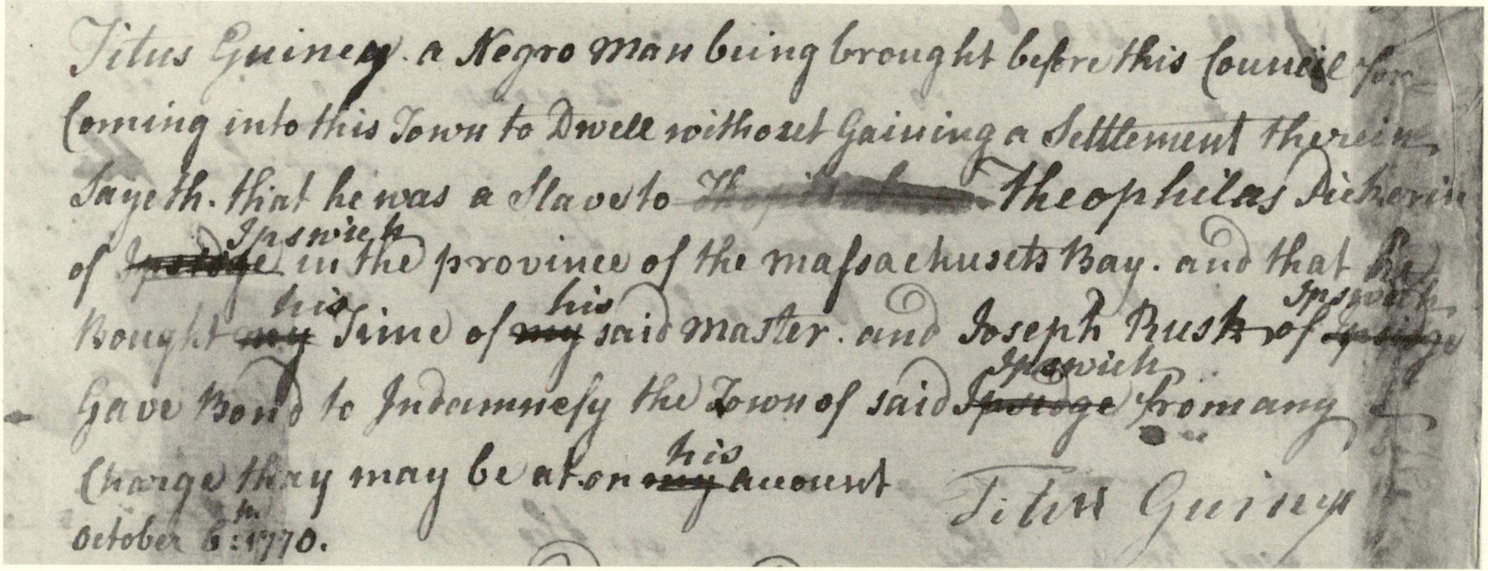

Titus Guiney a Negro Man being brought before this Council for Coming into this Town to Dwell without Gaining a Settlement therein Sayeth that he was a Slave to Theophilus Pickering of Ipswich in the province of the Massachusets Bay. and that he Bought his Time of his said Master. and Joseph Rusk of Ipswich Gave Bond to Indemnefy the Town of said Ipswich from any Charge they may be at on his account

Titus Guiney

October 6th:1770.

Figure 1. Susannah Guinea's father Titus lived as a slave in Massachusetts until 1769. Soon after gaining his freedom, he moved to Providence, where town authorities questioned him on 6 October 1770. Guinea left this signature on his testimony. Source: PTP 2:38, neg. no. RHi (x3) 9396. Courtesy of the Rhode Island Historical Society.

and Binah Pearce continued to live in Providence. Perhaps they saw Susannah regularly, since the two towns were adjacent to each other. But in October 1789 the town council ordered Guinea—now ailing and "likely to become chargeable"—removed to his supposed hometown of Ipswich, Massachusetts, where his last master had pledged to take financial responsibility for him. After more than two decades of living, working, and being part of a community in Providence, Susannah's father was sent out of range of regular visits to his daughter. As for Binah Pearce, she continued to live in Providence, where she formed a new attachment, perhaps because Titus Guinea had died. In 1791 she gave birth to a baby she named Samuel, "a mulatto boy, an illegitimate son," brother to Susannah. His fate suggests what probably happened to Susannah: in 1797, the Providence town council bound out six-year-old Samuel Pearce as an indentured servant to Samuel Budlong of Warwick, who promised to teach the lad "reading, writing, and cyphering as far as the rule of three." Writing and cyphering were not usually taught to children of color, and their inclusion in Samuel's contracts suggests that Binah Pearce—or, more likely, the putative father—commanded some respect from officials.

Susannah's removal from her mother at age four was not an unusually early separation for children of poor parents. Eighteenth-century law and officialdom did not assume that a young child belonged with its mother, and councilmen sometimes concluded that even a nursing child should not stay with an "improper" mother. Of some 700 children placed in apprenticeship indentures by Rhode Island town officials during the latter part of the eighteenth century, over 40 percent were under the age of six at the time of binding.[7] Once a child was no longer a "nursling" child like Anthony Hathaway, officials assumed he or she would profit from being moved to a more "respectable" household, where material needs could be better met and more "suitable" training begun. Susannah Guinea's story underscores the fragility of poor, transient families, prone to being dismantled by watchful authorities armed with settlement law.

Jerusha Townsend

Abandoned children were perhaps the most pitiable of young transients, suffering the double blows of parental desertion and then their own displacement. When parents left their children behind, neighbors usually took over essential care until town authorities made more formal arrangements by binding out the children as indentured servants. But if the children belonged to a different town, then local officials lacked the authority to bind them out; instead, they sent the children, in care of a town sergeant and hired hand or nurse, to the town where they had a legal settlement. This is what happened to Jerusha Townsend and her sisters when their parents abandoned them.

William Townsend was a goldsmith, trained in one of the most elite crafts in early America, making his living by fashioning jewelry, decorative housewares, and carriage fittings for well-to-do customers. He lived and worked in Newport, where a concentration of merchants, ship captains, and professionals maintained households that required such articles. Then in 1774, Townsend, his wife Jerusha, and their three little daughters—six-year-old Lydia and her younger sisters Anna and Abigail—"removed" to Providence, which rivaled Newport as a locus of wealth and power in the colony. Townsend apparently found business in Providence, and there Jerusha had a fourth baby, another little girl, who was named after her mother.

Then, in August 1775, William and Jerusha Townsend "departed" Providence and "left their said children without anything to support them." The four little girls were apparently cared for by neighbors until the council issued a warrant for the removal of the four children to their hometown of Newport. It is not clear why the council concluded that Jerusha, "recently born" in Providence, was nevertheless an inhabitant of Newport like her older sisters, but the Newport authorities did not dispute the judgment. Constable Gideon Young hired a "nurse" to help him with the task of removal, "conveyed" the children to Newport, and delivered them to the home of John Pittman, overseer of the poor of Newport. Young's charge for "my trouble and expenses with the nurse and children" was greater than the cost of renting "the horse and chaise" for the trip; the total bill of £5 5s. made for a very costly removal. It must have been a trying time, with four young, confused, and helpless children being taken by strangers on an unwelcome journey.

There is no evidence of the Townsend parents' fate or that of the daughters as a family unit. In 1775 and 1776 it would have been difficult for separated children and parents to find each other in Newport. Tensions between New England townspeople and English authorities were high, and the British warship *Rose* patrolled Narragansett Bay, trying to discourage

Americans from smuggling goods and otherwise evading customs laws; several towns were bombarded by gunfire when they refused to provision the troops aboard the ship. In December 1776 a major British invasion force sailed into Narragansett Bay and headquartered itself at Newport. A majority of the townspeople fled and sought refuge inland. The four Townsend daughters had probably been folded into the households of relatives in Newport by this time and would have fled the town with their new families as part of the general exodus, perhaps going back to Providence, which became the magnet for Newport refugees during the war years.

Jerusha Townsend definitely did make her way back to Providence. She reappeared there in the 1790s as a young woman and "resided for some time" in the household of James Arnold, a man of wealth and status in the community who had been elected town treasurer of Providence every year since 1771. He may have been a kinsman, or perhaps an employer. But Jerusha did not prosper and came to the attention of the town council in 1796, when she fell so low as to require poor relief and seemed "likely to become further chargeable to this town."

The council questioned Jerusha Townsend, now twenty-one years old, but she "appear[ed] unable to render a satisfactory and intelligible account of herself," perhaps because she was distraught or confused by the confrontation. The councilmen instead consulted James Arnold, who reminded them of Jerusha's history as an abandoned child twenty years before. The council then issued a warrant for her to be taken back to Newport, where she still had a legal settlement by virtue of her father's former status. Within five days the young woman had been delivered to Henry Peckham, overseer of the poor in Newport.

Jerusha Townsend returned to Providence one more time. She was there in the late summer of 1797, when a yellow fever epidemic swept through the town, killing scores of inhabitants who were too poor to leave and seek sanctuary in a more healthful environment. The last mention of her name in the records is a poignant listing of her having died of the "infection" on 3 September 1797.

Susannah, James, John, and Isabel Brown

The four children of "troublesome" Roseanna Brown became the responsibility of Exeter, the town where they were born, when she was declared "not capable of taking care of herself" or her offspring. The children had lived together with their mother up to that point, but they were separated from her and from each other when town authorities made new arrangements for their upbringing. Brown could visit her sons and daughters in their new households, but she no longer had practical custody of them.

Roseanna Brown, "a black woman" living in Exeter, was very "troublesome" to the overseers of the poor and had necessitated an outlay of poor-relief money from the town treasury. By June 1797, when the latest "complaint" about her was brought to the ears of the councilmen, she had four children—Susannah, James, John, and Isabel—but no husband present to take responsibility for them. After hearing the complaint, the Exeter council summoned and questioned Roseanna's father, Prince Brown, who "inform[ed]" them "that the said Roseanna was born in South Kingstown." The Exeter council promptly ordered a warrant for her removal, and within five days Roseanna Brown was delivered to one of the overseers of the poor for South Kingstown.

The South Kingstown council considered the situation, concluded that South Kingstown was *not* Roseanna Brown's "proper place of settlement and residence," and decided to "appeal from said order." In their judgment, the Exeter officials had made a mistake because they had failed to question Brown directly, and when the South Kingstown officials followed that basic procedure they discovered that Roseanna Brown claimed to be married to an Exeter man:

Q: Was you ever married?

A: Yes, to Phillip Whitford, a black man belonging to Mr. Amos Whitford of Exeter.

Q: Who married you?

A: Elder Whitman.

Q: At what house was you married?

A: At a house in Coventry then improved by my father, Prince Brown, said house belonged to Robert Godfrey, as I supposed.

Q: Who was present when you was married?

A: Prince Brown, Adam Brown, James Brown, and Deborah Watson.

Q: How long since you was married?

A: I believe about eighteen or nineteen years.

Roseanna Brown Whitford, it seemed, belonged to Exeter after all, by virtue of having married a man of Exeter.

The case of South Kingstown v. Exeter was a washout; both parties appeared with "the best counsel" they could get, but the case was first continued (1797) and then dismissed the next spring (1798). Apparently the marriage between Roseanna Brown and Philip Whitford was not indisputably valid. The South Kingstown councilmen were forced to accept Roseanna Brown as their responsibility, and they issued her a certificate "acknowledging her as legally settled in this town" when she wanted to move back to Exeter in 1799.

Meanwhile, Exeter authorities were rearranging the lives of Roseanna Brown's four children, Susannah, James, John, and Isabel. Roseanna Brown herself might be South Kingstown's responsibility, but her children were Exeter's, by virtue of having been born there. In October 1797, soon after Roseanna had been sent to South Kingstown, the councilmen bound out eleven-year-old Susannah Brown, "a black girl" and "daughter to Roseanna Brown," as a servant to Leonard Ainsworth and his wife, who were obliged to teach the girl "to read" but not to educate her any further or teach her any particular work skills.

Three years later, in the summer of 1800, the Exeter council took action regarding the other three children. James Brown, "son to Roseanna Brown," was put under the guardianship of Exeter townsman Job Wilcox; this action indicated that the boy had property of some kind—perhaps an inheritance left by a relative—that would come to him when he turned twenty-one. As guardian, Wilcox was responsible to see that James received the necessities of life, had a proper place to live, and was trained for adulthood.

A little later the same summer, John and Isabel Brown were both bound out as indentured servants to Stephen Allen of West Greenwich. Twelve-year-old John, "a black boy, son to Roseanna Brown," had apparently exhibited a restless and independent spirit, for the terms of the indenture stated that the "the said Allen agrees to give said apprentice ten dollars and the interest thereon from the date of this council if said boy serves out his time, to be paid when said boy is 21 years old; if said boy runs away before he arrives to the age of twenty-one years old, then said boy is not to have neither money nor interest." Six-year-old Isabel also was promised "ten dollars at the end of said term of time if said apprentice serves out said time." Both children were to be taught "to read and write, if the schoolmaster thinks [them] capable of learning." And both children were to be provided with "sufficient meat, drink and lodging, and comfortable wearing clothes for everyday wear and a decent suit of clothes at the end of said term of time." The council clearly felt that Allen was getting a better deal than the children were, for they required that Allen pay the town "ten dollars in money for the privilege of having the two apprentices"; presumably that ten dollars would be used to pay any support costs the children had already incurred.

By the end of the summer of 1800, the four children of Roseanna Brown had been placed in three different households, under different living and working arrangements. Because Roseanna continued to live in Exeter, it seems likely that she maintained a relationship with them. Her intention of staying in Exeter seem clear; in July 1808 she renewed her certificate from the South Kingstown town council "acknowledging her to be legally settled in this town." The law may have said she belonged to South Kingstown, but her livelihood and her children lay elsewhere.

2. Family Life

*T*HE NARRATIVES in this chapter focus on the ways poor transients organized themselves into families, which were sometimes quite ordinary and traditional and other times quite the opposite. Officials frequently were dismayed by "improper" households: men and women lived together without being legally married, women gave birth to children who were legally "bastards," faithless men abandoned women and children to manage for themselves, women clustered together to raise children as an extended household with no adult males present, former bound servants and slaves lived lives unregulated by "proper" masters. While town leaders often tolerated such households within their community, they could—and did—intervene to remove the offenders if the household caused complaint.

In eighteenth-century New England, the terms "family" and "household" were used nearly interchangeably, referring to all who lived together as a unit based as much on economic survival as on affection and kinship ties. A traditional Anglo-American family was ideally headed by a man and often consisted of more than parents and children or stepchildren; it might include other kin, bound servants and slaves, and hired hands or day laborers. Authorities looked upon these household members as part of a man's *family*. One newly arrived resident reported to Providence authorities "that he *hath in family* himself, his wife, four children and a Negro girl." Another was fined for "having received *into his family*" a transient woman without notifying the town council.[1]

This chapter opens with the narratives of the Pike and Butler families, which were organized along fairly traditional, patriarchal lines, just as half of transient families were. In these cases, it was not household organization but poverty and illness of particular family members that prompted town officials to take action. These stories are included because they illustrate how some families coped with poverty, transience, and the threat of being warned out. By acting as a coherent unit, they demonstrated an important line of defense for those without a legal settlement: relying on those who constituted family.

The rest of the narratives in this chapter focus on families whose unorthodox organization drew official attention and resulted in warning out. Families who did not fit the traditional patriarchal pattern were numerous, making up fully half of the transient households in this study. At the heart of some of these families were a man and a woman whom I have termed "mates": authorities recognized them as a couple, but since the pair could not produce evidence of a legal marriage, they did not merit the protection of a shared legal settlement. This was the case with the parents of Susannah Guinea (Chapter 1), and it was the case with Judah Hazard Wanton and Lambo Wanton (this chapter). These couples may have considered their relationships binding, but however strong their personal commitment, it carried no official weight and could not prevent forced separation through warning out.

Other households had at their heart a woman who managed a family without the economic and social support of a husband. Sometimes these women claimed to be married, other times not, but all took responsibility for children and grandchildren who lived within their households. Indian women Mary Fowler and Sarah Gardner (this chapter) each bore many children without officials accepting their mates as legal spouses. Wait Godfrey (this chapter) also produced a large number of children with "husbands" who were always absent, but officials took the children from her and placed them as indentured servants so speedily that she never managed an extensive household as Fowler and Gardner did.

Still other transient families centered around mates in relationships that had neither legal protection nor social advantages. Abigail Foster accused Christopher Stocker of bigamy and had a detailed story to back up her claim. Nathaniel Whitaker never stayed long in any relationship, being given to two-timing his wife or current mate. Robert Fuller ran away from his wife and children when they were at a moment of great need. Thomas Field became so abusive toward his ex-wife during their divorce that he was jailed and then forcibly transported by officials.

Transient women in nonpatriarchal families such as these posed a problem for authorities whose primary objective was to put people where they "belonged." If councilmen were uncertain of a woman's status as wife, they were also unsure where her hometown was. Clerks added many an "alias" to a woman's name in the record to indicate that a mate rela-

tionship fell short of legal certainty. "Mary Fowler *alias* Cummock" had
been James Fowler's mate for decades, but the relationship did not qualify
as marriage under Anglo-American law; consequently the clerk added her
mother's name—Cummock—as the parent whose hometown might be
liable for any charges Mary Fowler incurred. Similarly, "Margaret Bowler
alias Margaret Fairchild" (Chapter 4) and "Judah Wanton *alias* Hazard"
(this chapter) indicated official doubts that these women were legally married; the names of their former masters (Major Fairchild, Jeffrey Hazard)
were included to indicate men whose towns could be held responsible for
the women's welfare.

The variety and number of nonpatriarchal families underscore how
frequently transient women were thrown on their own resources. Half of
the transient heads of household questioned by Rhode Island authorities
were women, many of whom were separated from their mates and raising
children single-handedly (see Appendix Table A1, p. 206). That separation
often made them vulnerable to economic distress and family dissolution,
for local officials stayed alert to signs of need and rapidly intervened in
moments of crisis to place the children in more "proper" households as
indentured servants (Chapter 1).

Of course, not all nonpatriarchal families were an economic or social
problem either for authorities or for the persons within them. Women
sometimes lived separately from their mates out of choice, as each one
pursued a particular livelihood. In southeastern New England, poor white
men and men of color often found jobs as soldiers and sailors, occupations that necessitated their long absences. Other poor men went off to the
western or northern frontier to carve out a rough homestead before taking
along the rest of the family. The women who anchored the families and
raised the children often grouped themselves together for mutual support.
Patience Havens (Chapter 4), Sarah Gardner, and Mary Fowler each
formed extended households with their adult daughters and their children. Some women ran boardinghouses for other women without their
mates, as did Margaret Bowler (Chapter 4). And aging widows sometimes
shared living space and expenses, a household form that officials themselves occasionally followed when arranging poor relief, as with Elizabeth
Stonehouse (Chapter 5).

The wide range of nonpatriarchal household forms revealed in the
transient narratives shows how traditional bonds of obligation and depen-
dence were beginning to break down as the basis for household formation

in southeastern New England in the latter part of the eighteenth century. People were being cast adrift from their former connections to propertied families, they were moving away from the places where they had once been rooted by custom and bondage, and they were creating new ways to organize their households to achieve economic competency and social support. Their efforts were not always successful, resulting instead in the unwelcome attentions of authorities who had different ideas of what constituted proper families.

Clarke, William, and Sanford Pike

The Pike family illustrates how transient poor families, not tied to a community by ownership of land, moved around the region as kin and work connections drew them. For William Pike and his sons, opportunity did not lie to the west or north or on the sparsely populated frontier. Their resourcefulness showed in marriage to women with family resources, and in geographic mobility that took them from one seaport town to another in order to take advantage of kinship connections and work opportunities. Accordingly, three generations of Pikes moved around southeastern New England, never sojourning far from the sea and always within reach of family.

William Pike was born and raised in Connecticut, but he migrated to Newport around 1720. There he labored as a "cordwainer," a shoemaker who made shoes and boots to order. Although shoemaking was among the lowest-ranking trades, Pike must have plied his craft with special skill or otherwise impressed those for whom he did "bespoke" work, for he prospered enough to marry Anna Clarke, daughter of Henry Clarke, "who owned a real estate in said Newport." This marriage, a source of long-lasting pride in the Pike family, prompted them to name their first son Clarke, conferred the title of "Mr." on both sons in their senior years, and became a ready reference point in the narrative of William Pike Jr. decades later. In 1782, William Pike—by then in his eighties—was still in Newport, still identified as a "cordwainer," and still heading his own household. His small family included himself, two elderly women (his wife and her sister, perhaps), and one "Negro" servant or slave. A shoemaker who had his own servant or slave must have had access to family money, and it seems likely Anna Clarke Pike was the source of such money.

Clarke Pike and William Pike Jr.—William and Anna Pike's two sons—grew up in Newport in the 1720s and 1730s. William Jr., at least, received enough literacy training that he and his son after him could sign their names. And both sons received practical training in some marketable skill. Whatever resources their mother brought to the marriage did not eliminate the need for the boys to be bound out as apprentices, but such binding came late and was short-lived. William Jr. did not begin his apprenticeship until he was sixteen years old, in 1741. The trade he learned is not mentioned in the record but was most likely his father's own business of shoemaking. William Jr.'s master, John Perry, died about a year after the indenture began, at which point Perry's widow "sold his indentures" to another John Perry, probably a kinsman, who lived in Swansea, Massachusetts. For another eighteen months William Jr. continued his indenture in Swansea, and then master Perry "gave up said indentures" for some undisclosed reason. William Jr. continued to live and work in Swansea, and then he followed in his father's footsteps by marrying above his station; he "intermarried with the sister" of his former master.

William Pike Jr. and his wife lived in Swansea for "about twelve years" and then "removed" to neighboring Bristol, Rhode Island around 1760; there apparently were no children born of the union. In Bristol Pike's wife died, and Pike married a woman named Martha. William and Martha had two sons: Sanford, born in Bristol in 1763, and a younger boy. The year that Sanford was born, Pike and his new wife and son moved back to Newport; Pike exchanged the family connections of his first wife for those of his birth family. For seven years he and his family lived close to his parents in Newport, and then, in 1770, they moved to Providence. He may have been drawn by other family connections; his brother Clarke Pike was in Providence and so was another kinsman—Jonathan Pike, who was respectable enough to be named master of a twelve-year-old indentured servant in 1785 and to be named joint guardian of son-in-law Gaius Davis when the man became "disordered in his mind" and was declared "non compos mentis" in 1786. Jonathan Pike may have been the family anchor for William and Clarke Pike in Providence.

Clarke and William Pike Jr. found work and community in Providence for twenty years. William Jr. and his family—wife Martha and two sons—appear on the 1782 census, but Clarke Pike apparently never married and must have been a boarder in someone else's house. Neither Clarke Pike nor William Pike Jr. was prosperous enough to show up on the tax lists in the 1780s, but they did not show up on the poor-relief lists, either. The family money that had kept William Sr. rooted in Newport did not lift the sons to fully respectable status, but it kept them from falling into abject need.

That all changed in 1790. Clarke Pike was "taken sick" and needed town support. Pike was "in such a situation that his examination cannot be taken," but the council gathered "the best information" they could and determined that Newport was the town with legal responsibility for him. They ordered his removal "as soon as may be," but the illness was more advanced than the councilmen realized; the very next day, Job Danforth was put to work making a twelve-shilling "coffin for Mr. Pike," who had not lived to be taken back to Newport.

Three years later Providence authorities focused on the Pike family again. This time it was Sanford Pike, twenty-seven-year-old son of William Jr., who was in trouble. Five years earlier, Sanford Pike had left his father's household, "intermarried with Sally Tew of Newport," and started his own family. Like his father and grandfather before him, he had produced two sons: five-year-old James and thirty-month-old Henry. In the spring of 1793, Sanford had gotten a serious "sore in his hand" that rendered him "unable to do business" and left "his family in a suffering condition." The overseer of the poor had given him ten shillings "for present relief" and two weeks later another ten shillings because he was "lame and unable to work." Since Sanford Pike was already thus "chargeable" to the town, the councilmen questioned him about his hometown. After hearing his testimony and verifying that neither he nor his father had purchased real estate anywhere, they concluded that Newport was his hometown. The council then questioned sixty-eight-year-old William Pike Jr., perhaps to see whether this father was "of ability" to support his son and grandchildren. These official interviews convinced the councilmen that William Jr. and Sanford had enough resources to render removal unnecessary. Officials recorded their testimonies and ruled that Newport was the responsible town, but they did not warn the men out, as they had done to Clarke Pike three years earlier.

Sanford Pike proved the councilmen right in their judgment. He recovered from his ailments, did not receive any further poor relief, and actually was paid by the town five years later for "services" that he and his wife had provided in "attending" Providence woman Esther Seaver "in the time of her distraction." It seems that Sanford's weeks of illness in 1793 were only a short interlude of need; otherwise, he relied successfully on his own labor and his family connections to sustain him and his household.

Patience and Abner Butler

Patience Butler directed the course of the Butler family, in fact if not in law. When her elderly husband Abner became ill and was not able to fend off the interfering arm of town authorities, Patience set the tone of the family's resistance. She thwarted the councilmen's attempt to get her signature on her testimony, and she organized the disappearance of the family when the town sergeant came looking for them. Assisted by her grown sons and daughter, she was able to avoid a removal for twenty months; in the end, she and her children left in their own time, not at the behest of town authorities.

Patience Borden, the daughter of Richard Borden, was born and raised in her father's hometown—"Freetown in the commonwealth of Massachusetts." She was considerably younger than Abner Butler when she married him in 1771—he was already over forty and she was a young woman. They were married in Abner's hometown, Edgartown, Massachusetts, on the island of Martha's Vineyard; it may have been a second marriage for Abner, for he was well established and "owned a real estate" in Edgartown. The couple had four children in the first ten years of marriage: Thomas, born in 1771, Joseph in 1774, Ruth in 1777, and Jonathan in 1779.

By 1782 the family had relocated to Bristol, Rhode Island, where Abner maintained an independent household and merited an entry in the 1782 census. Clues in the record suggest that he was a miller, a trade that was in demand in every New England community. Sometime in the 1780s the family moved once again, to Providence. The last child, Sarah, was born in 1786, in either Bristol or Providence.

Providence appealed to the Butlers and they settled into a neighborhood; the 1790 census lists all seven members of the family as still living together. By that time, they had rented a windmill and Abner was maintaining his milling business with the assistance of his wife and nearly grown children. They also brought in some income by renting out part of their house; in 1790, the town treasurer paid Abner Butler £2 8s. for "house rent" and other maintenance for Patience Ingraham, an infamous woman whose considerable property had been appropriated and managed by the town council because she had operated a bawdy house and been involved in several unsavory incidents of rioting and other unruly behavior. That the Butlers served as Ingraham's landlord suggests an association between the two Patiences that would shed some light on Patience Butler's later hostility toward town officials.

The Butler family became of particular concern to Providence authorities in 1793, when Abner, now over sixty years old, became ill. Patience, however, was in her forties, and not in the least frail, so rather than question Abner in his condition the councilmen summoned his wife to speak for him. While they did not question the accuracy of the information she provided about her family, they did object to her attitude: "Patience Butler, after the preceding examination was taken and read to her in the presence of this council and numbers of others present acknowledged the same to be true, and being required to sign the same, utterly refused to do it." Since they could not intimidate Patience into signing the document, three of the councilmen had to make a special trip to Abner's bedside to get his account, which (fortunately) corroborated his wife's.

The councilmen named Edgartown as the family's legal settlement and ordered that a warrant be prepared for them to be transported "as soon as they can conveniently be removed." But Abner's health made it impossible to send away the entire family at that moment, so two weeks later the council amended the warrant: Patience and the five children were to be removed "immediately" to Edgartown; Abner would be moved "as soon as his health will admit." Then a difficulty arose over finding transportation to Martha's Vineyard, and the council let the matter lapse for over a year, suggesting that there was no urgent need in the Butler family and that officials were content to let the family remain until another crisis occurred.

On 4 August 1794, the council again ordered the entire family to be removed to Edgartown "by water" and stipulated that it should be done "as soon as an opportunity can be found to convey them by water." Within the next few weeks, the removal warrant was carried out—in part. The Providence town sergeant spent ten days "looking after a vessel for the removal of Abner Butler" and making the round trip by which Abner Butler, still frail, was transported to Edgartown; he was handed over to two selectmen there on 12 August. This expensive removal had cost £9 9s. As for Abner's wife and children, they had "eluded the execution" of the order by "absconding beyond the reach of the officer." On 3 November of that year the council ordered the town sergeant to arrest Patience and the children—if he could find them—and "cause them to be confined in the workhouse." There is no record that this order was carried out; Patience Butler and her children seem to have melted out of official sight. They do not appear in the Providence records again.

Patience Butler and her five children may indeed have voluntarily traveled back to Edgartown to be with their elderly and ailing husband and father. However, their initial resistance to removal suggests that they had had good reasons for leaving Edgartown in the first place and were unwilling to go back. Providence seemed to offer them better opportunities for work and community. Patience and Abner may well have worked out how they would resist having the entire family transported back to Edgartown and how Patience and the children would maintain themselves out of sight of town officials. While Abner did not have the strength to fight for his family's freedom of movement, his wife did, and she successfully guided her children through the family's brush with authority.

Judah Hazard Wanton

Judah Hazard Wanton's story illustrates the fragility of the families of former slaves. Although Wanton was released from slavery as an adult, she was not truly free to live where she wished and as she pleased. When she fell into need, she was ordered back to the place where she had once been a slave, and the family she built with another former slave was splintered by the warning out. Poverty and race proved to be constraints as effective as legal slavery.

Sometime in the 1730s, perhaps earlier, Judah was born as a slave child in the household of Jeremiah Hazard, the owner of a large estate in North Kingstown. When Judah was "about three years old," she was relocated to a new household as part of a wedding dowry, "given by the said Hazard to his daughter Mary, who married Jeffrey Hazard," a distant relative and a man of wealth and status in North Kingstown. When the couple married, Jeffrey Hazard assumed legal control of the slave girl Judah, a not uncommon transfer from wife to husband under the legal custom of coverture. Judah grew from toddlerhood to adulthood in Mary Hazard's household, probably alongside Mary's children. In 1753 Judah gave birth to a baby girl, named Urania or "Raney." Raney's father may have been Lambo Wanton, the "Negro" man (and former slave) who was clearly associated with Judah in later years. The birth actually took place in Newport, where Judah apparently had kin. Raney later testified that "as soon as her mother got well of her lying-in sickness, she with her mother went [back] to said Jeffrey Hazard's."

When Jeffrey Hazard died, both Judah and Raney came under the control of his oldest son and heir, Jeremiah Hazard, who transferred them back to his mother Mary Hazard, now a widow. These various transfers, which Judah later traced with care, insured that Judah stayed with Mary Hazard, suggesting that Judah was a prized personal servant to Mary. Mary then "gave" Urania to William Barker, a gentleman of West Greenwich; very likely, Raney was a wedding present to one of Mary's daughters, perhaps perpetuating a family tradition of sending a toddling slave girl to accompany the bride to her new home. As for Judah, she was manumitted by Mary Hazard "three years after she received her" from her son. Perhaps Mary was about to remarry and did not want Judah to become the property of her new husband. Perhaps Mary wished to reward Judah for years of faithful service. In any case, Judah became a free woman sometime in the late 1750s.

Judah Hazard moved to Newport, a place where she had long-term connections and where a strong community of free black people offered shelter and opportunity. After a time, Raney also moved there, her master having allowed her to "go out to work upon shares" in Newport. The language indicates that William Barker hired out his slave girl to work for a household in Newport, and that Raney was allowed to keep some "share" of her earnings while the remainder went back to Barker. Judah and Raney doubtless were reunited in Newport, perhaps living together in rented lodgings and laboring. Judah's presence in the town may have persuaded Barker to grant young Raney the "liberty" to work there, since his slave would be under the supervision of her mother. Both Judah and Raney probably earned their livings as washerwomen or domestic servants in the households of the propertied merchants, landed gentlemen, and other elites who kept substantial houses in Newport. During this time, Judah began her long-term association with Lambo Wanton. After Judah and Raney had lived and worked for many years in the town, "the enemy" arrived and occupied Newport in December 1776. Judah fled the town (as did many others) and moved to Providence; Raney followed within the year.

Providence officials, nearly overwhelmed with a flood of refugees from the British occupation during the Revolutionary War, nevertheless took pains to document the presence of newcomers. These records indicate that Judah Hazard and Lambo Wanton, having relocated together from Newport to Providence, were recognized by officials as mates. They were summoned together to town council to be questioned, and Judah's name was rendered "Judah Wanton alias Hazard." Slavery assigned each member of this small family a different last name—Lambo Wanton, Judah Hazard, Raney Barker—as a perpetual legacy from their former masters.

Judah Wanton, now in her fifties, and Raney Barker, in her mid-twenties, soon fell into difficulties in Providence. Lambo Wanton, who escaped official interrogation, may have been a seafaring man, as were many free men of color in eighteenth-century Providence. His absence at sea may have been what made his mate and her daughter vulnerable to disaster. By January 1780 Judah and Raney had become inmates in Providence's workhouse, where the most destitute lower sort residents lived on town welfare under the management of an overseer. In their eagerness to warn out all the workhouse inmates who had hometowns elsewhere, the Providence councilmen tried to trace Judah's background, even questioning Lambo Wanton's former master, who presumably knew something of Judah's and Raney's histories. Eventually the councilmen questioned the two women directly and under most unusual circumstances. Instead of having some dozen unsavory workhouse inmates crowding into their meeting room, the councilmen sent one of their own number to interview all the transients on-site at the workhouse. Judah proved to be a troublesome witness, refusing to sign her testimony with an "x." The frustrated councilman who conducted the interview wrote this on the document: "The above named Judah refused to sign the above examination, assigning for reason that she never did sign any writing." He then took his dozen written testimonies back to council meeting.

After reading her testimony and hearing of Judah Wanton's behavior, the councilmen ordered that she be removed to North Kingstown; they named her "a person of bad character and reputation," a judgment that appears to have been prompted by her refusal to sign her testimony. The council sent twenty-seven-year-old Raney Barker to West Greenwich because she also was deemed "a person of bad character and reputation" as well as someone who was "likely to become chargeable" to Providence. Under settlement law, these women technically "belonged" to the hometowns of their masters, whose names they bore.

There is no record of Judah's fate, but a Providence constable later submitted his bill for "removing" Raney to West Greenwich and delivering her to one of the overseers of the poor there. Very likely the same thing happened to Judah, despite her remarkable assertiveness in refusing to sign a document written by an official she had no reason to trust. One wonders if this mother, daughter, and father were able to reunite and maintain a household together, despite official pressures to divide and dislocate them. Their former slave status had pursued them into freedom, visited them with poverty, and rendered their family life fragile.

Mary Cummock Fowler and Mary Fowler Champlin

Mary Cummock Fowler, "Indian woman," and her adult daughter Mary Fowler Champlin made it clear that Anglo-American conventions of marriage were not firmly in place everywhere in New England. Both women were brought before the South Kingstown council and questioned about their mates so that officials might determine where their hometowns were. Both Marys described long-term spousal relationships that they realized did not conform to the marital institutions of whites. The councilmen certainly agreed that these were not marriages within *their* meaning of the term, and they carefully appended "alias" to the women's names to indicate that their attachments did not have the protection of Anglo-American law.

The two Marys had come to the attention of the councilmen in April 1796, when Mary Fowler Champlin and her children appeared to be in great need; the councilmen ordered the overseer of the poor to provide "suitable necessaries" for the family while they investigated where they belonged. They were summoned to town council at the same time and questioned together, indicating that they had formed a household and that the elder Mary might shed some light on the legal settlement of her needy grandchildren.

"Mary Fowler alias Mary Cummock"—the elder Mary—had no written documents of her birth, her marriage, or her children's births; she relied on oral tradition in the manner of her people. Her mother, Sarah Cummock, was "one of the tribe of the Indians in Charlestown." Mary herself was born in South Kingstown, "as she has been informed," and she, in the manner of so many Indian children, grew up in "an apprenticeship to Caleb Gardner Esq. of this town by indenture and served out all her apprenticeship." After becoming free, Mary lived with James Fowler, "a mustee" man, for thirty years and "had ten children by him," but "never was married to him in the manner white people are married in these parts."

The South Kingstown councilmen designated Mary Fowler's adult daughter as "Mary Fowler Jr. alias Champlin alias Mary Cummock," pointing to the younger Mary's father, husband, and mother in that order. Mary Fowler Jr. was also born in South Kingstown, "as she has been informed," but she escaped the usual fate of indentured servitude. As an adult, however, she forged a trail similar to her mother's, in that she "hath lived with a person of the name of John Champlin, a mustee man, as his wife eleven years . . . and has had six children by him, but never was married to him according to the form used by the white people in these parts." Six years earlier, the 1790 census had shown John Champlin, a "Negro" man, living in South Kingstown with four other nonwhite "free persons"—Mary and three children, in all likelihood—in his household. Three children had been added since then, and the condition of the youngest ones was of particular concern to town officials.

Settling the extralegal status of these long-term partnerships still did not clarify the location of the two Marys' legal settlements and left the councilmen confused about where to send the needy children. Perhaps Mary Cummock Fowler belonged to the Narragansett tribe, or to the town of Charlestown, as her mother did, or to the town of South Kingstown, as her former master did. Mary Fowler Champlin, it seemed, might belong to South Kingstown, where she had been born, but she had lived in Exeter long enough to give birth to two children there. And in any case where did these women's mates belong and could the children legitimately be sent there? Unable to determine where to send the two women and their children, the councilmen decided to let the matter drop, by "continuing" the investigation to a future date, which never arrived.

One year after the examination, in 1797, Mary Cummock Fowler (already the mother of ten children and surely at least in her middle forties) gave birth to a child whom officials labeled a "bastard"; when the boy was four years old the councilmen ordered that he be bound out as an indentured servant. In a generational footnote, in 1838, the South Kingstown council bound out as an indentured servant a girl named Lydia Champlin, "daughter of a colored woman, late Mary Champlin, since married to a man whose name is unknown." Lydia Champlin's mother may have been Mary Fowler Champlin, who could have given birth to a child in the early 1820s; it is just as likely, however, that Lydia's mother was the namesake daughter of Mary Fowler Champlin, and that the girl bound out in 1838 was the granddaughter of Mary Fowler Champlin and the great-granddaughter of Mary Cummock Fowler. Like the names that parents passed on from one generation to another, indenture was visited upon the grandchildren and great-grandchildren of children earmarked for servitude.

Sarah Gardner and Her Daughters

Sarah Gardner, "Indian woman," is a fine example of a transient whose steady persistence in returning enabled her to carve out a life for herself and her family in a town where officials did not want her. Drawn to opportunities for work and community in Providence, she moved herself and her large family of children there in the late 1760s, and although town authorities ordered her out on five different occasions, she returned four times and continued to maintain a home there. Her household, which was always bursting with a changing mix of growing and grown children and grandchildren, suggests that Sarah Gardner adapted the traditional native role of matriarch so as to govern and protect a family struggling to survive culturally and economically in a society dominated by whites.

Sarah Gardner was born on 16 January 1730, the daughter of Thomas Gardner, an Indian man who, she later recalled, "owned a house and land" in Warwick, Rhode Island. As was the case with most Indian youngsters, Sarah was bound out as a child to work and live in a more prosperous household; she "served her time" with David Greene, one of Rhode Island's wealthiest and largest colonial landlords. After she gained her freedom, probably around age nineteen or twenty, Gardner built an independent life for herself.

Although she never married according to white convention, Sarah Gardner bore twelve children in the 1750s, '60s, and '70s. Eight of them were still living in 1780: Mary, Margaret, Kit, Thomas, William, Sarah, James, and Lydia. All Gardner's children were born in Warwick, and she raised them there for a number of years, probably with the support of her own extended family and others in the native community that still survived in Warwick. It is also likely that she had an Indian mate who supported the children offstage and out of sight of white officials. Only once did town authorities intervene in this household that appeared to have no husband and father present. In 1762, when Gardner had seven children and seemed particularly needy, the councilmen ordered that the four oldest be formally bound as indentured servants to the men with whom they had been informally placed by their mother, thus giving the masters official control over and responsibility for the youngsters. The councilmen also arranged for the overseers of the poor to rent "some house" for Gardner and the three youngest children "to live in this winter," lest they "become chargeable to the town" in the cold lean months of the year. The provision of a house suggests that Gardner did not live in English-style structures as a matter of course, but rather maintained a more traditional native wigwam or lodge, as did many native people living near whites.

In 1767, when she was thirty-seven years old, Gardner decided to uproot herself from Warwick. She and the children living with her moved briefly to Smithfield and then on to Providence in 1768 or 1769. Perhaps she was drawn by a desire to be near the unnamed son who had been bound out to a "Mr. Sterry of Providence" in 1762 and was nearing his age of freedom. Very likely she was also attracted by the growing community of free people of color there and by the potential for jobs for her many children. By 1770, her Providence household included "six children," some of whom had completed their indentures or had otherwise been released from them.

Sarah Gardner and her family were not welcome in Providence. When the councilmen first questioned her, in March 1770, they ordered "a warrant to remove the said Sarah and six children to the town of Warwick" if they did not leave "in three weeks." But Gardner returned to Providence and in February 1772 was found "in direct violation of the law . . . returned again to this town." The councilmen ordered her to leave once again and ordered her to be "publicly whipped eleven stripes on her naked back by the town sergeant" if she was found in the town after 10 April. This two-month allowance of time suggests that there was no immediate material need in the family, rather that someone influential had prompted the warning-out by complaining about them; it also suggests that authorities were aware of the native rhythms of Gardner's life and did not want to force the family into moving until warmer spring weather had arrived.

After this 1772 warn-out from Providence, Gardner remained in Warwick long enough for officials there to become concerned about one of her sons and take action. In June 1773 the councilmen bound out William to a man in Coventry. At sixteen years of age William Gardner would have made a prize servant. An indenture at that age was unlikely to indicate a child's need for shelter, food, and clothing; rather, it suggests that William had offended neighbors and was being bound out as a method of punishment or control.

After William left the household, Gardner moved back to Providence with some of her other children and resumed residence there. At this point she apparently also bound out her son James to Providence man William Bowen. In October 1778 James ran away from his master, and Bowen advertised in the *Providence Gazette* for "James Gardner, an indented Indian servant, about 17 years of age." James, born in 1771, would have been one of the youngest of Sarah Gardner's twelve children—she named him next to last in her list of children "now living" in 1780. Even if Bowen did not know where his servant was—"It is supposed he is gone towards Boston"—Sarah at least had enough information about him to know that he was alive. The family network doubtless formed a refuge for the runaway servant, and he may very well have been living in Providence when his master thought him headed into Massachusetts.

In 1780 Gardner once again came to the attention of Providence officials. Rather than whipping her in consequence of their 1772 dictate, the councilmen simply questioned her, ascertained that she had eight children "now living," and then officially declared "the said Sarah Gardner and all her said children" were not inhabitants of Providence. She was questioned in company with several other women that day, and it appears they resided near each other or at least were associated with each other in the councilmen's minds. The question of a "bad house" seems to loom over these interviews. A month later the council reconsidered their tolerant attitude—perhaps because they had received a specific complaint by neighbors—and officially warned out Gardner and the children who were living with her, "daughters Mary, Margaret, Sarah and Lydia," all of whom were "of bad character and reputation." The language here clearly suggests that Gardner and her daughters were suspected of prostitution.

If the Gardners left, they soon returned. In July 1782, when a mob "pulled down" Margaret Fairchild Bowler's house (see her narrative in Chapter 4), the council also summoned Sarah Gardner to be questioned along with the inhabitants of Bowler's house, all of whom had been accused of "whoring and misbehaving themselves." Gardner, it seems, was sufficiently associated with Bowler's house and occupation to justify an official appearance to answer questions about the riot. Six weeks later Gardner "and her four daughters" were officially warned out to Warwick again, very likely as part of the cleanup in the wake of the riot, an effort requested by the deputy governor, who wanted "other bad houses [to be] surprised" and "order and virtue" to be restored to the town.

Gardner returned once again, but she and her family lived quietly for five years, without attracting council attention again. Then, in 1787, the council reopened Sarah Gardner's case, probably in response to a complaint. The council issued a warrant for the removal of Sarah and her daughters Mary, Margaret, and Lydia, all to Warwick. Lydia escaped the net, but on 17 October 1787, "Sarah Gardner the mother and Mary Gardner and Margaret Gardner, her daughters" and "her grandson Christopher" were all delivered to one of Warwick's overseers of the poor.

With this fifth removal, Sarah Gardner, then fifty-seven years old, apparently ended her career as irritant to the Providence council. She did not appear before Providence authorities again, nor does she appear in the Warwick records. Her daughter Lydia, who had continued to live in Providence, was finally warned out in 1796, but Sarah herself is not mentioned.

For her twenty years in Providence, Sarah Gardner was clearly persona non grata. Not only did she have a large family, some of whom were clearly causing complaint among neighbors, but she herself persisted in returning after being warned out and consorting with other women who were of concern to the town council. In two instances she was questioned in the company of other women of color, and the implication in the record is that these women had formed a community of support. But however strong her common cause with her neighbors, Gardner had greater common cause with her own children. She was never alone in her removals and returns, but always in company of daughters and grandchildren. The adult Gardner women seemed to anchor a household that provided refuge and sustenance for others in the family, such as runaway James, who never were in town long enough to attract official attention. Sarah Gardner and her adult daughters were the most visible, but clearly not the only ones, in this large and resourceful family.

Wait Godfrey alias Whitney alias Grafft

Rhode Island town officials wanted to know the marital status of Wait Godfrey Whitney Grafft, but they were never sure they had it figured out—hence the "alias" between her names in the official record. This concern was more than just a passion for order in their communities and in their books; officials needed to know whether she was legitimately married because those marriages may have resulted in new legal settlements for Wait. Furthermore, each child she bore (there were a goodly number) prompted an official inquiry about the father, the legal settlement, and then arrangements for poor relief or an indenture. Wait complicated things further because she "misrepresented facts" and gave different versions of her history at different times and places. While it is possible that she was genuinely confused and gave erroneous information with honest intentions, it is more likely that she sensed the advantages of supplying information strategically in order to help influence her fate at the hands of authorities.

Wait Godfrey was born in the middle 1740s in East Greenwich, where her father, John Godfrey, had a legal settlement. At her first interrogation by the Providence councilmen in 1780, Wait reported that her parents died when she was young, but her father was certainly alive when Wait moved on her own to Providence in 1765; in fact, he was warned out of Warwick the next year. At her second examination she reported that her father had moved to Warwick when she was six years old, in the early 1750s, and that she had lived with him in Warwick "about five or six years."

At age eleven or twelve, when many young people were bound out as apprentices, Wait moved to the first of many places where she would work as a young servant in her teenage years. First she was "some little time" with Edmund Andrews in East Greenwich. Then she was "bound to Miss Tanner, widow to William Tanner, in North Kingstown," for "some time." Then Tanner "signed over" the indentures to Deliverance Cleveland of West Greenwich for "two or three years." Then she was sent to Joseph Nichols's house in East Greenwich for "about six months." Then she spent "two or three years" with Caleb Allen on Prudence Island in Narragansett

Bay. Finally, in 1765, she moved to Providence and "lived a considerable time in the family of Benjamin Lindsay," very likely as a domestic servant.

In May 1773, when she was around twenty-eight years old, Wait Godfrey went back to East Greenwich—to be with relatives, perhaps—and there had a daughter she named Polly, the "bastard" child of a man named Pearce. In August 1777, when she was around thirty-two years old, she gave birth to a second "bastard" child—George, son of a man named Parker—in Providence. During the Revolutionary War she met and "married" Lemuel Whitney, a soldier in the Continental Army. She seemed quite clear about the legitimacy of the marriage, reporting that it was "published in Mr. Snow's meeting in Providence," that it took place on 15 February 1779, and that it was performed by "Major John Porter of Col. Wigglesworth's Regiment in the Continental Army." Furthermore, she reported that her husband had been born and raised in Sudbury, Massachusetts, where he probably still had a legal settlement. After the marriage she went back to Providence, and in December 1779 she had another baby, apparently the legitimate son and namesake of Lemuel Whitney. Her husband disappeared into army life and never surfaced again.

Now with three young children and no husband, Wait Whitney came to the attention of the Providence overseers of the poor. She was brought before the council in March 1780, when baby Lemuel was just three months old. Apparently she had some means of supporting herself and her children, for the council did not warn her out; they did not even make a determination about her place of legal settlement. Perhaps they wanted to gather more information from other sources. But Wait took it upon herself to return to East Greenwich without a removal order; perhaps she found that a more congenial place to raise her children. Soon she added another child to her growing family: son John was born in East Greenwich in the summer of 1782. During the lying-in period, when she needed assistance, the overseer supplied her "with sundry articles as she may want, to the amount of £2 8s. real money."

When baby John was about six months old, Wait Whitney seemed to be living on the edge financially, and the East Greenwich councilmen assessed the claims she had on the town. After questioning her in January 1783, they concluded that her hometown was in Warwick—perhaps her father had established a settlement there when she was a youngster—and they ordered her to be sent there. They also ordered her children to different locations. At this point her oldest child, ten-year-old Polly, was no

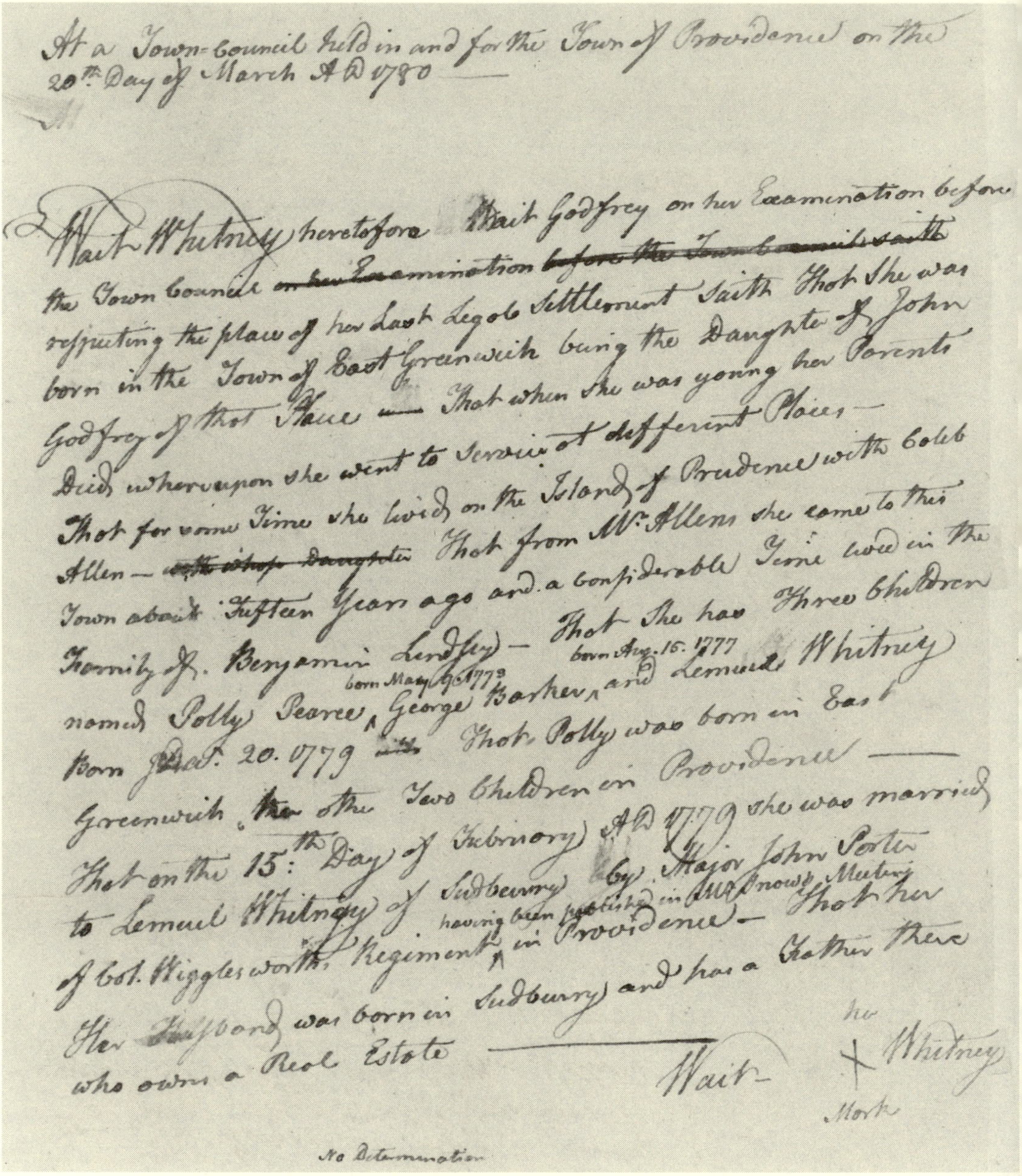

Figure 2. Wait Godfrey Whitney left this mark on her first testimony given before the Providence town authorities on 20 March 1780. Town officials simultaneously questioned Whitney and Sarah Gardner; the two women were probably neighbors. Source: PTP 5:40, neg. no. RHi (x3) 9398. Courtesy of the Rhode Island Historical Society.

longer living with her mother and was probably in an indenture, as Wait herself had been when she was a youngster. Son George Parker was to be removed to Providence, where he belonged by virtue of his having been born there as a "bastard" child. Son Lemuel was to be removed to Warwick with his mother, apparently because his father's legal settlement was ambiguous. And baby John, having been born in East Greenwich, would stay there as one of the poor of the town. Not willing to have her family split up, Whitney immediately went to the Providence town council and asked for "a certificate acknowledging the said two children to be inhabitants of this town," so that she and her sons could live together in Warwick without being warned out.

At this point Wait gave some indication that her marriage to Lemuel Whitney was bogus. The Providence officials declared that "doubts have arisen respecting the validity" of her marriage. Instead of trying to find Whitney and determine his legal settlement, they simply shouldered the responsibility of the son, resolving that "the said two children [George and Lemuel] be and they hereby are acknowledged as inhabitants of this town." But the East Greenwich councilmen refused to allow the boys to stay, even with a certificate; three weeks later they ordered the town sergeant "to carry George Parker and Lemuel Whitney, sons of Wait Godfrey alias Whitney to the town of Providence, that being their legal place of settlement." Since Wait indicated that she would follow her sons to Providence, they also granted a settlement certificate for "John Godfrey alias John Whitney," the baby then nearing one year old, "owning it a proper inhabitant of this town."

Since East Greenwich officials would not let her Providence-born sons live in their town, Wait had to return to Providence to keep the three boys together. But there her family was split up despite her efforts. As soon as she arrived in Providence in July 1783, the councilmen ordered Lemuel and George bound out as indentured servants, the usual fate of poor and illegitimate children whom authorities wanted to place in more proper households.

Wait lived a year without incident in Providence, but then ran afoul of the Providence councilmen, probably because she was once again pregnant and "likely to become chargeable." The councilmen referred to their earlier 1780 interrogation of Wait and concluded that East Greenwich was the legal settlement of this "spinster"; they sent her there, in the care of constable Rufus Sprague, who delivered her to Andrew Boyd, East Greenwich overseer of the poor, in August 1784. East Greenwich sent her back and advised the Providence councilmen of their error. On 1 November, the Providence councilmen ordered Wait removed to Warwick, her "real" place of legal settlement. The removal was delayed for two months, perhaps because Wait gave birth and could not be moved for a while. In January 1785 she was finally delivered to Warwick.

Wait seemed determined to live in Providence. By June 1786 she had returned once again, and once again was about to give birth. This time she represented herself as married to the father of the child she was about to deliver—someone whose last name was Grafft—and the Providence clerk rendered her name "Wait Godfrey alias Wait Whitney alias Wait Grafft." The councilmen, noting that she had "misrepresented facts" about her history, ordered her removed to Warwick "immediately." This quick action had the desired result: baby Sophia was born in Warwick.

Wait, who would have been forty years old at the time of Sophia's birth, stayed in Warwick, perhaps tired of moving around. In 1787 her son John was taken from her by the East Greenwich town council and bound out to William Weaver. She did not follow him to East Greenwich, for she had yet another child, Elisabeth, on the way. Sophia and Elisabeth were bound out as indentured servants by the Warwick authorities, in 1789 and 1790 respectively. Sophia's indenture was complicated by the fact that someone (Wait?) "misrepresented" the child's age to prospective master Bennett Low, who thought he was getting a servant who was nearly four years old, instead of nearly three years old, as Sophia actually was. Until children were seven or eight years old, they could do little significant labor to contribute to the household economy, and masters who took on orphaned and bastard children as young as Sophia usually were paid a "premium" out of the town treasury to cover the costs of supporting the child until it could "earn its keep." Within a month of taking Sophia into his home, Low realized that the premium he received would not cover the cost of feeding, clothing, and housing her until she was capable of useful labor, and he demanded that the indentures be canceled. The council then upped the premium substantially to attract another master for the child.

In 1798 Wait made it into the Warwick records once again. Now fifty-two years old, Wait shed her "troublesome" image and performed a useful service for town officials. She took in ailing Susannah Booth, a poor Warwick inhabitant who was being supported by the town, for five weeks; thus Wait's last recorded official act was to receive $2 in payment from town officials.

Nowhere in the many references to Wait Godfrey in the town records of Providence, East Greenwich, and Warwick is there any hint that she was suspected of prostitution. Yet she gave birth to at least six children and there are suggestions in the record of several others. In 1771, for example, a little girl named Susanna Godfrey was bound out as an indentured servant by the East Greenwich town council. Wait would have been around twenty years old when the child was born (in the mid-1760s), and that may very well have been her firstborn, but she never mentioned Susanna in her three examinations by authorities. In any case, giving birth to at least six illegitimate children right under the noses of authorities is an impressive record. Officials never bound out Wait to a master who would keep her to work and curb her sexual activity, nor did they censure her and warn her out because of "lewd" or "evil" behavior. She seemed to get into relationships that at first promised some kind of permanence but never delivered on that promise.

When Wait was in her fifties, her hometown authorities—who knew the sweep of her life—represented her simply as "Wait Godfrey" in the official record. Her supposed marriages were forgotten, her children were bound out in indentures, and all the "alias" terms had disappeared from her name. She had produced at least six children who were scattered around the state, bearing different names and working in the homes of different masters, but in the end she herself was simply "single woman" of Warwick.

Christopher Stocker and Abigail Harris

Abigail Harris came to Providence in 1786, looking for the man who had called himself "William Foster" when he pretended to marry her six years earlier. She found the person she was looking for, but that man now called himself Christopher Stocker, was now legally married to someone else, and firmly denied that he had ever pretended to marry Abigail Harris. The uproar caused by Harris's accusations and Stocker's denials landed both of them before officials in what must have been one of the most interesting council meetings of the year. The image is compelling: a warm August day, with windows thrown open; councilmen gathering in a room at a conveniently located inn for their usual meeting on the first Monday of the month; a lineup of nine transients to question and perhaps to warn out;

heated testimony from Harris and Stocker, the fourth and fifth transients to be examined, by now in the middle of the day; customers at the inn and passersby straining to hear the questions and answers. In 1786, bigamy was a rare and interesting scandal, and the Harris-Stocker dispute must have provided dinner conversation for many days.

Abigail Harris told her story first. She "was born in Newent, [Connecticut] about fifteen miles from New London" sometime around 1750. Her father, James Harris, moved from Newent to New London "when she was very young" and lived there "about twenty-five years." Still unmarried in her middle twenties, she moved west to the town of Saybrook, on the Connecticut River, to "keep house" for Capt. James Harris, a mariner who was "a relation of hers." In 1780, while housekeeping for Captain Harris, she met and "married a person who called his name William Foster." Her hope of husband and family vanished quickly, however, for her new husband "soon after [the marriage] took all the property she had and ran away and left her." For six years "she made constant inquiry after him," but learned nothing until July 1786, when she "heard he was in Providence and went by the name of Christopher Stocker and that he now lives with a woman who has taken his name." Accompanied by two "Irishmen" who had recently arrived in the United States, she made her way to Providence, "expecting to obtain some support and assistance" from Stocker. She had arrived "yesterday" and was able to "see" Stocker at his dwelling "near the millbridge," but had "made no settlement with him" as yet.

Stocker then told his story. He "was born in New-Castle, in Northumberland County in England" in 1751. He did not come from wealth or privilege and received no specialized training. Until he was sixteen he "worked sometime at the farming business," probably as a farmhand, and perhaps in a servitude contract. At age sixteen, he "joined the British army," just in time to participate in the revolutionary crisis in North America. In 1774 he "came to North America with the British troops" under General Gage; in 1776 his unit, "the 43rd British Regiment," was stationed in Newport. On 25 April 1777, he "deserted from that regiment at Newport and passed Howland's Ferry and joined the Americans."

For six months after his defection from the British line, Stocker "tarried" in Providence and then, in November 1777, he "enlisted into the American Army," collecting a "bounty" from and fulfilling a quota for the town of Swansea, Massachusetts. He claimed to have "served about six years" in the army and to have been "discharged" in 1783, "peace having taken place." But when the councilmen pressed him about his service record he admitted that he left the army for "about two years" from 1779 to 1781, when he "went to sea in a privateer fitted out from New London," following a course taken by many ablebodied men who were lured away from army service by the hope of sharing in prize money from captured enemy ships. During this hiatus, Stocker "assumed the name of William Foster," and it was then that he met Abigail Harris, who lived in the seafaring town of Saybrook, not far from New London.

This much did Stocker tell the Providence councilmen in 1786. He might have said much more. His service record obligingly offers a physical description of him—five feet, nine inches tall, "light" complexion, and "black" hair—and also reveals that he had a notorious career of "repeated desertion and reenlisting" and "changing his name." His two-year disappearance to go privateering was only one of many such deceptions. Under the name Christopher Stocker he enlisted for Boston early in the war, deserted, and later resurfaced and enlisted for Swansea; military officials eventually realized that there were other enlistments under other names such as "William Foster." When his commanding officers caught on to what he was doing, they court-martialed him and sentenced him to "100 lashes, with twenty-five lashes administered on each of four successive mornings." His American military career developed no more favorably than his British career had.

After being discharged from the military in 1783, Stocker moved back to Providence, where he secured jobs of "common labor" in the busy port city; in 1785 he appeared on Providence's tax valuation, but with so little property that no value was set beside it. He married, this time legally, and seemed prepared to settle down. And then Abigail Harris "Foster" appeared.

After hearing Abigail Harris and Christopher Stocker tell their tales, the councilmen warned them both out of Providence. Since Harris was from Connecticut, where the supposed marriage had taken place, and Stocker was from Massachusetts, Providence officials were under no obligation to judge the validity of the couple's union. In this case, Providence was simply the site where a Massachusetts-Connecticut squabble was aired. The councilmen gave Harris "one week" to leave voluntarily for Newent, her birthplace. Stocker they judged to be "not of good fame and reputation" and ordered him out immediately.

Abigail Harris complied and left Providence; she does not appear again in the town's records. Having located Stocker and unloaded some portion of six years' anger, she apparently found other ways of making him pay for his fraudulent behavior. Stocker, however, persisted in his efforts to live in Providence. When forcibly removed from Providence, he went to Swansea, but they "refuse[d] to receive him" and disputed Providence's decision to send him there; perhaps they felt no obligation to him, since he had taken their bounty money and then deserted the army before he completed his tour of duty. Stocker then "went to New York," but things did not go well there, either, "circumstances not permitting him to live there"; perhaps his reputation had preceded him. Exactly one year after he had been ejected from Providence, Christopher Stocker came back.

The Providence councilmen were not inclined to be lenient with Stocker. As soon as they heard of his return, they ordered the town sergeant "to make diligent search" for this unwelcome resident and "commit him to the cage in the workhouse," a special cell for troublemakers. After that, he was to be whipped or fined and removed once again. Two months later, from some undisclosed location, Stocker sent a petition to the Providence town council. First he apologized for his return to Providence: he had "supposed the objections to his living in Providence were removed," since his legal wife lived there and since Abigail Harris "had no legal title to him, neither could she produce any." After a year of exile, he "ventured to return to Providence in hopes he might be permitted to continue there, as long as he behaved in a becoming manner, and there appeared no danger of his becoming a town charge." Second, he pled that he needed to be in Providence for his very livelihood. He was "extremely unhappy" about leaving town, because only there could he pursue the work he knew how to do—"common labor, or on board of vessels, or following the seas." Outside Providence, with its port work opportunities, he was hard pressed to find a job, since he was "unacquainted with farming and has not any trade whereby he might obtain an honest living." Returning to England was impossible because on that side of the Atlantic he was considered a deserter. Finally, he appealed to the Providence councilmen's pride, praising the "civility formerly received" there and declaring that he was "peculiarly attached" to the town and that his "wife's relations" lived there. He promised to be "a peaceable inhabitant" and "behave himself agreeable to the laws of the town and state." If Providence authorities checked back on Stocker's testimony a year before, they would have found that he had claimed to have "worked sometime at the farming business before he joined the British army." Stocker, it seems, had a little trouble keeping his stories straight. But, in any case, the seasoned Providence councilmen were not easily taken in by a hard-luck appeal. They voted that his petition be "not received."

That was not the end of the story, however. Stocker did return to Providence eventually and apparently conducted himself sufficiently "peaceably" to persuade the councilmen that he should be permitted to stay. The 1790 census listed him as living there with two females—his wife and a daughter perhaps. That same year, the Providence town council granted a liquor license to "Mr. Christopher Stocker," thus permitting him to run a tavern out of his dwelling house. To all appearances, he had settled down in Providence, suggesting that someone had intervened on his behalf, perhaps by assisting him in the purchase of real estate or by posting bond guaranteeing that he would behave in a "becoming" manner and avoid the kind of controversy that had brought him to official attention in the first place. Whatever the conditions, Stocker, at age forty, was given a second chance in Providence.

Nathaniel Whitaker

Nathaniel Whitaker seemed unable to maintain a permanent relationship with a woman. Each time he was summoned before the Providence town council, he was in a different relationship, and the relationship was seriously troubled. The disputes he had with his various mates apparently occasioned complaint by neighbors and resulted in his being warned out. The last time they sent him away, the Providence councilmen described him as a "person of bad fame and reputation." Doubtless his castoff lovers had other names for him as well.

Nathaniel Whitaker was born in 1759 in Rehoboth, Massachusetts, the son of Nathaniel and Mary Whitaker. He had an older sister named Mary and one five years younger than he, named Patience. In 1767 Nathaniel Sr. moved his family across the border into Barrington, Rhode Island, and then, in 1769, on to Providence, where the family "lived in the house of Major Ebenezer Thompson at Tockwotton." He never prospered enough to purchase real estate in either Barrington or Providence, so the family lived as transients, with a "hometown" in Rehoboth, where he had owned land.

In the early 1770s Nathaniel Jr. began an informal apprenticeship with Reuben Potter, a "caulker" who worked building and repairing ships in Providence. Nathaniel Jr. was not bound formally—"there never was any indentures given of him to the said Reuben Potter"—and in 1778 at age sixteen he left Potter and "enlisted for a year" in the army during the Revolutionary War. After his tour of duty was up, he returned to Providence and began work, probably as a caulker like his master.

The war years were troubled ones for the Whitaker family. Nathaniel Jr.'s older sister Mary became pregnant in 1777, when she was "in the nineteenth year of her age," and the Providence authorities warned her out to Rehoboth so that her illegitimate child would be born in the town that had financial responsibility for her. Nathaniel Sr. died during or shortly after the war, and his widow returned to her home in Rehoboth. Nathaniel Jr. remained in Providence.

Nathaniel Jr. married Mary Potter sometime in the 1780s; she was the daughter of Samuel Potter, who was probably a kinsman of Whitaker's former master, Reuben Potter. The marriage was deeply troubled, perhaps because the couple never had any children, but more certainly because Whitaker began a long-term adulterous relationship with another woman, Martha Spears, who lived in the neighboring town of North Providence. For several years he "kept company with" Spears while married to Mary; in 1790 he and Spears had a daughter, Lisbon.

Nathaniel Whitaker and his wife Mary were both white, but Whitaker's mistress was almost certainly a woman of color. This is indicated not only by the name Martha Spears gave to her daughter by Whitaker—"Lisbon," a name associated with slavery—but also by officials' lack of outrage at Whitaker's duplicity. Other situations that involved white men committing adultery openly with white women drew down the condemnation of town leaders, as when the Providence council issued a warrant for the arrest of Timothy Brownell, who had shamed and neglected his wife Mary when he in a "most wicked and scandalous manner accompanied with other women and hath with them expended much of his time and estate." No hint of such criticism entered the council's proceedings concerning Nathaniel and Mary Whitaker and Martha Spears. A long-term dalliance with a woman of color apparently did not offend proprieties to the same extent.

After the birth of Lisbon, Mary and Nathaniel Whitaker's marriage seemed to unravel. In December 1790 Whitaker came to the attention of the overseers of the poor in Providence, because he "had his feet, etc., frozen in this inclement season" and was "unable to procure a competency" to support his family. The overseer gave him nine shillings "to purchase necessaries," and reported him to the council, who summoned and questioned him on 3 January 1791. On learning that his hometown was in Rehoboth, they ordered him and his wife Mary to leave "by Thursday next," unless they wanted to be forcibly transported. That was the last mention of the couple together in the town records; they divorced soon afterward.

Nathaniel Whitaker pursued his relationship with Martha Spears in North Providence, and they had another child, James, in 1793. But Whitaker never married Spears, even when he was free to do so, again suggesting that Spears was not white and that Whitaker felt no compelling obligation to legitimize their relationship or their children. Sentiment in fact went against such regularization, although it was not until 1798 that the state legislature officially ruled that no minister or justice of the peace "shall join in marriage any white person with any Negro, Indian or mulatto, on penalty of two hundred dollars."[2] So Whitaker left Spears and their children vulnerable to economic distress and forced separation by authorities in times of crisis.

Those times were not far off. In 1795 Whitaker came to the attention of the North Providence town council; at that point he was coupled with yet another woman, Rebecca Nichols, who was ordered to appear before council along with Whitaker. Whitaker, it seems, was two-timing both Spears and Nichols, and it may have been Spears's discovery of his infidelity—and the resulting scene—that brought the couple to the attention of North Providence authorities. Instead of responding to the council's summons, both Whitaker and Nichols left North Providence, apparently going in two different directions and ending their liaison. Whitaker moved back to Providence, and Spears followed him. Four weeks later, the two had caused some kind of disturbance in Providence—probably a noisy dispute—and were brought before the town council. After being questioned, they were given until "tomorrow morning at nine o'clock" to leave the town, the usual punishment of transients who had "broken the peace" of the community. Providence authorities had had enough of Whitaker's scenes.

Whitaker kept a low profile for four years. Then, in 1799, his thirty-three-year-old sister Patience was brought before Providence authorities. By this time, Patience had "been twice married" and was twice either widowed or divorced. She was now single, but someone had accused her of prostitution. After questioning her and ascertaining that Rehoboth was her hometown, the councilmen ordered her to leave immediately or to be sent to the Bridewell, the jail for minor offenders; this, it was hoped, would limit her activities.

In 1801 Nathaniel Whitaker, now nearly forty years old, came to the council's attention again. He had been living in Providence for some time, and that town had tolerated his presence as long as he stayed out of trouble. But he got himself embroiled in another crisis with a woman. This time he had gone across the state border to Rehoboth to marry nineteen-year-old Peggy Mason. Some eighteen months previously, Mason had left her lawyer father Sampson Mason in Dedham, "on account of some difficulty between them." She had run away to Providence, met Whitaker, and then married him in July 1801, in a service conducted by "a transient person at the house of Reuben Thurber in Rehoboth" without previously publishing any notice of the impending marriage. That legal precaution might have resulted in Mason learning something about Whitaker's infidelities beforehand, and it might have revealed the questionable standing of the official who performed the ceremony. Now, two months later, during an official interrogation by the Providence town council, Mason learned that Whitaker "was divorced from" his former wife Mary Potter (who was now married to another man) and that her own marriage to Whitaker was invalid, a sham ceremony conducted by an uncertified person under questionable circumstances.

The council ordered both Whitaker and Mason to depart within "one week." Whitaker they sent to Rehoboth; Mason (whom they never referred to as Peggy Whitaker) they sent to Dedham, underscoring the invalidity of the marriage, which did not entitle Mason to Whitaker's legal settlement. Mason left right away, probably returning to her parents' home in Dedham. Whitaker, however, stayed on in Providence, perhaps thinking he was in the clear now that Mason was gone. He was wrong. When the councilmen learned that he was "still residing in this town" some three weeks later, they ordered a warrant to have him "removed to the said Rehoboth as a person of bad fame and reputation." They were no longer tolerant of this troublesome transient.

In the space of fifteen years, Nathaniel Whitaker had married once, pretended to marry another time, and been involved with two other women whom he did not marry but whom officials recognized as his mates. He fathered two children, for whom he took no responsibility after his relationship with their mother ended. His periodic summonses to council meetings coincided with crisis points in the termination of these various relationships, suggesting that Whitaker was given to public brawling or disputing that alerted the neighborhood to his troubles. When the Providence council warned him out in 1801, their judgment of "bad fame and reputation" was based on three previous tumultuous episodes, first with wife Mary Potter, then with mate Martha Spears, then with "wife" Peggy Mason. Between the alienated women and the irritated officials, word of Whitaker's character doubtless spread throughout the community and made it difficult for him to live anywhere in the Providence region without the sharp eyes of officials fastened on him. Whitaker was most certainly—and with reason—an "unwelcome" resident.

Robert Fuller's Family

Robert Fuller ran away from his wife and children when he was being forcibly transported to the town he claimed as his home. In fact, it was not his hometown and he had no claim there; when Providence officials took him at his word, they opened themselves up to dispute and expense that could have been avoided. Actually, Fuller was in trouble before he was ordered out of Providence, and his desertion of his family at a moment of crisis was not the first instance of "misbehavior." Robert Fuller was by no means the first New England man to run away from his wife and children, but his "escape" at this strategic moment highlighted the problems local officials faced when trying to get transients back home where they "belonged."

Robert Fuller was born in Attleboro, Massachusetts, where his father—so said the son—"owned a considerable real estate." As it turned out, Robert's father, Timothy Fuller, had left Attleboro "before the late war with Great Britain," when Robert was still a child, and never returned there; his long absence had canceled his settlement in the town. Robert Fuller himself drifted toward Providence; he was there in 1790, according to the census, married and with one young son. Another child was born in the early 1790s. Then in September 1796 he came to the attention of Providence authorities, apparently because of some troublesome behavior— perhaps a public dispute or drunkenness. At first the councilmen gave him "one month" to leave the town, but he pled for this judgment to be reversed, probably promising good behavior, and they relented. Then, in November, Robert Fuller "forfeited [the council's] indulgence" by some "recent instances of misbehavior," and the councilmen ordered an "immediate" removal of the family to Attleboro.

Robert Fuller never arrived in Attleboro. The town sergeant of Providence delivered the family to Gideon Ray, one of the constables of North Providence, who was supposed to pass the family along to the town sergeant in neighboring Attleboro. But Robert Fuller "made his escape" from constable Ray, so that only Fuller's wife and the two children were actually delivered to Attleboro authorities.

The Attleboro overseers of the poor rejected the Fuller family as legal inhabitants of their town. In a lengthy letter to the Providence councilmen, they explained that Timothy Fuller, Robert's father, had left Attleboro more than twenty years before and had died without ever returning to the town. Furthermore, they pointed out that the Massachusetts settlement laws had been revised in 1790 so that no one could "gain habitancy in any town in this state by taxation." They declined to investigate the matter—"we do not think it our business at this time to search for the place where the said Robert and family legally belong"—but offered their assistance with further information.

The Attleboro officials kept the Fuller family for three weeks before sending them back. This gave them time to "cleanse" them from "their lice and dirt," to provide them with "necessary" clothing, and otherwise to remedy their "most destitute and disagreeable circumstances." In their letter the Attleboro overseers scolded the Providence officials for having "imposed on" them by sending them "the most abandoned and worst of characters," and they demonstrated proper procedure by returning the wife and children "in much better circumstances . . . than they were in when they came here." They also sent along a bill for the costs of boarding the family; providing shirts, shifts, shoes, and stockings; and "killing their lice and cleansing them from their dirt." They carefully deducted the value of "Miss Fuller's work" during the time the family stayed in Attleboro. The bill must have been as strong a rebuke as the letter, indicating that the Providence councilmen had gravely neglected their responsibilities as town fathers to those who needed their oversight and care.

The Providence authorities were subdued by the settlement information in the Attleboro authorities' letter, if not by the admonition of their colleagues. They "received" the Fuller family into the town and paid most of the bill for their care in Attleboro ($20.60 out of $22.48). There is no indication in the record that they located some other town with responsibility for the family; they may have given up and put Fuller's wife and children in the workhouse, where they would be managed by the overseer of the facility and kept to work to help pay for their food, clothing, and lodging.

After his family was returned to Providence, Robert Fuller also returned. And later that year, when a yellow fever epidemic spread through the town, Fuller was one of the victims. He and several other Providence residents died on 18 August of "the putrid fever." Because of the "highly contagious" nature of the disease, the Providence council made an unusual ruling regarding the disposition of the dead bodies. First, they recommended that "no more persons attend said funerals, than are necessary for the interment of the deceased." Second, they advised that "the corpses of said deceased persons be conveyed to the place of interment through the most private avenues leading to the same." For his last earthly journey, Robert Fuller was whisked to his grave in a clandestine manner ironically appropriate for someone who had worked so hard to avoid official hands less than a year before.

Thomas Field

The marriage of Thomas Field and Mary Justice ended in a public, noisy spectacle that must have been the subject of many an indignant conversation among respectable inhabitants of Providence in the spring and summer of 1789. Mary Justice was a Providence inhabitant, but her husband, Thomas Field, was a transient who had no legal home in North America. Field's belligerence and refusal to cooperate with authorities during the breakup of his marriage (apparently including abusive behavior toward Mary) resulted in his being warned out of Providence twice, put in solitary confinement in jail and then in the workhouse cage, and finally forcibly put aboard ship and taken to New York. Thomas Field was clearly one of the most unwelcome people of the decade, not just for ex-wife Mary Justice but also for Providence officials.

Thomas Field testified that he was born in 1763 in Londonderry County, Ireland. As a young person he was "put apprentice" to a man named Captain Thompson, "who followed the sea as his business." In 1783, six months short of the end of his indenture, Field left his master's service, by mutual agreement perhaps, or perhaps because Field ran away. He made his way to New London, which was "the first place he landed at in America"; from there he "sailed on several voyages for nearly three years." In 1787 Field came to Rhode Island, settled in Providence, and there met and married Mary Justice, who operated a tavern out of her home and probably also took in boarders.

In April 1789 Thomas Field caused a great disturbance, drawing the attention of authorities. Field's marriage was unraveling, and his misbehavior apparently involved a public fight with his wife—perhaps also destruction of their household goods. The Providence councilmen questioned Field and listened to his story, but concluded that something was amiss with his narrative. They wanted correct information and more of it, but badgering Field seemed to get them nowhere. He wanted to keep his secrets even more fiercely than they wanted to pry them out of him.

After hearing Field's story on 9 April, the Providence councilmen summoned and questioned several respectable inhabitants of Providence about "the conduct and behavior of Thomas Field." What they heard convinced them that Field was "a very disorderly person and unfit to have the management of his family and effects." In a highly unusual move, they declared Thomas Field "non compos mentis," a step ordinarily taken only when people were insane or senile. They appointed "Mary Field his wife" to be his legal guardian and gave her "charge of his goods and estate." This may have been a deft move to make sure Mary did not lose any property in the coming divorce, and it also suggests that Field's "disorderly" behavior related specifically to the couple's possessions.

The next day, after "having taken into consideration" Field's testimony, the council officially warned him out, declaring New London—where he first set foot in North America—to be his place of legal settlement. Mary Justice was not warned out with her husband, as would have been the case if officials considered the marriage to be in force. Instead, this removal seems to have been implemented as a way of protecting Justice from the destructive behavior of her soon-to-be-ex-husband. Field was put in jail for three days, until the removal could be organized, further evidence that the council did not trust Field loose on the town.

A little more than two weeks later, Thomas Field had returned to Providence, which must have dismayed both Justice and the town council.

After declaring him to be "an idle person of bad fame and an unsuitable subject to be let loose," the councilmen ordered that the town sergeant keep him "in close confinement" in jail until the cage in the workhouse was "in sufficient repair to receive him." After two weeks of this treatment, Field asked to address the council. The councilmen may have hoped that a chastened Field would finally penitently cooperate with the council by providing truthful information about "the place of his birth, his life or travels, by which his legal place of settlement may be ascertained." But in fact Field's objective was simply to make work for the council and bring them together so he could defy them collectively and refuse to answer their questions once again. The angry councilmen declared him "an obstinate, malicious, unruly subject" and "an unwholesome member of society" who was "not suitable to let loose or run at large." He was sent back to jail "till further orders."

Two months later, in July 1789, Field proposed a solution: if the council would release him, he would leave town and not return. He gave his word, and the town sergeant conducted him "to the bounds of this town." Doubtless the councilmen were relieved to be rid of the costs of boarding him at 4 shillings and 6 pence per week. But Field's word was not his bond: he came back to Providence within a couple of days and once again "behaved himself in such a manner that this council are of opinion that it is dangerous to the safety and welfare of this town." They ordered the jail keeper to "confine him in irons in close jail" and "suffer no person to have communication" with him.

Mary Justice was probably the one most at risk from Field, even though the two were divorced and she was now "Mrs. Mary Justice, late the wife of Thomas Field." But she herself offended the council by unspecified actions that were "unbecoming and imprudent," perhaps some public scene prompted by the return of her ex-husband. The councilmen declared her "non compos mentis"—hinting that she had behaved in some "lunatic" fashion—and appointed Providence gentleman Joseph Peck as her guardian. Ten days later, the council found "satisfactory" cause to lift the judgment and she was "hereby restored to all her rights and privileges." By that time, Field was back in jail and presumably no longer a threat to her.

Two weeks later, in early August 1789, the councilmen ordered Field to be transferred in irons from the jail to the newly repaired cage in the workhouse, and there he sat for the next four weeks. Finally, at the very end of August, the councilmen settled on a more permanent solution to the Field problem. They worked out an arrangement with one of the captains of the packets that plied the North American coastal trade, agreeing to pay the captain to "take [Thomas Field] on board" and "land him in New York or in the west part of Connecticut," far enough away that he could not return without significant trouble and expense. They ordered that on "the same day the packet sails," the town sergeant was to "safely convey him on board and there tarry with him until she sails."

This stratagem seemed to work, for there is no further evidence that Thomas Field returned to trouble either Mary Justice or Providence residents at large. But it was without question a devious way to get rid of an unwelcome transient. Instead of another proper warrant and removal to New London, the councilmen resorted to an under-the-table deal with a sympathetic ship captain. This arrangement was not recorded in the official town books but only in the town sergeant's papers, suggesting that the ship captain was expected to draw his own conclusions about what to do with Field in an era of impressments and disappearances at sea. Indeed, officials in "New York or in the west part of Connecticut" would have been incensed to learn that an "unwholesome" and "unruly" transient had been dumped on their shores in such an improper manner. Providence officials had few options for getting rid of a man who posed a continual threat to the peace of a community, who had not yet committed a crime but seemed likely to do so at any time. This was their way of protecting Mary Justice—and the rest of the town—from Thomas Field.

3. Work Life

TRANSIENTS did not have legal inhabitant status, but they provided essential labor for those who did. In every New England town, transient residents worked in kitchens, fields, and shops, enabling legal inhabitants to maintain their households, farms, and businesses; these arrangements often stretched over such long periods that employer and employee both forgot that one of them did not legally "belong" in the community. When need or trouble put such long-term employees in jeopardy of being warned out, surprised employers sometimes resisted authorities. Providence gentleman and tavern owner Esek Aldrich, for example, tried to prevent the removal of his valued "mulatto" servant Sarah Mason, by "secreting and withholding the said Sarah & by otherwise obstructing the officer" who came to remove her.[1]

Employers such as Aldrich were under no obligation to secure the labor of their transient employees in contracts. They could, if they wished, simply hire workers for a short period of time and let them go on their way—or be sent away by authorities—when their services were no longer needed. Thus employers could avoid taking responsibility for the laborers on whom they relied; they could count on the warning-out system to remove beggars from their door.

Town officials tried to prevent blatant exploitation whereby some employers lured workers into a community for a time. If they knew that poor transients had arrived in a community in response to a job offer, they required the employer to post bond or immediately send away the workers. When West Greenwich man Samuel Reynolds was caught trying to import transient labor, he "confessed that he did hire and entertain ye said [Philip] Palmeter and his family"; Reynolds was fined forty shillings, and the luckless Palmeters were warned out "forthwith," before they could fall into need. Portsmouth authorities required that gentleman Abraham Redwood of Newport post bond because he "hath brought into this town" Caleb Cornell and his family from Dartmouth, Massachusetts, and "settled them in his dwelling house" on his farm. But officials could not monitor the comings and goings of all transients, especially in populous towns, and so employers could take advantage of the pool of transient labor that lapped perpetually against their doorways.[2]

Transient people performed all kinds of work in southeastern New England in the eighteenth century. A few people without legal settlements had been trained in respectable professions such as clerk or schoolmaster or surgeon, but they had fallen on hard times and were unable to establish themselves as inhabitants. Another small cluster of transients were skilled artisans who ranked at the top of the hierarchy of crafts, such as goldsmith John Treby (this chapter). A much greater number were artisans whose humbler skills put them among the lower sort, like shoemaker William Pike (Chapter 2) and blacksmith Latham Clarke (Chapter 5). The greatest number of transients, however, supported themselves and their families as unskilled laborers—sailors, domestic servants, hired hands. Often they had been indentured servants or slaves during their youth and had not been trained to take up any skilled occupation as adults. Nathaniel Williams, a transient who brought his family to live in Westerly, told authorities that "he depends chiefly upon his hands for a living"; he spoke for many.[3]

The range of occupations mentioned by transients demonstrates that misfortune could visit anyone, but the predominance of unskilled laborers shows that they were at greatest risk. Although the work they performed was essential to the maintenance of households and communities, their labor did not always secure them a safe place in the town or even supply them with the essentials of life. Transient work opportunities were constrained in several ways. First, they frequently lacked training in those skills that brought good wages. Second, local officials often acted as gatekeepers to prevent especially unwelcome groups from staying in town long enough to secure a job—a particular problem for people of color, who were often called before authorities and warned out within days of arriving in Providence. Third, community prejudices sometimes made it difficult for them to keep jobs they obtained, for a well-placed complaint by an influential inhabitant could easily result in warning out.

This chapter begins with the narratives of transient women, whose hard manual labor was most poorly recompensed, although their work of baking, spinning, and washing put clothes on the backs and food in the bellies of hundreds of settled inhabitants. Phillis Merritt Wanton had been a slave and Mary Carder and Olive Pero had been indentured servants; as free people, all three labored in domestic service in Providence. Elisabeth Hodges had been neither servant nor slave and had once had a small piece of property, but need forced her to bind out her daughter as an indentured servant.

The transient men in this chapter illustrate a wider range of work skills. Cato Freeman, former slave, and Mark Noble, common laborer, both sought opportunity as soldiers during the Revolutionary War. Peter Norton spun out his whole life as "hired man." In contrast, John Treby was a skilled goldsmith and Nathaniel Bowdish was highly literate, versed in law, and apparently made a living dispensing advice and acting as clerk for others less educated.

These narratives underscore the economic problems of a fluid social hierarchy in early America. In England in an earlier era, these workers would all have belonged somewhere, at least in theory—to a monastery, a manor, or a guild—where they and their dependents would have been supported in times of desperate need. In the absence of such institutional structures in the eighteenth century generally, and particularly in the English North American colonies, these people, whose labor was given low status and compensation on the economic scale, found they belonged nowhere. Although many had been slaves, servants, and soldiers in the past, they could not claim the care of their former masters when they fell into need. Well before the Industrial Revolution began in New England, these "lower sort" people formed a "working class" who felt, through inadequate wages and insufficient social security, the pinch of economic exploitation that was totally foreign to the propertied class.

Phillis Merritt Wanton

Phillis Merritt Wanton's story emphasizes the difficulties and limitations faced by women of color, who found that race and poverty shut the door to skilled labor, so that they had to support themselves and their families by working as servants and washerwomen in white households. Wanton was clearly a woman of strength and resourcefulness, yet on a daily basis she performed the tedious and unsavory physical labor that others did not want to do for themselves. At the same time, she married, raised children, and built connections in several different communities, thus doing the double duty of work abroad and work at home so familiar to poor women across time.

Phillis was born a slave in Attleboro, Massachusetts, "in the house of Mr. Robert Sanderson," to whom she "belonged." When she was "about five years of age," Sanderson "went for England" and "left her" with Mr. John Merritt of Providence, whose "servant or slave" she became, and whose name was attached to her own. She grew up in Merritt's household, probably under the management of his wife, laboring at the myriad domestic responsibilities of maintaining a gentleman's family. When "Master Merritt" died, the estate executor sold Phillis "for one hundred dollars" to "Mr. John Field of Boston, a leather breeches maker," who wanted a domestic servant; accordingly, she moved from Providence to Boston. After an unspecified period, Field sold her and "went away out of the country." Phillis was now the property of "a Mr. Peck" of Boston. In 1774, "about the time of the blockage of that place by the British," Peck told her "to seek and provide for herself," apparently a kind of informal emancipation.

Free to "go and get her own living," Phillis returned to Providence, where she had grown up, and there she supported herself by "go[ing] out to washing." She lived "at different places, particularly with Mrs. Goodwin on the west side of the river, whose house she made her home." After a time she met misfortune, perhaps in the form of illness or injury, and she became "chargeable to the town," that is, she needed poor relief. The overseer of the poor who learned of her trouble and assisted her then informed the town council; they questioned her in February 1784 and warned her out to her legal hometown of Boston, where her last master had lived.

If Phillis was actually removed to Boston, she returned to Providence fairly soon afterward and continued to work as a washerwoman. Six years later, in 1790, she once again drew council attention; she had just given birth to a son, and her temporary debility may have been what caused concern among officials. Although the councilmen did not know it, Phillis had married by this time and her place of legal settlement was no longer Boston. But the councilmen did not question Phillis again; rather, when they learned of her need, they simply renewed a warrant for her removal to Boston. They also sent the town sergeant to remove her forcibly, but Phillis hid from him and he spent "near half a day" looking fruitlessly for her. Clearly she had some network of support that town officials knew nothing about—people who cared for each other out of sight of white authority. Rather than pursuing her, the councilmen dropped the matter, and she remained in Providence.

Two years later, in 1792, Phillis came to official attention once again, this time as the wife of Jack Wanton, "a Negro man," who seemed unable to support his family adequately. In his testimony before the Providence councilmen, Jack "saith that he was an African born." Brought to Newport by ship captain John Goddard, Jack had been sold to John Wanton of Newport and had lived with him "about 15 years." In 1791 Jack's master "gave him his freedom." By that time Jack had married Phillis and the couple had "one child named Squire," the baby born in Providence in

Figure 3. Phillis Merritt Wanton was ordered out of Providence for the second time in June 1790. Town sergeant Henry Bowen, tasked with making sure she left town, spent "near half a day" looking for her without success; he later charged the town 2 shillings for his efforts, as this account illustrates. Many transient people, like Wanton, avoided removal by hiding from the authorities. Source: PTP 13:101, neg. no. RHi (x3) 9401. Courtesy of the Rhode Island Historical Society.

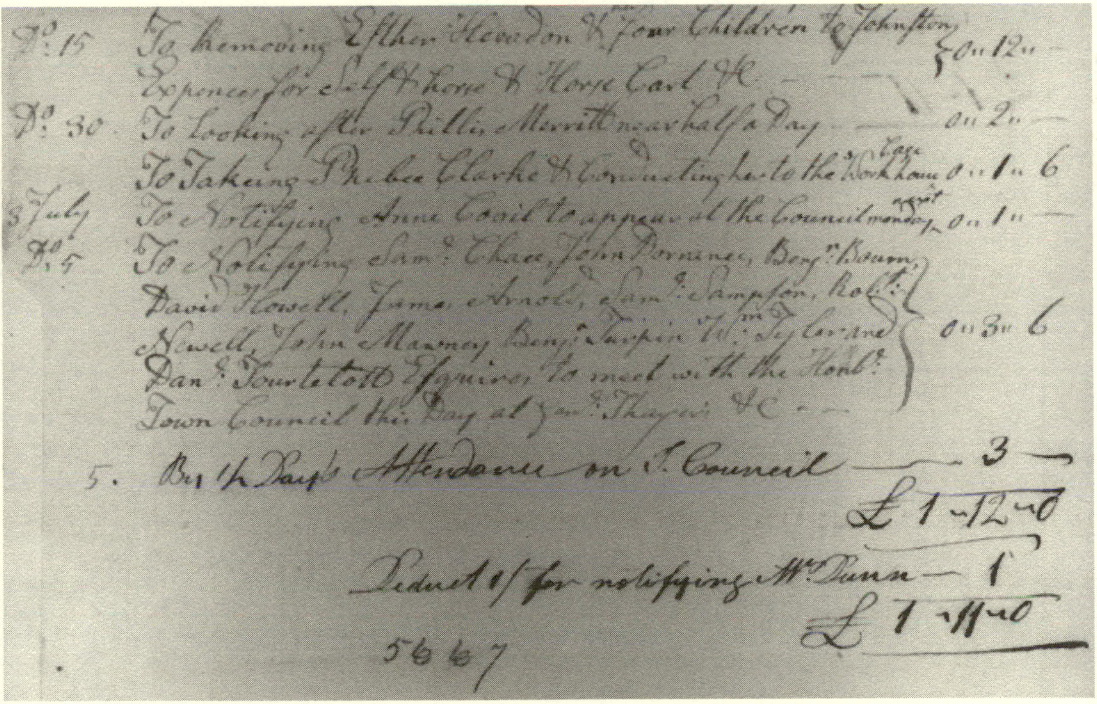
Do. 15 To Removing Esther Hevardon & four Children to Johnston
Expences for Self & horse & Horse Cart &c — } 0 .. 12 ..
Do. 30 To looking after Phillis Merritt near half a Day — 0 .. 2 ..
To Taking Phebee Clarke & Conducting her to the Work house 0 .. 1 .. 6
3 July To Notifying Anne Covil to appear at the Council monday next 0 .. 1 ..
Do. 5 To Notifying Saml. Chace, John Dorrance, Benjn. Bowen, David Howell, James Arnold, Saml. Sampson, Robt. Newell, John Mawney, Benjn. Turpin, Wm. Tyler and Danl. Tourtelott Esquires to meet with the Honble. Town Council this Day at Jam. Thayer's &c — } 0 .. 3 .. 6
5. By 1/2 Day's Attendance on T. Council — 3 —
£ 1 .. 12 .. 0
Deduct 1/ for notifying Mr. Dunn — 1
£ 1 .. 11 .. 0
5667

1790. Since the child's status followed that of the mother, Squire would have been born free, even though his father was still enslaved. Judging that the family was likely to need poor relief, the councilmen ordered Jack, Phillis, and Squire to be removed to Newport, Jack's hometown, "as soon as may be."

Eight years later, in October 1800, Phillis once more faced the Providence councilmen; she had fallen into need again, probably as a result of illness or injury. Now clearly recognized by officials as Phillis Wanton, she told of marrying and bearing three children: ten-year-old Squire and seven-year-old Marianne were "bound out [as indentured servants] in the town of Foster"; and Vina, "a girl about four years of age, is now with her." Jack Wanton was absent; he was back in Newport, probably in the work-house, because he was "at times insane."

Without manumission documents or other written proof of her free-dom, Phillis was at a disadvantage in her dealings with the Providence councilmen. In her second testimony she emphasized the way Mr. Peck set her free just before the Revolutionary War began. She also underscored her free status by reminding officials that she had "lived in the family of Moses Brown," the prominent and wealthy Quaker abolitionist. If anyone could successfully vouch for her status as a free woman, he could.

The Providence councilmen did not record any doubts they may have had about Phillis's status as a free person. Instead, they ordered her and her daughter Vina, now "likely to become chargeable," back to Newport, where they belonged by virtue of Jack Wanton's settlement. Three days later, one of Newport's overseers of the poor took in Phillis and Vina, who had been brought to his door by the Providence constable. He probably sent them to live in the workhouse until Phillis could once again labor for her own maintenance.

Phillis, who had no formal "schooling," was unable to sign her name; she left only "x" marks on the transcripts of her testimonies. But she knew how to live as a free black woman in a society organized by well-to-do white men. She supported herself by her own labor, and she arranged for her children's support when her husband proved incapable. She knew how to tell her life story effectively, with plentiful references to influential peo-ple and revolutionary events that might stir sympathy among the council-men. She knew how to hide from the town sergeant when her livelihood depended upon her staying where she was. That she lived independently for over twenty years by the strength of her arms suggests she had built a network of support among white employers as well as among the community of color. Phillis was well educated in the art of survival.

Mary Carder

Mary Carder, who was identified in town records as "mustee" and "Indian," experienced two of the worst aspects of servitude: family instability and sexual exploitation. By the time she was sixteen Carder had lived in five different households as daughter, indentured servant, and free laborer; by the time she was eighteen she had two children. Such a childhood was no shelter from hard work or adult concerns.

Mary Carder, nicknamed "Moll" in some of the records, was born in 1757 in the town of Warwick. Her mother, Abigail Carder, was not married and was almost certainly a woman of color herself, though no racial designation is given in the records. When Mary was four years old, her mother bound her out to "Manna Burman, a free Negro man," in the town of Providence. At four, Mary Carder was considerably younger than most children apprenticed privately by their parents, but it was a typical age for very poor and orphaned children to be bound out in public contracts by local officials. The young age suggests that Abigail Carder was quite poor and unable to support her daughter; in this case, the "binding out" was not to educate and train the little girl but simply to provide her with the necessities of life—food, clothing, shelter. Thus Mary was placed in a labor contract as soon as she was no longer physically dependent on her mother and could be expected to perform some useful labor in another household. Under the daily supervision and guidance of Burman's wife, even four-year-old Mary could contribute to the family economy in small ways: feeding the chickens, weeding the garden, rocking the baby, and generally assisting older children and adults in their labor, while she learned how to take on increasing responsibility.

Mary Carder remained in the Burman household "about five years," and then her master "dismissed [her] from his service" and returned the indenture to Abigail Carder. The language suggests that Burman initiated the breaking of the contract, perhaps because he was not satisfied that the little girl would be a productive worker in his household, or perhaps because he was moving his household and was reluctant to take the young girl away. Nine-year-old Mary then "went and lived with Jacob Harris, a tenant of David Harris's, and his wife Deborah." This was not an apprenticeship indenture, for Mary "was not bound." But it was a common enough arrangement when parents could not afford to purchase an official indenture or when they were reluctant to commit a child to a master in a formalized fashion. Mary probably assisted Deborah Harris in her management of the household and continued to learn the business of housekeeping. If Mary was healthy and strong, her labor would have been perceived as a substantial contribution to the family economy by this time.

For two years Mary Carder worked in the Harris household, and then she "went to the Town of Warwick and stayed there a few days." Apparently eleven-year-old Mary went to be with her mother for a time. Perhaps she ran away from the Harrises; perhaps she was dismissed by her master: her ambiguously worded testimony provides no explanation for this break in the pattern of service. Then, after those "few days" in Warwick, Mary "returned with her mother and was left in the care of Mr. Edward Thurber." Once again Abigail Carder had located a place of service for her daughter, this time with a substantial householder in Providence. Mary was "not bound" in the Thurber household, once again laboring without the benefit of a formal contract. By this time, her work would have been valued nearly as highly as an adult's. She would be expected to participate significantly in the running of the household: spinning, sewing, cooking, gardening, dairying, preserving meat, and the myriad other responsibilities of providing food, clothing, and daily care for a family.

For two years Mary Carder worked in the Thurber household; then she returned to her mother in Warwick once again. This thirteen-year-old girl was about to have a baby ("like to have a child"). After two weeks in Warwick, her mother located a place for her to stay in Cranston during her delivery and recovery. After giving birth to a daughter, Mary "lay in" at Colonel Waterman's house in Cranston, probably for two weeks or so, while she and her baby gained strength. Despite her youth, she seems to have recovered well from labor and delivery, and the child also survived.

Mary Carder then worked in Captain Samuel Aborn's house in Warwick for three years. Aborn's family would have expected a thirteen-year-old servant girl to perform nearly all the adult female tasks of running a household, although the presence of the baby must have limited Mary's labor to some extent. But her stint in the Aborn household ended as it had in the Thurber household: with her becoming pregnant and leaving to have a child. This time sixteen-year-old Mary "kept house in Warwick" for the weeks leading up to and following childbirth, the commonly used phrase indicating a kind of independent existence; perhaps the father of the baby or someone else was supporting her through this second birth. Mary's mother is conspicuously missing from the narrative at this point, suggesting that she had died, moved away, or become dependent, unable to manage her daughter's care any longer.

After giving birth to her second daughter, Mary Carder "lived at different places for about two years," moving around frequently and working in short-term jobs, probably as a house servant, perhaps among a network of householders associated with her former employers. Some of those places were in Providence, which bordered Warwick to the north. In February 1775 she came to official notice in Providence, and the councilmen questioned her. It was the middle of winter, and eighteen-year-old Mary and her two children were apparently in need. The Providence councilmen judged that she was headed for disaster: a free woman of color, with no husband, father, or master to govern and support her, was raising two young children on intermittent servant wages. These officials ruled that her hometown was Warwick, the place of her birth, and they ordered her removed there "together with her two children." Providence town sergeant William Compton carried out the council's order, delivering Mary and her daughters to the overseer of the poor in Warwick.

Moll Carder still wanted to live in Providence; soon after being taken to Warwick, she petitioned the Warwick council for a settlement certificate, saying she had "a mind to live in the town of Providence." Armed with the certificate, she returned to Providence and apparently was permitted to stay there without official harassment, for she does not appear again in the Providence records. But nine years later, in 1784, she applied to the Warwick councilmen once again for a new settlement certificate, this time to Scituate, where new job opportunities, perhaps, awaited her.

In that second settlement certificate, issued in June 1784, the clerk described Mary Carder as "Negro," in contrast to her earlier descriptions as "Indian" or "mustee." At that time, an increasing number of former slaves were gathering in Warwick and Providence, building a community of people of color. And in March of that same year, gradual emancipation legislation took effect, so that all children born to slave women after 1 March would be free when they reached the age of majority. Slavery, freedom, and race were on many people's minds. And the clerk who looked at Mary Carder across the council table didn't trouble to ask if she was Indian or check back to the previous records which clearly identified her as such; he simply decided that this poor, free laboring woman was "Negro." Thus, before she was thirty, Mary Carder had undergone the indignities and oppressions of class, gender, and race prejudice: shunted from one menial labor situation to another as a child, sexually exploited at a tender age, and finally designated as a former slave on the basis of physical appearance. While she was never legally a slave, Mary Carder must have felt that she had lived a slave's life.

Olive Pero

Olive Pero, described as "mulatto" in the warrant for her removal, exemplifies well the plight of free women of color whose domestic skills brought them only meager financial rewards without any job security. If such women fell sick, as Pero did, they had no resources to fend off desperate poverty.

Olive Pero was born sometime in the 1740s in Rehoboth, Massachusetts, to parents who could not support her. Perhaps she was an illegitimate child; perhaps her parents died; perhaps they were ill and could not labor sufficiently to keep their family together. In any case, the town selectmen of Rehoboth stepped in and took over responsibility for her. They bound her out as an indentured servant to David Peck, who lived across the border in Warren, Rhode Island. Peck may well have been one of the community of wealthy merchants who lived in that thriving seaport on Narragansett Bay; he was apparently happy to obtain inexpensive long-term labor through such a contract, which bound Olive Pero to live with and labor for her master until age eighteen. She would have been under the daily management of Peck's wife, who directed the girl's work of washing, cleaning, cooking, and other labor of maintaining an upper-class household. Pero "served till she was eighteen years of age," indicating that Peck had no cause to terminate the contract or her service prematurely.

Freedom brought a precarious existence for Olive Pero. She moved about nearly continuously, staying a few days or weeks in one place and then another. First it was five weeks with Captain Joseph Olney in North Providence, then "about one week or a fortnight" in Daniel Marsh's household, then back to Olney's house for two weeks. Finally she settled into service at Charles Brown's house in North Providence, long enough to see her through a momentous occasion: the birth of "my bastard child that is now with me, called Rebecca."

Work continued to be intermittent and unreliable after Rebecca was born. Keeping her baby daughter with her, Pero worked "one summer" in a place called Feather Hall, the last place she would consider "home" for some time. After that, she said, "I had no proper home but worked from house to house where I could get employ." She did not specify how long this unsettled time lasted, perhaps as much as a year. Eventually she moved to Smithfield "and tarried with my aunt about three months." Then, in June 1766, she returned to North Providence to work in familiar territory—first a few months with the Chaltee household and then five weeks at Mercy Squibb's house.

At this point Olive Pero became ill and could no longer labor enough to support herself and her daughter. "I being sickly went from house to house," she reported, describing apparent attempts to obtain assistance from former employers. To no avail. In December 1766, as cold weather set in, she became desperate. She went to Rehoboth and appealed to the overseers of the poor "to take care of me," but they "refused so to do." One of the overseers, Obadiah Carpenter, "gave me money to pay my ferriage" across the Providence River and "ordered me back from whence I came."

Having been rejected from Rehoboth, Pero went to the Providence home of a "Mr. Wheaton," perhaps someone who had previously taken her in when she was in desperate straits. This may well have been Ephraim Wheaton, who would later serve as one of the overseers of the poor for Providence. He took her in for "one night" and then sent her on to "the widow of James Brown," one of the most prominent mercantile families in the town, who also took her in for a night. While she was there, John Brown, son of James Brown, heard her story and ordered her to "apply to [Daniel] Tillinghast, one of the overseers of the poor."

Tillinghast had a word with the Providence councilmen, his colleagues and peers, who convened a council meeting, questioned Pero, and decided to remove her to Rehoboth, despite that town's recent rejection of her. In the warrant for her removal, drawn up the day after her examination, the town sergeant was directed to "deliver" Pero to one of Rehoboth's selectmen or overseers of the poor. This was to be done "at her own charge if able to pay it, otherwise at the charge of the town of Providence who send her." Pero was indeed unable to pay for these expenses, and the sergeant later submitted a bill to the town council for a total of nearly sixteen shillings, more than Pero could have earned in a full week of domestic labor. He listed the following charges of removal:

6 shillings for his own "trouble" of transporting her;
8 pence for the costs of the ferry across the Providence River;
3 shillings and 9 pence for rental of a horse;
3 shillings for rental of a "sleigh";
1 shilling for getting a copy of the warrant to leave with Rehoboth officials;
1 shilling and 6 pence for transporting Pero's child to North Providence.

Daughter Rebecca, having been born in North Providence, was a legal inhabitant of that town, regardless of her mother's settlement, and so to North Providence she was sent.

Olive Pero's story reveals the grimness of poverty and transience. The list of her temporary employments is extensive, highlighting the dependent status of a woman who lived perpetually on the edge of disaster. In the six months before her examination by the Providence councilmen, she was going from bad to worse, probably seeking shelter and food each day in return for her labor. When she reached rock bottom and appealed to public officials in her hometown, she was rejected by them. When she found a more sympathetic audience in the Providence overseers and councilmen, she was separated from her only child, who would probably be bound out as an indentured servant to a household in North Providence. Pero herself, if she lived, probably ended up in a workhouse or in bound servitude in Rehoboth.

Olive Pero's story is not altogether dismal. She demonstrated persistence in appealing to employers and seeking support from town officials. She seemed to understand settlement law and went directly to her hometown authorities when she fell into desperate need. Finally, she left a unique impression in the Rhode Island records at the time of her interrogation. When asked to "sign" her transient examination, this illiterate woman drew a careful hieroglyphic—a backward "P"—that is both beautiful and distinctive. Pero's artistic, highly personal mark, which appears in Figure 4, suggests that she understood the function of a signature in the world of government and bureaucracy: to attest to the truth of a document. Though uneducated in the skill of writing, Olive Pero would know her own mark if she saw it again.

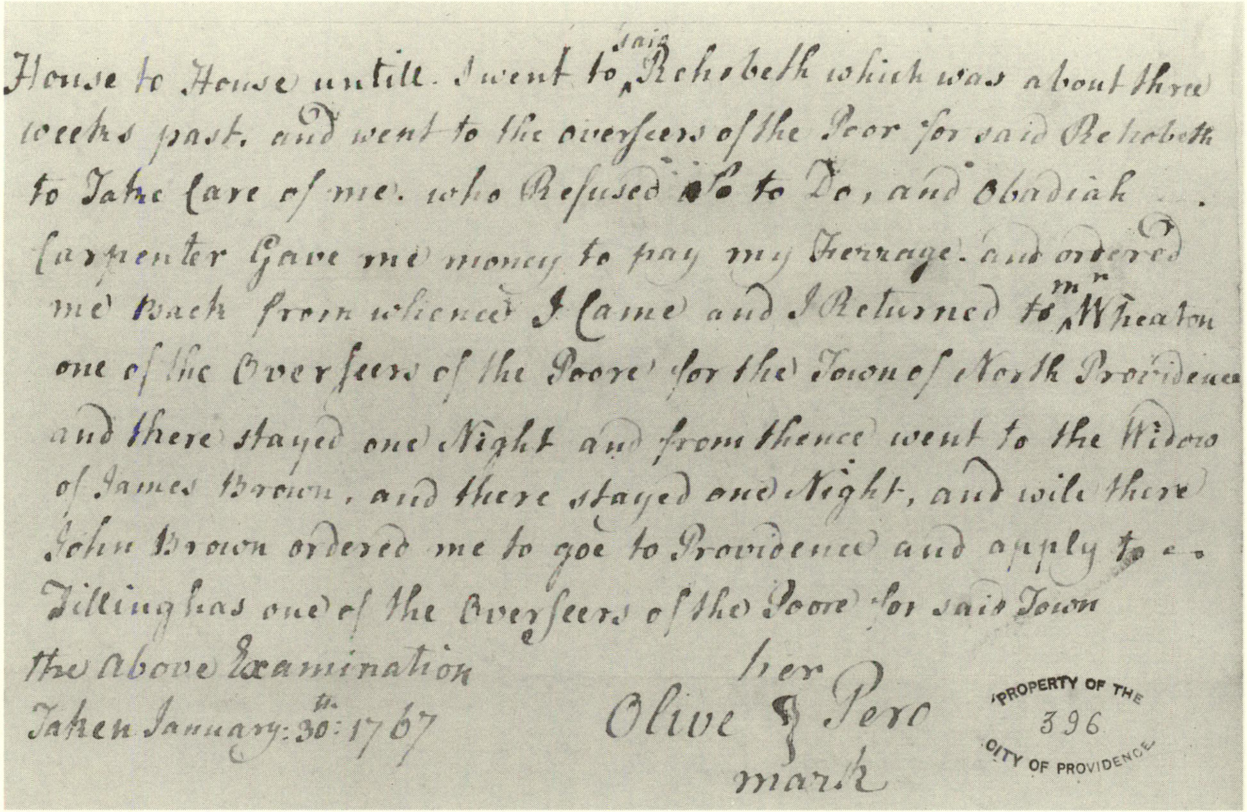

House to House untill I went to said Rehobeth which was about three
weeks past, and went to the overseers of the Poor for said Rehobeth
to Take Care of me. who Refused to Do, and Obadiah
Carpenter Gave me money to pay my Ferrage and ordered
me back from whence I Came and I Returned to mr Wheaton
one of the Overseers of the Poore for the Town of North Providence
and there stayed one Night and from thence went to the Widow
of James Brown, and there stayed one Night, and while there
John Brown ordered me to goe to Providence and apply to
Tillinghas one of the Overseers of the Poore for said Town
the above Examination
Taken January 30th 1767

her
Olive Pero
mark

Figure 4. When Olive Pero was interrogated by Providence town leaders on 30 January 1767, she "signed" her testimony with this backward "P". Instead of making an "x" mark, some illiterate transients left a unique hieroglyphic. Source: PTP 2:22, neg. no. RHi (x3) 9395. Courtesy of the Rhode Island Historical Society.

Elisabeth and Molly Hodges

Elisabeth Hodges was a single mother, never married, and—for a time—with enough resources to raise her daughter Molly without the assistance of a husband and without the interference of the overseers of the poor. She does not mention her own work, which may have been spinning, housewifery, washing clothes, sewing, or some other female task that drew wages in a busy seaport town like Providence. Whatever her labor, it did not provide her a "settlement" or buffer her and her daughter from forced removal, once her resources failed her and she fell into need.

In 1746 Elisabeth Hodges crossed the border from Rehoboth, Massachusetts, into Providence, Rhode Island, where she gave birth to Molly, an illegitimate child. In all likelihood, Hodges had friends or relatives in Providence, for she "tarried about four years" after Molly was born, apparently supporting herself and her child by her own labor or by managing her resources carefully. In 1750, when Molly was four years old, Hodges moved back to her hometown of Rehoboth and lived there seven years. During that sojourn, she "acquired a real estate of eight or ten acres of land" in Rehoboth, a piece of property that might have been worth a great deal or very little, depending upon the location of the acreage and the use to which it was put. The modest size of the tract suggests it was a bequest from a relative, although it is possible that Hodges purchased the property on her own.

Elisabeth Hodges chose not to live on the land, instead probably renting it out to someone who would farm it or otherwise use it to obtain a living. Hodges herself moved back to Providence in 1757 and then prepared eleven-year-old Molly for independence by placing her as an apprentice with Baulston Brayton and his family in Smithfield, the town adjoining Providence to the north. This private arrangement probably cost Hodges a good sum, and the land Hodges owned may have been the source of the money needed to secure Molly's contract.

Elisabeth and Molly Hodges thus separated in 1757, adolescent Molly going to live with the Brayton family in Smithfield and Elisabeth staying in Providence, working at whatever employment had sustained her for the previous decade. Mother and daughter doubtless visited on numerous occasions, their places of residence not being far distant, and Elisabeth probably kept close track of Molly's progress. Molly would have been under the daily care of Brayton's wife or other female relative who managed the household work—and that woman may have been a relative or friend of Elisabeth Hodges, with whom Hodges could place her daughter with confidence. Under this tutelage Molly would have learned the work of a farmwife. "Keeping house" on a farm was an enormously varied occupation that included the manufacture of cloth and clothing; the cultivation of a kitchen garden of vegetables and herbs; the preparation of butter, cheese, salted meat, and other foods; and countless additional chores that kept a household running—all on top of caring for young children.

The terms of Molly's contract were likely typical elements of an apprenticeship indenture. Brayton was obligated to provide Molly with lodging, food, clothing, medical care, a rudimentary education, and training in some useful skill. Girls' contracts rarely specified any education more than "reading," but it seems that Molly was among the more fortunate of apprentices in this regard. She learned how to write—and proved it by carefully signing her name to her testimony when she was seventeen years old. Clearly her mother was not her teacher, for Elisabeth Hodges was illiterate and signed her testimony only with an "x." It may well have been this anticipation of her daughter's literacy that prompted Hodges to seek an apprenticeship with Brayton.

Then something went awry. Molly was bound "to serve until she was eighteen years of age," the traditional age of adulthood for white women in eighteenth-century New England, and then the master was obliged to send away the servant with some sort of "freedom dues" as payment for her years of otherwise unrecompensed labor. This payment was most often one or two new suits of clothing and perhaps a small sum of money. But Molly never received any payment. A year before the contract would have been completed, Elisabeth Hodges and Baulston Brayton "agreed to exchange indentures"; that is, they canceled the contract and returned the copy each held as proof of the arrangement. In September 1763 seventeen-year-old Molly was released from apprenticeship and returned to Providence "to dwell with my mother."

Elisabeth Hodges may have agreed to end the contract because she was unhappy with some aspect of her daughter's situation and was willing to forgo the significant material advantage her daughter would gain by finishing her apprenticeship. Equally possible is that Elisabeth Hodges had no choice but to agree to end the contract because Molly had violated its terms in some way. Circumstantial evidence suggests that Molly may have become pregnant, a circumstance that would have prompted her master to terminate the indenture. Three years later, in 1766, when Elisabeth was warned out of North Providence, she was accompanied by "her child." "Child" is an unlikely description of Molly, who would then have been twenty years old, but it would be a very appropriate description of a three-year-old grandchild whom Elisabeth raised.

Whatever the reason for the contract's termination, Molly returned to her mother in September 1763, and two months later the two were summoned before the Providence town council and questioned individually. Elisabeth was rejected as an inhabitant, it being clear that she owned land and had a settlement in Rehoboth, but the councilmen needed to think about Molly's situation, for the young woman had been born in Providence and might claim settlement there in consequence. The council let the matter rest for three weeks, and then ruled that Elisabeth and Molly both "belonged" to Rehoboth and ordered them out. One month later, by the very end of December 1763, Elisabeth and Molly had come back to Providence and were spotted by officials, who had them removed to Rehoboth once again. The Hodges' persistence in coming to Providence suggests that their livelihood depended on being there. But the town councilmen were even more persistent, perhaps anxious to have Molly safely in her hometown when her baby was born. Elisabeth and Molly do not appear together again in the Providence records, and only one other mention of Elisabeth and "child"—being warned out of North Providence in 1766—provides further clues. Perhaps Molly was ailing and was put under the care of the overseers of the poor in Rehoboth. Perhaps Molly died in childbirth, leaving Elisabeth with a grandchild but no daughter. Elisabeth's disappearance from the Rhode Island records suggests that she, too, ended up back home in Rehoboth, her time of limited independence having come to a close.

Cato Freeman

The narrative of "Negro man" Cato Freeman underscores the economic vulnerability of former slaves. Although Freeman was emancipated during the Revolutionary War, his years of labor as a slave and then as a soldier did not provide him the means to obtain a good "competency" for himself and his family. Without the resources to strike out on his own, he could not take advantage of available land to the west. Instead, he migrated within a limited geographic area and worked at menial jobs that were all too familiar to someone who had been a slave.

Cato was raised from birth as a slave in the household of Captain Ebenezer Stedman of Cambridge, Massachusetts, in the mid-1700s. Very likely involved in the manual labor of maintaining a household, Cato probably performed a wide variety of traditionally male tasks—chopping wood, caring for horses, running errands—and perhaps also served as a valet to his master. The great event of his life came when his master "gave him his freedom at the time of the Bunker Hill Battle" (June 1775), influenced, perhaps, by the revolutionary rhetoric of liberty. Cato then shed his master's last name and gave himself the name Freeman to mark his new status.

One of Freeman's first independent acts was to join the Continental Army, serving, by his own reckoning, "six years and three months"—the entire duration of the war. As a soldier, he probably performed many of the same servant tasks as he had as a slave, as was the fate of many African Americans who enlisted in the Continental Army. But being in the army gave him certain opportunities he did not have as a slave. His military service gave him mobility, and he traveled widely with the army during the war. He was at Valley Forge the winter of 1777–78, at West Point in the spring of 1781, and on "boat service" in the summer of 1781. His service record also shows that he and two comrades solved a serious problem of food shortage in a very practical way during the starving winter of 1781–82: Cato Freeman, Backus Barton, and Cicero Sweat were court-martialed and convicted of stealing and killing a cow that belonged to a civilian inhabitant in the area where the army was camped; their punishment was 100 lashes and a fine of forty shillings to help cover the cost of the cow, an amount probably withheld from his already meager and intermittent pay.

When Freeman left the army he also left Cambridge and moved around freely in southeastern New England. He found an agreeable place to settle down in Rhode Island, where in August 1785 he married Katherine Greene, probably a free woman of color, in a ceremony presided over by Mr. Joseph Snow, probably a minister. The couple already had a daughter, Alice, born early in 1785; it may have been her birth that prompted the couple to formalize their relationship in a ceremony conducted by a white official.

In 1787 Cato Freeman came to the attention of the Providence councilmen, who questioned him and ordered him to "remove himself within one week" to his hometown of Cambridge. Freeman did indeed remove himself, but not back to Massachusetts; instead, he tried to settle in Cranston, the town adjoining Providence to the southwest. But Cranston officials learned of his presence and sent him to Cambridge. The persistent Freeman then asked the Cambridge selectmen for a certificate verifying his legal settlement there—his passport to residency elsewhere. The selectmen complied, writing a detailed and polite letter rather than the usual brief certificate. The letter, signed by Cambridge town clerk William Winthrop, represented Freeman's desire to live in Rhode Island, "supposing he can better support himself & family there, than he can here." It also assured the Cranston councilmen that the town of Cambridge would "reimburse the town of Cranston for whatever supplies they may advance for the support of the said Cato," as long as the supplies were truly necessary and the Cambridge selectmen were informed by "earliest notice."

Thanks to this letter, Cato Freeman and his family were able to settle down in Cranston for a year or so. When Freeman learned of a better opportunity in Providence, the family moved there. The Cranston council forwarded the Cambridge letter to the Providence council as evidence of Freeman's settlement, and Providence officials allowed him to live there on the strength of it.

But not for long. In 1790 Freeman and his growing family again came to the attention of the Providence council. The 1790 census lists Cato Freeman as having four other people in his household—his wife and three children, in all likelihood; it may have been the arrival of the youngest child that threw the family into need. For laboring families with a marginal income, the cessation of the wife's wages when a baby arrived could well push the entire family into serious trouble. Cato was summoned to the council in May, and the entire family was ordered out in July. In April of that year, Freeman had been issued a land warrant for 100 acres in the transappalachian territory that the United States had gained in the treaty ending the Revolutionary War; this was back pay for his services as a private during the conflict. But possession of this warrant could not keep him from present need. The official warrant for their removal to Cambridge declared that they were "likely to become chargeable." The forced trip back to his place of slavery must have been extraordinarily difficult for Freeman, who had spent six years in the army and an equivalent number as a transient laborer, trying to secure the fruits of freedom. Despite his efforts, he and his family were once again heading back under the rule of a master—this time the officials of Cambridge, Massachusetts.

Perhaps Cato Freeman and his family moved west to take up the opportunity provided by those 100 acres of reserved land. Perhaps. Unfortunately, many veterans were unable to take up such opportunities because the start-up costs were so great: tools, seed, transportation west, and maintenance for the first year, before the crop could be harvested. Given Freeman's economic marginality, it is just as likely that he sold his land rights to a speculator and stayed in New England, eking out a living in the region where he and his wife had work and community.

Mark Noble

Mark Noble lived a humble and troubled life as a common laborer. Orphaned as a child, he was raised as an indentured servant, and then charted an erratic course as a soldier and as a laboring man who did odd jobs in different places. His family did not flourish and eventually wound up in debt. Without skills, persistence, or social connections, Noble never moved beyond his modest beginnings. His three appearances before the Providence councilmen have a dreary note about them, as though officials themselves were baffled by Noble's failure to thrive. Noble's main limitation, it seems, was his reluctance to exert himself.

Mark Noble had an unusual start in life; on 6 July 1753, he was "born near Boston on board a vessel when his parents were removing to this country," probably from England. His parents appear to have settled in Rhode Island, for a man named Mark Noble served as an officer in the Rhode Island Regiment during the French and Indian War and accompanied the expedition to Crown Point in 1756. The senior Mark Noble may have died during the war, for his name disappears from the military records after 1757, and the junior Mark Noble later reported that both his parents died "when he was young." It is possible that Noble's widow moved to Boston in search of employment for herself and support for her child, and there she died too. At any rate, young Mark was in Boston when he was completely orphaned, at which point town officials took charge.

In February 1760, when Mark was six years old, the Boston overseers of the poor bound him out to Moses Marsh, a "gentleman" who lived in Hadley, Massachusetts. The contract obligated Marsh to teach Noble the work of "husbandry," basic labor tending livestock and planting crops that occupied the great majority of Massachusetts inhabitants in the late eighteenth century; Noble later testified that he had been "educated at the farming business" by Marsh. Marsh was also supposed to teach Noble how to read, write, and do basic arithmetic. Since Noble signed his three testimonies only with "x" marks, it seems that Marsh did not fulfill the "writing" part of the indenture, or else Noble proved unable to learn this skill.

Noble later reported that he lived at Marsh's estate "near twenty years" or "till the late war broke out." The indenture was originally contracted to end on 6 July 1774 (Noble's twenty-first birthday), a year before hostilities commenced, but the indenture might have been lengthened if Noble ran away or otherwise violated its terms. After he became free, he worked briefly in Brookfield, Massachusetts, probably as a farmhand, and then, on 10 May 1775 he enlisted in Colonel Benedict Arnold's regiment, almost as soon as it was formed in the wake of the battles at Concord and Lexington. Apparently wishing to follow in his father's footsteps as a military man, Noble remained in the Continental Army for nearly the whole war, joining or being transferred to different units periodically. He was on the campaign into Canada to capture Montreal in 1775–76; he wintered at Valley Forge in 1776–77; he served four days aboard the brig *Freedom* in 1777. And one particularly momentous event: while stationed in Providence, Rhode Island, in June 1778, he married Mary "Polly" Moor. Noble was then twenty-five years old.

Unlike his father, young Mark Noble did not become an army officer; he never rose beyond the rank of private or seaman, and he created trouble by deserting in the middle of the war. He originally joined the army as part of the quota from the town of Pittsfield, thus receiving the enlistment bonus that town offered. When that three-year tour of duty was over, he reenlisted as part of the quota for the town of Hadley (his hometown) and received their bonus, which was probably significantly higher than Pittsfield's had been; as the war dragged on, all towns found they had to offer bigger bounties to entice recruits. Before that tour of duty was complete, Noble deserted, disappearing in July 1780. On 1 January 1781 he surfaced in Cranston, Rhode Island, and enlisted for military service with the Rhode Island Regiment for three years. He served seven months of his tour of duty before the Massachusetts military authorities learned of his whereabouts and demanded him back. On 1 August, he was sent back to the First Massachusetts Regiment, where he was court-martialed for desertion and punished with 100 lashes. He stayed with the Massachusetts troops for the rest of the war, mustering out in 1782. Later, in 1792, his military services were repaid by the issuance of a warrant for 100 acres of land in the new territory the United States had acquired in the peace treaty.

Meanwhile, his family was growing: a daughter was born in the late 1770s or early 1780s, and son Stephen was born in 1785. Despite his training in "the farming business," veteran Noble supported his family by following "the business of a laborer," work he characterized as "chopping wood, butchering, &c"—a brief, telling description of the backbreaking work necessary to warm and feed a household. It apparently was a good enough living to satisfy the Providence councilmen, who questioned him in January 1787 and permitted him to remain in Providence for the time being. Not until December 1787 did the councilmen actually warn him out. The removal seems to have been timed to evict the family as cold weather closed in. The harvest was in, the butchering done for the year; Noble may have found work scarce and been unable to pay for his family's lodgings, generating a complaint.

By 1790 he had moved back to Providence, and the census that year listed him, his wife, and the two children in the household. Then, in December 1792, when Noble was almost forty years old, he fell into difficulties again. Once again, though, it was the beginning of winter and work may have been slow and wages especially meager. In his testimony, Noble stressed that as a young man he had completed an indenture with a master in Hadley, and so the councilmen ordered Noble and his wife and children to be removed to Hadley "immediately." They soon returned to the Providence area and continued to live there, but quietly enough to avoid council action for the next few years. In this period, Noble saw his daughter "married to George Field, Jr.," a satisfying connection that Noble later reported to officials.

Mark Noble's work as a laborer did not bring his family a comfortable living. Relying on credit with shopkeepers, a usual form of exchange in the late eighteenth century, may have supplied the Nobles with the necessities of life, but it eventually got them into serious debt. In September 1798 Noble placed an advertisement in the *Providence Gazette*, divesting himself of financial responsibility for his wife: "All persons are hereby cautioned against trusting my wife, Mary Noble; as I am determined to pay no debt of her contracting, after the date hereof." The notice implies that the couple were living such different lives that Noble had no firm knowledge of his wife's activities; they may have been separated at that point. In any case, their relationship was certainly troubled by financial difficulties, a not surprising consequence of the small pay Noble earned as a common laborer.

A few months later, in January 1799, the family drew official attention once again. Without specifying a particular problem—but perhaps it had to do with their financial difficulties—the council warned out forty-five-year-old Noble, his wife, and their fourteen-year-old son Stephen. Since during this testimony Noble emphasized that he had enlisted in the Rhode Island Regiment for the town of Cranston during the Revolutionary War, the councilmen ordered the family removed there, believing that to be their hometown. Noble's claim to settlement in Cranston was false, of course, since he had enlisted there fraudulently while still under obligation to the First Massachusetts Regiment. But the warning-out order had the effect of temporarily removing a troublesome family from Providence, and the council did not pursue the matter.

There is no evidence to tell us where Noble went to continue his work as a "laboring man." He may very well have come back to Providence, where he seemed to have had work and community contacts. He and his wife seemed to live on the economic margin and probably had accumulated a fair amount of debt by this time. The wages he earned as a common laborer were clearly not sufficient to maintain his wife to the extent she desired, but unfortunately she left no record to tell her side of the story. Perhaps she struggled to keep the family afloat financially, harried by constant debt and her husband's inability to stick to a job. In any case, raising a family without trouble on such slim pay took more ingenuity and resourcefulness than the Nobles seemed to possess.

Peter Norton

In contrast to Mark Noble, Peter Norton was a laboring man who eventually won the favor of authorities. After being warned out of Providence, he came back and made a home for himself there in a somewhat mysterious manner. Officials dropped their objections to his presence, in all likelihood because he lived peaceably, worked hard, and formed a "proper" family with his wife and two sons. When he and his wife died suddenly, officials swung into action, treating his orphaned boys with unusual care and generosity, a tribute to the status that Peter Norton had finally achieved.

Peter Norton, called "Blue Peter" by some, was born in Lynn, Massachusetts, around the year 1725; "I there lived until I was twenty-three years of age," he told authorities later. Although his testimony does not mention his growing-up years, the limited skills and menial labor of his adult years suggest that he was an indentured servant as a child, learning the most basic manual work needed to maintain a farm and household.

In his early twenties, Norton left Lynn and moved about in south-eastern New England, working as a hired man. Many transient men earned their living this way, hiring themselves out for the day, the week, the season, or the year. Some worked as agricultural laborers on farms (clearing fields, building fences, helping with the livestock); others worked on the wharves and in warehouses (loading and unloading ships, moving goods); still others worked alongside their employers in shops and yards (butchering, chopping wood, sweeping streets). These casual laborers had no long-term job security; without permanent labor contracts, they worked for as long as the employer agreed to pay them, and looking for the next job was a regular part of their lives. These men were not part of anyone's household, as servants were; they usually had to "find for them-selves"—that is, provide their own room and board.

Norton began his career as a hired man by hiring himself out annual-ly to employers in Pomfret, Connecticut. Having employment for a year at a time was a relative luxury in the world of transient labor, as it ensured him of wages even during the winter months. His work year probably ran from December to December, for this was the traditional English work-ingman's labor year, ending at Christmas and resuming at the new year. After two years in Pomfret, his jobs followed a more seasonal trajectory; he hired himself out for "about eight or nine months" to an employer in Dighton, Massachusetts, and then for "about seven months" to an employer in Little Compton, Rhode Island. These periods of time suggest that he worked for farmers who wanted his labor for the crop cycle and did not employ him during the winter months. The insecurity implicit in such seasonal labor may have prompted him to find another way to sup-port himself; he moved to Rehoboth, where he "hired a house" and "dwelt" in it for two years, probably paying the rent and supporting him-self by growing some of his own food and doing occasional day labor to obtain what he could not grow or make. This, too, apparently was an unsatisfactory arrangement. Perhaps he could not earn enough to pay the house rent. In 1756 he moved to Providence, probably in search of more steady work, and here he seemed to manage better. For seven years, he lived and labored in Providence; when he finally came to the attention of officials there in 1763, he told them that he had been in the town "ever since the last war [French and Indian War] begun."

When Peter Norton was questioned by Providence officials in 1763, he was thirty-seven or thirty-eight years old, a free but poor man who labored with his hands and lived on the margin economically because he lacked the education, skills, and social connections needed for advancement. As his nickname suggested, "Blue Peter" Norton was probably a man of color; named with Norton on the same summons were "Glasco, a Negro man," "Prince Sweet, a Negro man," and "Patience Tew, a mustee woman." Their simultaneous appearance before authorities suggests they were neighbors or friends of Norton's. No particular "complaint" about need or behavior had been lodged about these transients. Rather, this seems to have been a "round up" day, one of several occasions when Providence councilmen summoned and questioned—one after the other—transient people of color who lived in the same neighborhood. Such days occurred when authorities questioned seven heads of household on 31 December 1757 and 15 January 1774, nine on 7 August 1786, ten on 20 March 1780 and 8 December 1785, thirteen on 24 July 1770, fourteen on 17 December 1795, and eighteen on 13 October 1797.⁴ Apparently the presence of a cluster of transients like Peter Norton—free people of color unregulated by bound service—was enough to attract official attention.

As a result of his interrogation, Norton was formally rejected as an inhabitant of Providence. He moved to the adjoining town of North Providence and tried to make a living there for a time, but in 1765, he was warned out of that town as well. He returned to Providence and established himself as an inhabitant by some means not revealed in the record. His life took on settled contours. He married, and he and his wife, Rose Norton, had two sons, both born in Providence, Peter in 1770 and Richmond in 1771. There is no obvious explanation for Norton's acquisition of settlement—perhaps he gained the patronage of an influential person or perhaps he was able to purchase a small piece of real estate, although he does not appear on the Providence tax lists in the eighteenth century—but it is clear that he had inhabitant status because, when disaster struck, town officials took over the management of his family instead of warning them out. This happened in 1776, when smallpox swept through Providence, infecting both Peter and Rose Norton. Neighbors supplied food (meat, cornmeal, and molasses) and essential clothing at town expense, including a "petticoat" and a shirt for Richmond, who was still being dressed in the traditional English-style gown of boys not yet "breeched." Both Peter (then about fifty years old) and Rose Norton died of the illness, and neighbors prepared them for burial: a few women "laid out" Peter Norton's body; one man built a coffin for him; another was paid six shillings from the town treasury "for digging Rose Norton's grave," and shortly thereafter another six shillings for "digging Peter Norton's grave."

After their parents' death, the Norton boys were bound out as indentured servants by the Providence town council, a typical action taken when poor children were orphaned. Richmond went to Moses Daniels of Mendon, Massachusetts, and Peter went to Job Smith of Providence. The boys, both described as "mustee," were bound until they reached adulthood (age twenty-one) in contracts that required the master to teach them "to read and write the English language" and enough basic arithmetic "so as to keep common book accounts." Richmond's master promised to "educate him as an husbandman" and Peter's to "teach him the trade of a cooper."

Peter Norton's hard manual labor brought him some success: he lived for years in Providence without being warned out; he made himself an accepted part of the town; he married and had children. While his meager earnings could not cushion his children from being separated and bound out when he died, those boys were placed in contracts that, in theory at least, gave them the opportunity to achieve a socioeconomic status higher than their father's. While Peter Norton was unable to write and signed his examination with an "x," his boys were supposed to be taught to write—and, further, to keep book accounts. If their masters lived up to the terms of the contracts, then young Peter and Richmond Norton could indeed have lived less on the margin than their father had.

John Treby

Goldsmith John Treby was an elite craftsman who made jewelry and decorative art objects, and fitted out carriages. He found Newport and Providence congenial places to ply this trade, where wealthy householders were concentrated, those most likely to want and be able to afford his labor. But some unspecified "misfortunes" brought him low and resulted in his forcible removal from Providence. His reduction in status indicates how even skilled craftsmen could be rendered highly vulnerable by vagaries of business in the late eighteenth century.

John Treby was born in the late 1730s in Newport. He was given a good start in life: trained in a highly skilled craft and given commensurate literacy training as well. He signed his name in a clear, educated hand on a number of documents, indicating his familiarity with pen and ink—a necessity for a good craftsman who kept his own accounts. Someone set him up in business with tools, a workshop, and potential clients. All this suggests parents who provided well for their son.

Treby probably either set up his own shop in Newport or teamed up with other craftsmen. In September 1761, he joined with thirty other Newport men, some of them quite wealthy and influential, to sign a petition—his was the last signature—asking the colonial legislature for permission to run a lottery, the profits of which would finance the "paving" of Thames Street. This was busiest and most congested part of Newport, where merchants and craftsmen had their shops, but where frequent traffic to and from the wharves created inconvenient and even dangerous ruts and cracks in the road. Enterprising men of business wanted the street smoothed and made more impervious to the mud, dust, ice, and snow that seasonally churned up the earth. For those in the production of luxury goods, good custom depended considerably on good roads.

After working in Newport for a year or two, Treby "moved to the Town of Providence and purchased a small real estate and dwelt some time" there in the mid-1760s. This was probably his attempt to establish himself independently as a goldsmith. During his five or so years in Providence, Treby married the daughter of Providence man Ebenezer Richardson, and it may be that Richardson had offered Treby a partnership or otherwise attracted him to Providence in the first place.

After his Providence sojourn, Treby moved back to Newport. In the late 1760s, he tried his hand doing "business in the character of a merchant" and was successful enough that he "paid town and colony taxes" in Newport. Something turned the venture sour, however; he described his disappointment as "meeting with misfortunes." Very likely the trouble related to his merchant enterprise. In June 1769, one of Treby's customers, William Richardson—perhaps one of his wife's relatives—petitioned the colonial legislature for permission to declare bankruptcy, an act that left Treby unable to collect the £32 he was owed by Richardson. A few such unpaid debts could easily have sunk a new merchant, and the incident apparently discouraged Treby enough to send him back to Providence and to the craft of goldsmithing.

He did not flourish in Providence. Although he was back in his wife's hometown, something went wrong there too. A health crisis, with family complications, appears to have prompted official action, and in July 1775 he was warned out to Newport, the town where he had been born and raised and where he had recently paid taxes. Treby also may have become alienated from his wife and her family, for Ebenezer Richardson apparently was unwilling to help out Treby and did not prevent his removal from Providence. Treby's wife and children are conspicuously absent from the removal order, indicating that they remained behind, perhaps with Richardson, while Treby alone endured the embarrassment of being "carried" to Newport by the Providence sergeant and "delivered" to John Pittman, one of Newport's overseers of the poor. This journey must have been an acute humiliation for Treby, who had once fashioned decorative tableware for well-to-do families like Pittman's.

In 1781, six years after being thus returned to Newport, Treby died, perhaps of whatever debilitating condition had prompted his removal from Providence. At Treby's death, Ebenezer Richardson was appointed guardian over the two children, Elizabeth Treby and Ebenezer Richardson Treby. This legal action indicated that the children stood to inherit property from someone, although probably not from their impoverished father; with their "natural" guardian now deceased, the grandfather took over administering their property until they came of age. The paper trail of Treby's wife and children ends here.

John Treby was among the most privileged of transients in this study, with his literacy, his fine skill training, his once-successful business, and his marriage into a respectable, property-owning family. But the "misfortunes" of mercantile business, his own bodily weakness, and his alienation from his wife reduced him to transient status and brought him the sting of official rejection. Before he was forty years old, this once-prosperous craftsman had become an unwelcome resident.

Providence ss To the Town Serjeant or to either of the Constables of the Town of Providence in the County of Providence in the Colony of Rhode Island . . . . Greeting

Whereas complaint hath been made unto Us George Taylor, Richard Jackson, Benjamin Thurber and Job Sweeting who constitute and make the present Town Council of the Town of Providence aforesaid that John Treby Goldsmith hath come in this Town to inhabit without gaining a Legal Settlement therein and Whereas it appears by the Examination of the said John Treby taken before the Town Council aforesaid that the Town of Newport in the County of Newport in said Colony was the last Place of the said John Treby's Legal Settlement — We do therefore adjudge the Lawful Settlement of the said John Treby is in the Town of Newport aforesaid

These are therefore in his Majesty's Name George the Third King of Great Britain &c to require you or either of you on sight hereof to apprehend the said John Treby and him convey to the said Town of Newport and him deliver to one of the Overseers of the Poor for the said Town of Newport — Together with an authentick Copy of this our Order: And you the Overseers of the Poor for the said Town of Newport are hereby Required to Receive and Provide for the said John Treby as an Inhabitant of said Town of Newport — Hereof Fail not and make true Return of this Warrant Given at a Town Council held at Providence on the on the 22.d Day of July in the Year of our Lord One thousand Seven Hundred and Seventy Five and in the Fifteenth Year of his said Majesty's Reign —

Signed and Sealed by Order and Behalf of said Council

By Theodore Foster Council Clerk

Figure 5. When goldsmith John Treby was warned out of Providence to Newport, the town sergeant who transported him also carried this official warrant for his removal, dated 22 July 1775. Source: PTP 2:151, neg. no. RHi (x3) 9397. Courtesy of the Rhode Island Historical Society.

Nathaniel Bowdish

Nathaniel Bowdish is something of a mystery. The many pieces of his story do not add up to a satisfying whole, so making sense of his experiences requires considerable speculation. Bowdish identified himself as a "gentleman"; supporting that claim is his unusual literacy and his expert understanding of legal procedure. But he also identified himself as a "poor man"; supporting *that* claim are the meagerness of his assets, his frequent financial problems, his transient status in several towns, and the trouble that seemed to spring up between him and authorities, who generally viewed him as a troublemaker. Between the documents that he himself generated and the ones that town leaders generated about him, Bowdish carved a distinctive and puzzling trail.

One plausible interpretation of the evidence is that Nathaniel Bowdish was an itinerant legal advocate who migrated throughout Rhode Island, supporting himself by selling his legal knowledge and clerical expertise on an occasional basis to ordinary people. By reading and explaining letters and documents illiterate people had received, by advising them of legal rights and opportunities, and by writing letters and petitions for them to send elsewhere, he might have functioned as a populist lawyer. But in doing so, he usurped the place of clergy, town officials, and the other local elites to whom uneducated people would normally turn for such assistance. As a literate, educated man outside the ruling order, his actions would have fostered an independent spirit on the part of people who traditionally had deferred to the "fathers of the town." This would explain the hostility those "fathers" displayed toward Bowdish.

Whenever he was questioned about the place where he "belonged," Bowdish claimed Preston, Connecticut—but he made this claim even after he had clearly gained settlement in Glocester, Rhode Island. Probably at one time he had belonged to Preston, and naming it became a convenient fiction once rooted in fact. His reluctance to name Glocester as his home may have sprung from his desire to protect his family and neighbors there.

He seemed to understand that his business would stir up hostility in other places and may have wished to prevent his relatives and friends at home from suffering any repercussions.

Nathaniel Bowdish was born and raised in Preston, Connecticut, according to his own testimony. The documentary record shows he married Elizabeth King in neighboring Glocester, Rhode Island, on 28 September 1745, by which time he was probably in his early twenties. They had at least two children: Nathaniel Jr. and Rachel, both born in the late 1740s. The family seemed to prosper in Glocester, for Nathaniel Bowdish purchased twenty acres of land and "a dwelling house" there in 1751. Then, in 1752, Elizabeth apparently died. In 1753, Nathaniel sold the house and acreage and purchased a much smaller tract of land; Elizabeth's signature was noticeably missing from the mortgage deed that confirmed this transaction.

Nathaniel Bowdish continued to maintain a home in Glocester, and his children grew up there. Rachel eventually married Glocester neighbor Gideon Eddy in 1769. Nathaniel Jr. became part of Glocester in time-honored ways. He served as a member of Glocester's special "alarm" militia at the beginning of the Revolutionary War, and he served for several years as part of Col. Archibald Crary's Rhode Island Regiment. He acquired land—forty acres worth £150 in 1778. He married and had four sons and three daughters, all born between 1781 and 1802. He became a voting member of the town meeting and served in minor public offices such as constable and surveyor of fences in the 1770s and 1780s. The Glocester councilmen periodically granted him a tavern license in the 1780s and 1790s, so that he might sell liquor by the drink in his home. In March 1788 he turned out for the popular referendum on ratifying the newly proposed federal constitution and voted "no" along with the majority of his fellow townsmen. (In this, the one state where ordinary voters were given the opportunity to express their opinion about the new constitution, they voted it down by a huge margin: 239 for and 2,711 against ratification.[5]) To all appearances, Nathaniel Bowdish Jr. was a solid, settled, trusted inhabitant of Glocester.

Not so his father. Nathaniel Bowdish forged an unconventional path after the death of his wife. If indeed he was an itinerant clerk and legal advisor, his career seems to have begun at this point. In 1752 he was warned out of Smithfield, a complaint having been lodged against him; the councilmen ordered the sergeant to "convey" Bowdish back to "ye

colony of Connecticut," which he had apparently given as his place of settlement. In fact, he returned to his home in Glocester and let the fuss in
Smithfield die down.

A few years later, he was offered an ensign's commission during the
French and Indian War, an honor that indicated he had some influence in
the community, since rank depended on a man's ability to raise troops.
Such a commission also hooked him into a chain of patronage with his
senior officers. This chain was tested and broken in 1758, when something
happened between Bowdish and the colonel of the Rhode Island Regiment
in which he served. At Fort Stanwix, Bowdish's senior commanding officer
stripped him of his commission without a court martial, which was clearly against Rhode Island's militia law. Being stripped of his commission—
the most drastic action that could be taken against an officer—suggests
that Bowdish had seriously offended his colonel and also that his colonel
knew that Bowdish did not have sufficient influence and power to fight the
illegal action. Bowdish tried, however. In a petition to the Rhode Island
General Assembly some months later, he complained that he had been
demoted "without any justifiable cause" and without the due process of a
court martial, which was "contrary to the militia law." He asked for his
ensign's back pay to be restored to him, along with the "expense of his
travel home from Fort Stanwix," where his demotion had occurred. The
General Assembly rejected his plea, which suggests that the commanding
officer had more political power and influence than Bowdish did.

In that revealing 1760 petition, Bowdish identified himself as a "gentleman," implying that he did not labor with his hands as did the farmers
and artisans who were his neighbors. The "manual" labor at which he
seemed most skilled was the business of crafting legal documents, for this
petition was written entirely in Bowdish's hand; the clear, regular writing
indicates his long familiarity with such documents, and the several cross-
outs and additions show how he fine-tuned his language to sharpen his
appeal.

In that petition, Bowdish also claimed that he was "a poor man" who
"cannot subsist without help" in order to care for his "large family." His
poverty, coupled with his education and expertise, suggests that he was
born to wealth and privilege but had come down from that high status.
Perhaps he was a younger son of a propertied man who devolved the bulk
of the property upon his oldest son and trusted a professional education
to see this younger son through. Perhaps his father was a lawyer himself

and had trained his son, but then the two had a falling out and Bowdish had been disinherited. Perhaps he had been apprenticed to a lawyer but had not stayed in business with his master, either because he chose independence or because his master did not want to work with him. In any case, Bowdish evidenced a kind of training that was unknown to middling and lower-sort men.

Bowdish's reference in the 1760 petition to a "large family" may have been a strategic exaggeration. The Glocester records confirm the existence of his daughter Rachel and his son Nathaniel Jr., but no others. Perhaps he was using "family" in an extended sense to encompass other relatives who had a claim to his care. "Bowdish" dots the Glocester records, and it seems probable that Bowdish trusted the raising of his own son and daughter to relatives while he was away plying his trade as a clerk or serving in the military.

In the 1760 petition, Bowdish identified his place of residence as West Greenwich, where he may have possessed enough property to justify his claim. The Glocester records show numerous small land transactions on Bowdish's part, suggesting that he might have been something of a land speculator as well. In any case, his primary settlement and principal allegiance continued to be Glocester, whatever he might have written in a calculated petition.

After his stint in the military, Bowdish returned to whatever business kept his family afloat back in Glocester, and he continued to surface in odd places, apparently pursuing his itinerant trade as a clerk and legal advocate. His most notorious sojourn occurred in Charlestown. In March 1771 he stirred up some kind of trouble there that drew the attention of authorities, who gave him one month to leave the town and return to Preston, Connecticut, his supposed hometown. He left Charlestown, but returned later that year and caused even more of a fuss. The councilmen sent the town sergeant "to make diligent search" for Bowdish (a "vagrant person") because he had returned "without the consent of this council." When Bowdish was brought before them within a matter of hours, the town officers asked him "why he voluntarily returned into this town without first obtaining leave of this council." When he did not give "any satisfactory reason," the councilmen ordered him to pay the statutory forty-shilling fine for violating the removal order. Since Bowdish could not pay the fine, the council had him whipped "thirty lashes upon his naked back" before having him removed once again. It is an unlikely "gentleman" who would submit to a public whipping rather than pay a fine, but perhaps this spectacle actually increased Bowdish's business among lower-sort people, who may have seen him as their champion.

Undaunted, Bowdish returned to Charlestown and was spotted there six weeks later. Although the council wanted Bowdish arrested immediately, the sergeant was unable to find him; he had disappeared from sight, perhaps hidden away by his clients. But he was not idle. That winter he initiated a lawsuit against Charlestown for improperly removing him. By the spring of 1772, Rhode Island's superior county court had granted Bowdish a writ of certiorari, which required the Charlestown councilmen to "send the records & proxes [votes] relating to the fining and whipping [of] Nathaniel Bowdish" from their council meeting of the previous October.[6]

After they received the writ, Charlestown authorities were less disposed than ever to permit Bowdish to stay in their community. They instructed the town sergeant to keep an eye out for him, and when he was spotted in town on 1 April 1772 they ordered that he be brought before them the same day. Anxious to substantiate their own case, the councilmen also summoned several Charlestown residents to give public testimony about Bowdish's behavior and intemperate speech since his last removal. According to these witnesses, Bowdish "did damn this council & say that he would stay in this town if they whipt him again, and hath frighted & abused some of the inhabitants of this town, by behaving himself in a disorderly manner." No doubt believing their case fully justified, the councilmen had Bowdish whipped once again, this time "ten stripes upon his naked back," and removed from town for the third time.

Two weeks later, in mid-April 1772, Bowdish was spotted once again in Charlestown, "lurking about this town in contempt of the authority of this council." The council gave the town sergeant a standing order to the effect that whenever he found Bowdish in town, he should arrest him immediately and notify the council, who would promptly convene to "deal" with him to the full extent of the law. At this point, Bowdish disappears from the Charlestown records and, presumably, from the community. Perhaps he was daunted by the councilmen's persistence in tracking him down and having him whipped. Perhaps he was satisfied to have created a legal headache for them and delivered himself of his load of invective in public. Perhaps his business with Charlestown residents was completed and he had no strong reason to remain.

The Charlestown councilmen's hostility toward and harsh punishment of Bowdish is understandable if Bowdish was indeed a populist lawyer who helped ordinary people gain some advantage over their social and economic superiors. The probable result of such activity could be glimpsed in a worrisome incident that occurred in Jamestown, a few miles to the east, during the same year that Bowdish troubled Charlestown. In the summer of 1771 someone helped "husbandman" Isaac Pierce write a sharply critical letter to council president Edward Hull, Esq., offering "several ungenerous and ungentlemanlike reflections" on the council in general and on the council president in particular. Pierce criticized the way these town fathers had "discharge[d] the duties of their office" and alluded to some controversial ruling they had made recently.

Although this letter was dated July 1771, Hull did not show it to his fellow councilmen until January 1772, perhaps because the letter would then give him some advantage in a local dispute or even in the larger conflict brewing between the colonies and the English crown. (Chronic tension over revenue patrols in Narragansett Bay reached a climax in June 1772 with Rhode Islanders burning the royal schooner *Gaspee* in Narragansett Bay a few miles north of Jamestown.) When the other councilmen read the letter, they were shocked. The very production of the document constituted a grievance for these men, who apparently had never seen its like. They ordered that the letter be "lodged on file" with the town clerk, who was instructed to "give copies thereof to any person" willing to pay the clerk's fee for copying documents. The town fathers, it seems, hoped that the unencumbered circulation of the letter would damage Pierce's reputation and bolster their own.

This was the sort of challenge to authority that Bowdish seemed to represent. With his skills in literacy and law, his contempt for authority, and his acerbic personality, he posed a danger to hierarchical order in the community. He encouraged others to resist their leaders and to criticize them. What happened to the Jamestown councilmen in January 1772 was probably known by the Charlestown councilmen by April, when Bowdish was chased out of town for the third time. Although no one directly accused him of instigating or authoring Pierce's letter, councilmen who knew Bowdish must have wondered.

From an official point of view, Nathaniel Bowdish was among the most troublesome transients to be sent away from a Rhode Island town in the latter part of the eighteenth century. His power against authorities

stemmed from his fearless and knowledgeable attitude. He had a fine
understanding of settlement law, had figured out how to position himself
so he could claim more than one settlement at the same time, and knew
that officials could do no more than whip him if he returned, which he did
more than once. He was not deterred by the threat of being whipped, thus
robbing the councilmen of one of their most effective discouragements of
transients: fear of painful corporal punishment and public humiliation.
And he had his own ways of irritating and humiliating the councilmen in
return. He used his tongue to criticize them publicly and strongly in a way
that touched their pride and honor; he initiated a court suit against them,
creating paperwork and bureaucratic headaches for them. It was a case he
could not win (which he probably knew), but it apparently gave him satisfaction to see them forced to defend themselves.

After his ejection from Charlestown, Bowdish seemed to stay closer
to home in Glocester. He may have moved in with his son Nathaniel Jr.,
bringing the household count to six males and four females, the report of
the 1790 census. Perhaps Nathaniel Sr. gave people legal advice over a
tankard of ale in his son's tavern room, a more attractive option for an
aging man than frequent travel and conflict with officials elsewhere. In
1785, the Glocester voters declared him exempt from taxes, perhaps in
recognition of his reduced activity and advancing years.

In the 1790s, Bowdish seemed to get a second wind. He got entangled
in a series of incidents which show him once again using his knowledge of
the law to gain advantage for himself or others. In 1792, he proved he "took
up and apprehended" Isaac Cottrell, who had stolen a horse; Cottrell was
subsequently tried, convicted, and whipped for the crime. Five years later
Bowdish petitioned the state legislature to receive $20 for his action, a
reward to which he was "entitled by the laws of the state." The lag time
between the event and his petition suggests that Bowdish belatedly figured
out how to profit from his good deed. The legislature granted this petition
and Bowdish got his $20 from the state treasurer.

Then, in June 1795, Bowdish did jury duty for the town of Glocester at
the Providence County court, in a trial that resulted in Rufus Peck being
convicted of receiving stolen goods. Peck later petitioned for a new trial,
perhaps at Bowdish's advising; Peck claimed that the jury had been intim-
idated in the original trial, and he brought Bowdish as a witness. Bowdish
testified that he "heard [fellow juror] Capt. Jencks say that a man that
would receive stolen goods was worse than a thief and that he ought to be

damned and that he ought not to live." According to Bowdish, Jencks made clear that he believed Peck to be guilty of the crime before the evidence had been presented.

In 1796 Bowdish sojourned in Providence, where his mere presence ("loitering about the streets") worried the councilmen, who judged him "an improper person to be tolerated here." When they questioned him, he "represent[ed] himself to belong to the town of Preston," avoiding his connections to Glocester in his usual manner. The Providence officials ordered that Bowdish leave the town within twenty-four hours or he would be forcibly evicted.

Then, back in Glocester, Bowdish's failure to pay his road tax resulted in the town council finally ordering him to "work out" his back taxes in the kind of manual labor needed to keep the unpaved "highways" clear for travel. The council directive that "Bowdish see the work is done" suggests they knew that this man in his seventies would not do the labor himself, but rather find someone else to do it.

That is the last mention in the town records of Nathaniel Bowdish, a most unusual transient. He identified himself as a "gentleman," and no authority ever contradicted that claim by identifying him as being in any trade or labor. Further, he was educated well beyond the norm for transient poor people, he repeatedly used the law to gain an advantage, and he dealt with authorities in an unusually assertive manner. On the other hand, he lived on the edge economically: he admitted to being a "poor" man; his assets were few; and he was unable to pay his taxes on at least two occasions. His activities seem deliberate actions based on shrewd calculations, not ignorance or impulse. He knew just how far he could push authorities, he knew what to do to accomplish his goals. Not surprisingly, his business caused authorities to bristle at his presence, and the Providence council's ruling that he was an "improper person" who could not be "tolerated" seems to sum up a series of official judgments over a span of forty-four years. Bowdish represented a threat to the "proper" class relationships within communities; his deployment of the law challenged the bonds of deference and paternalism that bound together so many townspeople. Whatever his gentlemanly origins, his business made him unwelcome.

4. Reversal of Fortune

WHEN IN 1764 John Bennett asked the Warwick town council to assist him in the construction of a house for his family, he pleaded that he "has the misfortune to be a very poor man." Many of the transients in this study could have said the same thing, for economic hard times, especially in the 1780s, made life even more difficult for people already struggling to get by. As if poverty were not sufficient misfortune, some transients were propelled into disaster by particular catastrophes. The narratives in this section illuminate the variety of misfortunes that complicated the state of poverty in which many transients existed.

Some catastrophes touched everyone in the community. Two wars dominated the political history of the latter part of the eighteenth century in Anglo-America: the Seven Years' War (1756–63) and the American Revolution (1776–83). In both eras, women and children became transients when they tried to follow or rejoin soldier fathers and husbands, and men became transients when they tried to pursue a livelihood in a new place where their army experience had brought them. In the Revolutionary War, transients were made by the three-year (1776–79) British occupation of Rhode Island towns on islands in Narragansett Bay (Newport, Jamestown, Middletown, and Portsmouth) and New Shoreham, on Block Island in Long Island Sound. Many of the residents in those towns fled to mainland towns to wait out the occupation, and the state legislature ordered mainland towns to shelter and support the arriving refugees (host towns would later be reimbursed from the state treasury). Some of those refugees preferred to stay in their host towns and did not return to their battle-scarred homes after the war was over. When they fell on hard times and needed assistance in the 1780s and 1790s, their host towns usually tried to send them back to their hometowns. Thus war was responsible for the dislocation of numerous transients, including Jerusha Townsend (Chapter 1), Judah Hazard Wanton (Chapter 2), Phillis Merritt Wanton (Chapter 3), and Benjamin Jones (this chapter).

Epidemic disease was another community catastrophe that visited southeastern New England regularly in the eighteenth century. Infectious disease made transients out of some people by causing death and disability in families and galvanized survivors into leaving their hometowns in search of another job, better fortune, or the support of relatives and friends. It also rendered resident transients highly visible to the official eye of town leaders, who were responsible for organizing community efforts to contain such diseases. In the atmosphere of worry and panic that gripped affected communities, transients could easily appear a threat to the town, and they could become handy scapegoats, charged with bringing a disease into the community or causing its spread by their poor and unhealthful living arrangements. Further, those transient residents who actually contracted the disease could expect to be forcibly removed to their home communities as soon as they were well enough to withstand the journey. An outbreak of infectious disease was good cause for all transients to worry about their future in a community.

Smallpox epidemics raged in Rhode Island towns six or eight times in the eighteenth century. It was by far the most feared of the contagious infections that Anglo-Americans of that era battled, and they looked to their town leaders to contain the spread of the disease and tend the victims. As soon as smallpox was detected, town councilmen met as often as necessary (daily or even twice daily at times) to cope with each new outbreak until the disease abated. Residents (often transients) who had an immunity to the infection (through prior exposure) were assigned to examine, nurse, and "cleanse" the victims and their household goods. Other residents were assigned to guard the quarantined houses where the victims stayed. Still others were assigned to be couriers of food, supplies, and messages to the victims. When smallpox was in the region, town leaders became particularly alert to transients in their community and were ready to warn out and forcibly remove any who looked likely to suffer or who had actually come down with the disease. The labor-intensive care of smallpox victims resulted in extremely high poor-relief costs if the victims were unable to pay for their own care; so every town was anxious to get poor transients out of town and into the hands of those who were by law required to support them in their poverty and distress. Peter Norton (Chapter 3) and his wife Rose left two young boys orphaned when they died in the smallpox epidemic that swept through Providence in 1776.

In the late 1790s, a new scourge, yellow fever, visited southern New England, brought into seaports aboard ships that had visited ports where the disease was present. The virulence and strangeness of the infection challenged town leaders in their efforts to contain both the infection and the hysteria that accompanied it. In Providence, where so many transients lived, town leaders met frequently to put into practice prevailing medical theory that disease flourished in an atmosphere of bad smells and that infection could be prevented by eradicating stenches. They organized special health committees whose members patrolled the streets with their noses in the air to locate those places where disease might fester and order offending residents to drain stinking water in ditches and cellars, throw lime in the vaults of their privies, and clean up the garbage that collected in walkways and alleys beside their dwellings. Legal inhabitants might have to be badgered, by fines and threats, to follow these orders, but poor transients could easily be ordered out if their shabby and smelly dwellings were considered a threat to the public health. Yellow fever panics occurred every summer and fall from 1797 through 1800, but the worst years were 1797 and 1800, when Providence officials issued weekly bulletins listing the names of victims and providing regular casualty statistics in an effort to combat exaggerated rumors about the extent of the epidemics. And in the falls of 1797 and 1800, not so coincidentally, Providence officials convened special meetings just to examine and warn out transients, particularly people of color, who lived in areas where officials suspected that the fever was breeding or spreading. Providence's transient poor had not only the disease to fear, but also the long arm of settlement law. Among the yellow fever victims in this study were Jerusha Townsend (Chapter 1), Robert Fuller (Chapter 2), and Patience Havens, whose story leads off this chapter.

Newport, Providence, and Boston, the largest and most commercialized towns in southeastern New England, bore the brunt of community-wide disasters such as war and epidemics. Providence, where so many transients were questioned and then warned out, was a typical eighteenth-century port city in North America. The misfortunes that brought transients into or flung them out of Providence were not unusual: other port cities along the east coast struggled with the same kinds of upheaval and experienced the same flow of dislocated, job-seeking, refuge-seeking people.

More personal misfortunes are the hallmark of other narratives in this chapter. Injury or sickness in the family, mental illness, or some peculiar twist of fate had left them without a stable and permanent place in a community. For many in eighteenth-century Anglo-America, such happenings were attributed to Providence, the hand of God that brought good and bad to people at every station in society, often beyond human understanding. For those who lived on the edge of ruin, a hard Providence tipped them over into disaster and then into being sent out of town by very human agents.

One of the most common reasons for transients to need poor relief was sickness or injury in the household. When the breadwinner was unable to work, the entire household suffered. But illness among children also brought distress, since it forced parents to abandon their jobs temporarily in order to attend their children, required medical care which poor households could not afford, and robbed the family of the economic participation (however limited) of one of its members. Often sick or injured transients could not be moved, and town authorities kept a running tab of expenses to present to the transients' hometown when they were finally removed. When overenthusiastic officials tried to move transients who were truly too ill to undergo transport, more compassionate residents sometimes objected, but eventually each incapacitated transient was removed to his or her town of legal settlement. In this chapter, the narratives of Elizabeth Springer (childbirth fever), Primus Thompson (broken leg), Benjamin Jones (crippled child), and Ann West ("underwitted") provide insight into the upheaval created by such personal misfortune.

The remaining narratives illuminate the kinds of misfortune brought upon transients by human behavior. Esther Heradon, Margaret Fairchild Bowler, Benjamin Champney, and Jacob Burke could all point to specific persons (sometimes themselves) whose actions precipitated tragedy. Heradon, abandoned callously by her husband, was further traumatized by two sets of town officials squabbling over where she "belonged," so that she and her four young children were dragged back and forth for weeks between Connecticut and Rhode Island. Bowler's house was torn down by an irate mob in the middle of the night, a mob fueled by the conviction that Bowler and her lodgers were prostitutes. Champney became such a notorious drunkard that town officials put him aboard a ship and under the care of a sea captain to keep him from creating further disturbance. Jacob Burke was convicted first of assault and then of rape, and only the petition of sympathetic men saved him from the gallows—but it condemned him to exile from the United States.

These narratives of misfortune are not success stories. Some of them, it is true, have a sweet undertone that stems from the sympathetic actions taken by family members, neighbors, and even some officials. But the central theme in each story is a hard one: that poverty and misfortune spelled catastrophe in eighteenth-century New England.

Patience Havens and Her Daughters

Patience Havens's story puts a personal face on the yellow fever epidemic that swept through Providence in 1797. It shows how transients were drawn to urban areas for work and community, how they built connections among themselves, and how disease and sudden death could fragment a household and an extended family.

Patience Havens was born in 1743, a slave to William Havens, a large landholder and slaveowner of North Kingstown. There is no mention in the records of Patience Havens being married according to Anglo-American ceremony. It seems likely, however, that she had a mate in North Kingstown, for she gave birth to at least five children: Nancy (Hazard), born in 1767; Deliverance, born in 1769; Deborah (Greene), born in 1775; Ruth, born in 1776; and Simon, born in 1786.

When William Havens died in 1786, he manumitted two of his slaves in his will: Lonnon and Cloe, two apparently old and faithful bondservants who were also granted rights to "enjoy" the Havens farm "during their natural life." Patience was not mentioned in the will, but she was listed in the inventory of Havens's estate as "one old Negro woman named Patience, about forty eight or fifty years of age, very infirm and liable to be supported," valued at £1. Since Patience, by her own testimony, was forty-three years old at the time of the inventory, it appears she exaggerated her age, perhaps to help persuade the administrators of the estate that she was past useful labor.

By virtue of being part of "all the remainder" of Havens's estate, Patience was bequeathed to Havens's wife Sarah. But Patience and her children had apparently already been manumitted in an informal way; some of them had migrated to Providence well before Havens's death in 1786. Sarah Havens apparently followed her husband's lead and affirmed the free status of Patience and her daughters without actual documentation; in any case, neither Patience nor her daughters ever produced any manumission papers.

In 1786, then, Patience Havens's master was dead, and she was able to live an independent life, however circumscribed by her limited laboring opportunities and abilities as a "very infirm" and "old" woman of color. And while her and her daughters' free status may have been ambiguous, that of her son was not. Simon, born in 1786, was free by virtue of Rhode Island's gradual emancipation law, which took effect in 1784. While the law freed no adults, it technically freed children born to slaves after 1 March 1784, although they stayed under the control of their mothers' masters until adulthood. Patience and her daughters were made free by the ambiguous actions of Havens and his widow, but Simon was free by statutory law.

Beginning in 1784, the family migrated one by one to Providence, found work, established families, and became part of the free community of color that mushroomed in Providence in the late eighteenth century. Deliverance was first, moving to Newport for a year and then on to Providence. She found employment doing domestic labor in the houses of prosperous residents, which encouraged her sisters to do likewise. Nancy followed in 1786 and probably entered the same sort of work. Nancy married Peter Hazard, and when that relationship foundered she lived with Cesar Greene "as his wife." She bore three children while in Providence: George, born in 1789; Chloe, born in 1791; and Phebe, born in 1796. Deborah was the next to move to Providence, bringing her baby daughter Sophia, born in North Kingstown. Deborah eventually married Ned Greene, a seafaring man who was frequently absent on long voyages, and gave birth to their son George in early 1796.

By 1790, Patience had followed her daughters to Providence, and the census that year placed her there as head of a household of eleven persons of color. In 1793, she was questioned by the Providence councilmen, who identified North Kingstown as her place of legal settlement but did not order her out. In that examination, Patience represented herself as having arrived in Providence that very week; perhaps she had moved back to North Kingstown between 1790 and 1793 and had just returned. In any case, the council was apparently satisfied that she had some means of support and that no one in her family was in desperate need. Patience Havens's household subsequently became the locus of an extended family that included her daughters, her son, and her grandchildren: it probably expanded from time to time to accommodate seafaring in-laws and other relatives who sojourned there. Ruth Havens was removed to North Kingstown by the Providence councilmen in December 1795, perhaps because she was ill or otherwise incapable of laboring toward her own support, but the remainder of the family continued to function as a key household in the Providence network of people of color. Their importance is attested to by the town council's recruitment of Patience to care for Nero Douglas, an inhabitant of the town who became ill in 1796 and required a caretaker approved by local authority.

In the summer and fall of 1797, the Havens household was ruptured. In August, when yellow fever began to spread through the town, the family came to official notice, probably because someone in the household was taken ill with the disease. On 7 August, seven-year-old Sophia Havens, granddaughter of Patience and the oldest child of Deborah, was taken from the family and bound out by the Providence councilmen as an indentured servant to "gentleman" David Vinton and his wife Mary until Sophia turned twenty-one. As an illegitimate child born to Deborah before she married, Sophia was subject to the management of the town "fathers," who could dictate such an arrangement if they judged that Sophia was "suffering" in any way under the care of her family. The contract specified that Sophia learn the work of "a house servant," and the term "apprentice" was carefully crossed out in the indenture form and replaced with the word "servant," foreshadowing Sophia's future as a domestic worker.

Three weeks later, at the end of August, Patience, Deborah, and Nancy were summoned before the town council and questioned about their place of legal settlement. This was part of a larger official effort to control the spread of yellow fever—or to provide a convenient scapegoat to blame for the epidemic—by warning out nearly thirty families of color. The way the women were questioned, one after the other, indicates they attended council together and also suggests that officials recognized them as an extended family. As a result of her examination, Patience was ordered to depart for North Kingstown within a week. Deborah was given one week to depart for Warwick, her seafaring husband's place of legal settlement. Nancy Hazard was allowed temporarily to stay in Providence, although the councilmen ruled that she "belonged" in North Kingstown.

None of the women actually left Providence, despite the council orders, but between the epidemic and official interference, the family was

This INDENTURE witnesseth,

That *The Town Council of the Town of Providence in the County of Providence*

~~strikethrough~~ and ~~strikethrough~~, and with the Consent of *Josphia Havens a poor girl Daughter of Deborah Havers, a black Woman*

doth put and bind *her an* Apprentice to *David Vinton Gentleman and Mary his Wife* *an House servant a servant*

to learn the Art, Trade or Mystery; and, after the Manner of ~~an Apprentice~~, to serve from *the Date ~~day of~~ hereof* for and during the Term of *fifteen years* next ensuing, to be complete and ended. During all which said Term, the said *servant ~~Apprentice~~ her* said *master & mistress* faithfully shall serve, *their* Secrets keep, *their* lawful Commands gladly obey: *she* shall do no Damage to *her* said *master or mistress* nor see it done by others, without letting or giving Notice thereof to *her* said *master and mistress* shall not waste *her* said *masters & mistress* Goods, nor lend them unlawfully to any: *she* shall not commit Fornication, or contract Matrimony, within the said Term. At Cards, Dice, or any other unlawful Game, *she* shall not play, whereby *her* said *master and mistress* may have Damage. With *her* own Goods, or the Goods of others, without Licenfe from *her* said *master* shall neither buy nor fell: *she* shall not abfent *herself* by Day or by Night, from *her* said *master mistress* Service, without *their* Leave; or haunt Ale-Houfes, Taverns, or Play-Houfes; but in all Things behave *herself* as a good and faithful Apprentice ought to do towards *her* said *master & mistress* and all *others* during the said Term. And the said *David & Mary* do hereby promife to teach and inftruct, or caufe the faid Apprentice to be taught and inftructed, in the Art, Trade or Calling, of *a House servant* by the beft Ways and Means ~~they~~ can. *finding and allowing unto the said servant good and sufficient meat Drink Washing Lodging & apparel, and to cause said servant to be instructed in Common School Learning such as reading & writing, and at the Expiration of said service to dismiss the said servant with a good and sufficient freedom suit of Cloathing with all decent parts of the Body*

12259

In TESTIMONY whereof, the Parties to thefe Prefents have hereunto interchangeably fet their Hands and Seals, the *seventh* Day of *August* Anno Domini *seventeen hundred and ninety five* and in the *twenty second* Year of *American* Independence. *1797*

Signed, Sealed and Delivered,
in the Prefence of

Wheeler Martin

David Vinton

Figure 6. When Patience Havens became fatally ill with yellow fever in August 1797, town authorities took her granddaughter Sophia from the household and bound her as an indentured servant to Providence gentleman David Vinton and his wife Mary. This formal contract, dated 7 August 1797, spelled out Sophia's obligation to work as a "house servant." Source: PTP 28:48, neg. no. RHi (x3) 9400. Courtesy of the Rhode Island Historical Society.

splintered. Patience died from "the malignant fever" in late September; a local laborer was paid $1.50 to dig her grave. When cold weather arrived, killing the mosquitos, the epidemic ended, but officials continued to target transients of color for removal that winter. In December, when poor laborers were most likely to need support, the council issued a warrant for Deborah's removal to Warwick, taking her out of visiting range of her servant daughter. Two months later, in February 1798, the council ordered out Nancy as well. She returned later that year, and was taken to North Kingstown once again in March 1799, when the Providence constable delivered her and her three children into the care of one of North Kingstown's overseers of the poor.

Patience Havens had been the anchor that held the family in place in Providence. With her gone, her adult daughters and their children were made more vulnerable to official action against transients, especially those of color. The removal of one key person by the misfortune of yellow fever ultimately reorganized the lives of everyone in that person's extended family.

Elizabeth Springer

"Betsey" Springer's tragic story could have served as a cautionary tale for young women of the late eighteenth century: it contained the dramatic elements of a young woman leaving her hometown, maintaining a marginal existence in another town, entering into a sexual relationship with a faithless lover, giving birth to an illegitimate child, falling sick, and dying in a place that was not home. Here was what awaited transient young women who sought their fortune in dangerous places. It is tempting to imagine her story being told to other restless young countrywomen to persuade them to stay close to home.

In 1760, Elizabeth Springer was born in Tiverton, Rhode Island, a quiet, pastoral township to the east of Narragansett Bay, where the majority of inhabitants made their living by farming, supplemented with fishing and boat-building. Lawrence Springer was thirty-five years old when his daughter Elizabeth was born, and he did not live to see her reach adulthood; rather than stay at home, Elizabeth decided to strike out on her own in 1776, at age sixteen. Her departure coincided with and was very likely prompted by the outbreak of revolutionary hostilities, which put Tiverton residents in danger, particularly those with property fronting Narragansett Bay, which British warships patrolled. As long as British troops were present in the bay, farmers' property frequently disappeared or was destroyed—fences torn down, orchards and pastures pillaged, livestock stolen. Elizabeth Springer, like so many others, sought safe haven in Providence.

Little was holding her in Tiverton, in any case. Her father was dead and the larger Springer clan, although numerous, was neither prominent nor prosperous. No Springer held an important office in the town in the eighteenth century, and none owned a notable amount of property. On the contrary, many Springers struggled to survive. For most of Elizabeth's childhood, her Uncle Thomas and his family were supported principally by poor relief, because he was permanently disabled and one of the children was perpetually "sick." The few Springers who appeared on the tax lists paid only a nominal amount. It is not surprising, then, that Springer left Tiverton to find a better way of life in the nearest "big city."

For sixteen years Elizabeth Springer lived in Providence without attracting the attention of the overseers of the poor. She never married, but she found work and supported herself; she had no reason to return to Tiverton. Then, in 1792, when she was thirty-two years old, Springer's life unraveled rapidly. She gave birth to an illegitimate baby, a child whose coming had not been heralded by ordinarily watchful neighbors or poor-relief officials. This was one case of town councilmen being caught flatfooted: a transient woman's baby born in Providence, with no opportunity to remove the mother to her hometown before childbirth. Springer must have lived a very quiet life, keeping her condition sufficiently disguised to avoid discovery in the last months of pregnancy.

Elizabeth Springer's baby was born 16 December 1792. At the last minute, she must have asked for and received assistance from a neighbor. The news spread rapidly, and within twenty-four hours the Providence councilmen convened to question the new mother. She was not well and must have been in considerable discomfort when questioned by the council so soon after giving birth. The council's insistence on "examining" her immediately indicates their sense of urgency about illegitimate births. They wanted both mother and child out of their jurisdiction as rapidly as possible, though they tempered this dictate by stipulating that the removal should take place "at whatever time the doctor employed by the town shall judge she can with safety be removed." Because she had never gained a settlement anywhere else, she was to be returned to the place of her birth, Tiverton.

The removal never took place, because Elisabeth Springer never got well enough to be transported. For three weeks following her examination, she was cared for in Providence in the household of Daniel Fenner, who later was repaid for the labor performed by his wife in keeping their charge fed, warmed, and provided with nursing care. To no avail: Elizabeth Springer died on 5 January, very likely of infection following childbirth, a condition probably not helped by her having to attend council the day after her delivery. Providence man Elihu Peck made a twelve-shilling coffin for "Betsey Springer"; Daniel Branch dug a grave for her and provided a "bier" for her last journey.

Meanwhile, Elizabeth Springer's baby was cared for in the home of William Spencer, whose wife or servant could wet-nurse the newborn. The infant was "very sick all the time" and required "more firewood, candles, and watchers" than was usual, making Spencer's bill "very expensive." Despite these efforts, the baby died on 21 January, at five weeks of age. Daniel Branch was called into service again, this time "digging a grave for a child of Elizabeth Springer."

Instead of paying for Elizabeth Springer's removal, Providence paid the costs of nursing, tending, and then burying a mother and baby. The total came to a little less than 100 shillings (£5). Because Springer was legally an inhabitant of Tiverton, the Providence councilmen may have tried to persuade Tiverton authorities to pay back this amount. But the Providence officials may also have chalked up these costs to common charity, one-time expenses caused by disaster overtaking the already unfortunate poor while they sojourned within the town's borders. Elizabeth Springer, buried in a pauper's grave two days' journey from her birthplace, had indeed experienced misfortune.

Primus Thompson

When Anglo-American settlement washed over Rhode Island in the seventeenth century, Narragansett Indians faced difficult choices. Many noncombatant Indians were massacred by white New Englanders at their winter village during King Philip's War, and many combatants who surrendered were later sold into slavery. This destruction of their people and their lifeways prompted many Indians to migrate west to Massachusetts, New York, and eventually Wisconsin, but others elected to remain in Rhode Island and try to eke out a living among white colonists. After 1709, a tract of land in southern Rhode Island was reserved for Indian habitation and use; but its small size and its distance from the coast did not permit the Narragansett to follow freely the agriculture, hunting, and seasonal migrations of their ancestors. Instead, a number of Indians left the reservation to seek a livelihood among whites, laboring as farmhands or domestic servants in most cases. This was the life followed by the mother of Primus Thompson.

"Indian man" Primus Thompson was "born at Captain Joshua Thompson's in the town of Westerly" in the early 1750s. His mother apparently was a slave or servant of Thompson's, for her child was considered part of Thompson's household. Primus grew up as an indentured servant who "served [his] time" with Thompson, doing whatever labor the household needed—chopping wood, planting and harvesting crops, maintaining fences and farm equipment.

When his "time was out" in the early 1770s, Primus Thompson decided to become a seafaring man. This was one of the few occupations open to men of color, and it particularly attracted Indian men in eighteenth-century New England. While at sea, they experienced a kind of community and freedom they did not often find on land—this despite the hard labor they performed and harsh punishment they often received from the ship captain. For several years, Thompson sailed in and out of Westerly; then, in the autumn of 1774, he moved from Westerly to Jamestown with William Wilbur. Wilbur took over the operation of a ferryboat between Jamestown (on Conanicut Island in Narragansett Bay) and the Rhode Island mainland, and he wanted Thompson's assistance to operate the business. Ironically, ferry work proved more dangerous than life at sea for Thompson; within three months of beginning his job, he met serious misfortune in the form of a severely broken leg.

The accident occurred on 26 December 1774, during the winter season when ice was an ever-present problem on an open-water wharf. Thompson "fell on [William] Wilbur's ferry wharf" and "broke his thigh," a serious injury that resulted in a substantial "doctor's bill" for "setting the bone of said Indian man's thigh" as well as "other necessary attendance" as Thompson lay helpless. None of these expenses could Thompson pay, having "no money by me" except for "a small matter [amount] that was charitably given me" by an unnamed benefactor. So William Wilbur paid the doctor's bill himself and then, in January 1775, "applied to the town" for "compensation" out of the town treasury. Unfortunately for Wilbur, town officials refused to pay the bill, since both Wilbur and Thompson were "uncertificated" transients who were not "inhabitants of this town nor freehold herein" and therefore had no claims on the Jamestown town treasury. If Wilbur had taken upon himself to take care of his unfortunate employee, he could not look to Jamestown for reimbursement.

Wilbur's request for payment had the effect of alerting the councilmen to Thompson's situation, and they convened a meeting on 20 January to question the injured man. Clearly anxious to move Thompson back to Westerly, they asked him, "Do you think your thigh is now so strong that you might be moved with safety, either on horseback or otherwise?"

"I cannot ride on horseback, but I do think my thigh is well enough for me to be moved with safety in a chaise or some carriage," he answered.

Satisfied that transport could take place immediately, the councilmen ordered the town sergeant to "hire a horse and chaise or other suitable carriage in Newport" at the cheapest price possible and remove Thompson "forthwith." After what must have been a painful and tedious journey across twenty-five miles of frozen landscape, Thompson was delivered to one of Westerly's overseers of the poor, who promptly placed him in the household of William Sweet Peckham, who took on the caretaking task of "keeping" Thompson until he had mended.

The accident on the ferry wharf was a setback not only for Thompson but also for his employer, William Wilbur. After losing Thompson's invaluable assistance, Wilbur was unable to operate the ferry; within three months he gave up the enterprise and returned to his hometown of Richmond. From there, in April 1775, he once again petitioned the Jamestown town meeting for payment for "his time and trouble, expense, and other necessary attendance" on Thompson, as well as his doctor's bill. Since both Wilbur and Thompson had left Jamestown and were safely back in Westerly by that time, the town meeting relented and "resolved" that about half of Wilbur's account "be allowed." Neither Thompson nor

Wilbur seemed likely to become a charge to the town, so some "common charity" would not go amiss.

Wilbur returned to Richmond, but he did not stay long. In 1780, he asked the Richmond council for a certificate so that he could move to Charlestown, perhaps to try another venture connected with seafaring. But his sojourn in Charlestown did not bring success, for in the census of 1782, Wilbur did not show up as heading his own household. Either he had moved out of Rhode Island or he was living as a dependent in someone else's household. The Jamestown misfortune had redirected not only Primus Thompson's life, but William Wilbur's as well.

Benjamin Jones

Benjamin Jones was well acquainted with misfortune. He never knew his father, who died right after he was born; he was unjustly convicted of theft while in the military; his business was disrupted and his family forced to relocate during the British occupation of Newport during the Revolutionary War; and then his nine-year-old son William, on whom he relied as assistant, was seriously crippled in an accident, eclipsing all previous troubles. As a man who lived on the economic margin, Jones relied on the cooperative efforts of his family members to maintain his bakery, and William's injury threw the whole enterprise into jeopardy. In desperation, Jones turned to the town for assistance, and although he was a transient resident with no legal claim to poor relief money, the voters came to his aid. In this unusual case of transient hardship, the town of Providence recognized its own liability in a debilitating accident, allowed a struggling transient family to remain in residence, and even assisted them with a special grant out of the town treasury.

Benjamin Jones's father, Thomas, "came from England" in the 1730s and pursued his occupation "as a master of a vessel" based in Newport until he was "lost at sea" in 1742, when Benjamin "was but a few days old." Benjamin grew up in Newport, first in his mother's house and then in the house of Thomas George, to whom "his mother bound him out an apprentice" when he was "about twelve or thirteen years old." Under George's tutelage, Jones learned the trade of "set work coopering," making small containers to hold liquids.

The indenture lasted "until he was twenty one years old," but Jones was not at work in his master's shop that whole time. For several campaigns of the Seven Years' War, he traveled back and forth between the colonial frontier and Newport, probably having been "volunteered" by his master to fulfill his own military obligation. It was not a completely positive experience. In 1761, at Fort Stanwix, when Jones "faithfully" assisted his commanding officer by making "cans and pails for the use of regiment," using "a pair of compasses" borrowed from "the King's stores," he was "unjustly and causelessly" accused of stealing that equipment and much more material that had disappeared. When a court martial "condemned" him to "pay for all the tools that were lost," he angrily "made his escape" from Fort Stanwix several days before the rest of the regiment broke camp. Two years later, he reconsidered his rash action and petitioned the colonial legislature for the wages he had missed by going home early.

As the Seven Years' War drew to a close, Benjamin Jones finished his indenture, left soldiering behind, and took up the work of a cooper, very likely drawing on the patronage of his former master's customers. Within a few years, he was doing well enough to marry; he and Susannah Weaver, from the town of Warwick, soon had two daughters: Alice, born in 1769, and Betsy, born in 1771. When British troops took over Newport at "the commencement of the late war," Jones moved his family to Providence for "about three years," and there, in 1778, son John was born. When the British left Newport, Jones and his family moved back home and continued to expand: daughter Polly was born in 1781, son William in 1783, and son Benjamin in 1785.

Newport never quite recovered from three years of stalled trade during British occupation, and it may not have been the most propitious place for Jones to resume his coopering. Or perhaps his three "refugee" years in Providence had given him new ideas and opportunities for business. In any case, when the family moved back to Providence in October 1786, Jones took up a new trade as a baker.

Within a year of his arrival, Jones was questioned by the Providence councilmen, who officially "rejected" him as an inhabitant and named Newport as his place of settlement, but took no action to remove him. Jones, it seemed, had his family and business in order, and there was no reason to warn him out. His enterprise must have been doing sufficiently well to support his large family, which continued to grow. In 1790, the Providence census showed Jones as heading a household of ten: himself, his wife, four sons, and four daughters.

In the latter part of the eighteenth century, bread making was carefully regulated by Providence councilmen, beginning with the first "assize of bread" in October 1771, establishing required minimum weights of one-penny "copper biscuits" and of two-penny and four-penny loaves made from either "good merchantable bread flour" or "superfine flour." Each Providence baker who retailed his product was to mark his products, which officials could then "examine and weigh" to verify that they complied with the assize; underweight loaves were seized for "the use of the poor." Occasionally, the town's bakers appealed collectively to the council that "the price of flour hath risen" so much that making bread according to the old assize could not be done "without loss," and the council adjusted the minimum weights of biscuits and loaves. As one of the town's bakers, Benjamin Jones was thus frequently under the scrutiny of town officials, and any complaints about his bread "falling short of just weight" would almost certainly have led to a fine and potentially to a warning out. That such complaints were never registered suggests that Jones plied his trade in a satisfactory and reputable fashion.

Then, after four years of supplying bread to Providence residents, a terrible misfortune befell the Jones family. On Saturday, 7 May 1791, Jones's son William, "about nine years old," was "greatly injured" when his right foot was run over by the town's machine for "taking persons from the upper parts of houses in case of fire." In the accident, "the ankle bones and bones of the foot were broken and displaced, and the sinews and cord so much injured, as to render him a cripple, probably for life." After a month of doctor's visits and treatments, Jones faced a mounting medical bill, and he petitioned the town meeting for "relief" in the form of a "grant out of the town treasury." He pled that he was "poor and unable to defray the expenses" of ongoing medical care, so essential to "prevent his said son from losing entirely the use of his limb." The voters responded by awarding him £6, the equivalent of six weeks' wages for a common laborer.

Benjamin Jones had also assessed the ongoing economic burden of a son who could no longer assist significantly in the bread-making business. Three months after the accident, in July 1791, Jones took on the indenture of a "poor boy" named Franklin Crouch, who was "not in a capacity to provide for himself." Crouch was very likely William's replacement: a new assistant and delivery boy. His arrival underscores the economic importance of each family member's contribution to the enterprise, even when that child was a nine-year-old.

For the next six years, Benjamin Jones maintained his bakery business without William's help. Then, in August 1797, Jones once again petitioned the Providence voters for relief, this time explaining that ever since the accident, William had been "incapable of earning his living, and there appears at present but little prospect of his ever being able to do so." Jones, despite "all his industry and economy," believed himself unable to provide for a "large family" that included a crippled sixteen-year-old son. In asking the voters to "commiserate" with him, Jones pled that "the hand of misfortune has borne heavy upon him without misconduct or blame on his part." The voters agreed, granting "the sum of fifty dollars" out of the town treasury to "William Jones, the son of Benjamin Jones the Baker," to be delivered in three equal payments over three months, and "distributed under the direction of the said Benjamin Jones." This payment, the equivalent of two months' wages for a common laborer, appears to be the last request Benjamin Jones, then fifty-five years old, made to the Providence voters.

It was not the end of Jones's misfortunes, however. In December 1799, Providence housewright Richard Burke sued him for an unpaid bill; Jones had paid a portion of the bill, but not all, because he believed that Burke had "overcharged above forty per cent." Because Jones, "being ignorant of the forms of proceeding in courts," had "put in no answer" on the case, the verdict went against him. At that point, Jones pulled out his pen and petitioned the state legislature for a new trial. In a judgment of Solomon, the legislature referred the dispute to a team of arbitrators and got the attorneys of both Burke and Jones to accept the team's judgment as "final and conclusive." Presumably, both Burke and Jones got some satisfaction.

Benjamin Jones's misfortunes had the effect of pushing him to the economic margin. In the wake of his son's accident, he struggled against debt so that the town's $50 grant came as much-needed relief; Jones immediately used the town's first one-third disbursement to pay off a long-standing obligation to George Benson "for value received of him." But although Jones was a transient and although he seemed extremely needy on several occasions, he never was warned out. His industrious labor as an honest bread maker no doubt helped his cause, but what decided authorities in his favor was the accidental crippling of his son. The voters' quick generosity on two occasions indicates that Jones and his family had become accepted members of the community and were considered appropriate recipients of communal charity that ordinarily was reserved for legal inhabitants. By dispensing that charity to Jones, Providence's freemen demonstrated that transients could indeed become virtual inhabitants of a town.

Ann West and Peter West

In every New England town there were some people who were not mentally capable of caring for themselves. Some were "underwitted"—of diminished intellectual ability—and some were "insane"—mentally ill. Other terms used in the record to describe peculiar behavior include "non compos mentis," "lunatic," "delirious," and "crazy." In an era before institutions or aggressive medical therapy for mental problems, people thus handicapped simply wandered around the community or were physically restrained indoors. The town-based system of poor relief recognized these problems as a burden on the family and household; many towns regularly provided financial support to cover the extra costs of doctor visits, caretakers, and the loss of the individual's labor. Town officials also appointed guardians over such underwitted and insane people, including those who became non compos mentis as they aged; this prevented the ward from buying or selling property and made the guardian legally responsible for the ward's behavior and treatment. Entire communities became involved in the care of mentally handicapped people, which could become an expensive proposition; in Warwick, for example, the care of the Carder sisters (white women unrelated to Mary Carder in Chapter 3), who were "very often non compos mentis," lasted eighteen years for Mary Carder and thirty-three years for Edith Carder. Town leaders were understandably anxious for such costs to be absorbed by the town with legal responsibility for such persons. Hence, transients who were insane or underwitted were quickly removed to their hometowns.

Ann West's story reveals the burdens of caring for a mentally handicapped person who was perpetually vulnerable to exploitation and abuse by evil-minded people. She came to the attention of the South Kingstown authorities in 1772, and they questioned her about her hometown. They soon realized she could not testify on her own behalf, "it appearing to said town council that said Ann is a person not capable to give a rational account of her legal settlement." Instead the council summoned her employer and then her father, and the testimony of these two men revealed her history.

Ann West was born in North Kingstown in the 1730s. She and her brother Benjamin were the children of Peter West, who "lived and owned an estate in North Kingstown." As a freeholder, he voted in town meeting, and as an able-bodied male, he regularly gathered with his neighbors for "training days." In 1736, he joined with forty other men to sign a petition to the colonial legislature, asking that the various militia "train bands" in Rhode Island be permitted to "nominate and elect their respective commission[ed] officers by a free vote" instead of having them appointed by General Assembly. The petitioners believed that such elections would quiet the "continual protest and murmurings" that characterized training days; West, apparently, was one of those murmurers.

During Ann West's growing-up years, Peter West shifted his residence five times. These moves seem to have been motivated by a desire to find a congenial environment in which to raise a mentally handicapped child who might unintentionally cause a disturbance or otherwise make authorities "uneasy" at her presence. With Peter West regularly gone from home to town meetings and militia training, someone else was caring for Ann on a daily basis. Although West's wife is never mentioned in the record, it seems clear that she—or another female relative—was taking primary responsibility for raising a young woman of diminished mental capacity. This meant a careful watch on her movements, lest she stumble into danger or irritate the neighbors by wandering into their houses. That the Wests always lived in rural, thinly populated areas suggests that the greatest dangers to Ann were "natural" ones: fire, bad weather, getting lost away from home, being attacked by predatory wildlife, which still presented something of a threat to livestock in rural Rhode Island in the mid-eighteenth century. But someone took good care of Ann, and she grew safely to adulthood.

The family's first move came when Ann was still a small child; West "exchanged" his land and house in North Kingstown for a similar "estate" in the western part of East Greenwich. There, in 1740, he and a number of his neighbors signed a petition, asking that a new township, "West Greenwich," be carved out of East Greenwich. They argued that getting to town meetings in the easternmost part of the township necessitated "considerable travel [and] trouble" and sometimes forced them to "forgo their several privileges" as freemen of the town. They wanted the seventeen-mile-wide township cut in half, so that no one had to travel more than eight or nine miles to do town business. The petition was granted, West Greenwich was carved out of East Greenwich in 1741, and Peter West and his neighbors set about the business of launching a new town. They still had a long distance to travel for militia training, however, and the next year, West and others signed a petition asking that another militia company be created, which would allow them to "do their duty and get home again the same day."

After a time in West Greenwich, West and his family "went back to live in North Kingstown." He did not purchase land there, but rather lived there as a transient, "under a certificate from West Greenwich." A few years later, the family moved on to Exeter. Again, instead of purchasing land and building a house, West first "hired a house of Robert Reynold and lived in it" and then "hired a house of Benjamin Reynolds and lived in it." Ann had grown to physical maturity by this time, and in February 1756 she came to the attention of Exeter authorities. The language of the warning-out order suggests that she was pregnant; the councilmen worried that this "single woman" would become a town charge "if not timely sent out." Because her father was "at present residing in the town of Exeter by virtue of a certificate from the town council of West Greenwich," Ann legally belonged to West Greenwich—and there she was sent.

The council's action to send Ann away seems to have galvanized West into settling down in Exeter. In April 1756, he "purchased land of Stephen Albro," a twenty-acre tract that cost West £154. As a result of this purchase, he eventually "was admitted a freeman" and "gained me a settlement there." He also brought Ann back from West Greenwich to live with him, and would later assert that "my daughter Ann always lived with me when I kept a family." His choice of settlement town was a lasting one. In 1763, he bought ten more acres of land and a "dwelling house" in Exeter from his son, Benjamin West, who was relocating to Providence. In 1773, Peter West was still in Exeter, "where I live to this day."

There is no evidence of what happened to Ann's child (if there was one); perhaps it did not live long, or perhaps it was bound out as an indentured servant. But Ann apparently was a good worker, sufficiently industrious to attract the attention of Peter West's friend Seth Eldred. In 1766, when Ann was nearing thirty years of age, Eldred approached West and "asked me if I was willing my daughter Ann West should go with him to live in South Kingstown," probably to help with the myriad domestic responsibilities of preparing food and clothing and raising young children. West agreed: "I told him if he would take good care of her, she might go if she was willing to live with him." West, having learned from experience that not every community would welcome a mentally handicapped person, asked Eldred "to acquaint me if ye town of South Kingstown was uneasy at her living here."

Ann was apparently willing to live with Seth Eldred's family and she moved to South Kingstown with them. All went well for six years. Then, in the winter of 1772–73, Ann came to the attention of South Kingstown officials, because someone had lodged a "complaint" about her. Perhaps she had become pregnant again, for the councilmen pointedly called her a "single woman and transient," which were the conditions that made a pregnant woman unwelcome. After questioning Eldred, the officials ordered Ann removed to North Kingstown, but before the order was put into effect, they summoned Peter West for confirmation of Ann's hometown. West clarified that Exeter, not North Kingstown, was his and Ann's legal settlement, thus saving the councilmen from an erroneous removal and subsequent dispute with North Kingstown authorities.

Ann West, now ordered out to Exeter, almost certainly went back to her father's house. West was a widower by now—he no longer "kept a family"—but he took full responsibility for his daughter's welfare. "[I] always have had ye care and oversight of her according to my ability, being a poor man, she being under-witted," he declared. "And I am and always have been willing to take care and provide for her as one of my family according to my ability."

The paper trail of Ann West ends with her father's willing assumption of responsibility for her at this second moment of crisis. West was in his sixties by this time and did not have long to live, but he seems to have spent his last years caring for a daughter whom he recognized as needing extra oversight. After her father died—he was gone by the 1782 census—Ann was probably folded into the household of her brother, Benjamin West, in Providence; in 1790, West's household included two adult males and two females, one of whom could well have been Ann. Whatever her situation, Peter West had probably made arrangements beforehand, as his last legacy to a daughter he regarded with tender concern.

Esther Heradon

Esther Heradon's story highlights what must have been a particularly horrible three months of her life, when she and her four young children lived on the road between Windham, Connecticut, and Providence, Rhode Island. Neither town wanted to take responsibility for this family that had been abandoned by William Heradon a few months before; each town scrutinized the settlements laws of its own state and arrived at very different conclusions about where the family belonged. The truly unfortunate ones in this intertown squabble were Esther Heradon and her four children. They were not only unwelcome, they were also overlooked in the process of warning out. Neither set of officials employed any language that would indicate any compassion or sympathy for five people who belonged nowhere.

Esther Bennett was born in Canterbury, Connecticut around the year 1760. She lived there for a few years and then moved with her family to Windham, Connecticut, where she grew up. When she was "twenty one or twenty two years of age," she moved to Norwich, Connecticut, where she resided as a transient with "a certificate from the selectmen of said Windham acknowledging her to be a legal inhabitant of said Windham." She lost that settlement a few years later when she married William Heradon in Norwich in September 1783, for by the laws of all New England states, she took on her husband's settlement. But where was William Heradon's settlement? Esther Heradon testified that "she does not know that her husband ever gained a legal settlement anywhere, that he has often told her he never had"; the implication was that William Heradon was an immigrant—not born anywhere in North America.

William and Esther Heradon had four children in six years of marriage: Elisha, James, Nancy, and "an infant unnamed" who was born in early 1790. They lived in Norwich for most of the time and then in October 1789, William Heradon moved his family to Providence. About the time that the last baby was born in Providence, William Heradon left his family in what appears to be an act of outright abandonment, for his wife did not know where he had gone. Esther Heradon not only had the care of four young children, one an infant, but she was new to Providence, having been there only a few months. Whatever resources she had soon ran out, and she came to the attention of Providence officials in May 1790.

After questioning her, the councilmen concluded that she belonged in Windham, Connecticut, the place of her settlement before her marriage. The Providence officials discounted her husband's settlement because she "has no certificate of her marriage"; and, in any case, her vanished husband did not appear to have a settlement anywhere in the United States. The very next day, 14 May, Providence town sergeant Henry Bowen, with the help of a "boy, horses and cart," transported Heradon and her children to the house of Cranston's town sergeant who in turn took the Heradons to the next adjoining town. The family was delivered to Windham several days later.

The Windham selectmen questioned Esther Heradon and did some checking of their own. On 7 June, they wrote to the Providence councilmen: "On enquiry, we find they belong not to Windham nor the state of Connecticut, and that they have been removed to this place by mistake." Their investigation turned up "a certificate from the person who married her" to William Heradon, which proved that the husband belonged to "some town in Massachusetts." Following the stipulations of Connecticut settlement law, they sent Esther and the children back to Providence, expressing a hope that the Rhode Island officials would "give us no further trouble on the subject" and instead "transport her to the place where she belongs" in Massachusetts. By 10 June, Heradon and her children were back in Providence, inmates at the workhouse.

Whatever proofs the Windham selectmen sent were not convincing to the Providence councilmen. Once again they issued a "warrant for the removal of Esther Heradon and her four children to Windham in the state of Connecticut," and now they directed the clerk to "write an answer to the letter this council has received from the selectmen of said Windham." On 15 June, Esther Heradon and the children began their second trip to Windham, arriving a few days later. The Windham selectmen promptly wrote a second, more irate letter and ordered it delivered, along with Esther Heradon and her children, to the Providence councilmen. "Your conduct is not justifiable," the selectmen scolded. The removals of the Heradons were a "nuisance" that gave "trouble and expense" to Windham. Point by point, the selectmen refuted the logic of the Providence councilmen's decision and pointed out that they were following Connecticut law when they returned the unwelcome transients yet again. "We are sorry to find that after you are informed of the truth of facts you adhere to your first error with an inflexibility which too strongly evinces an original intention to do us that injustice." They dismissed Providence's suggestion that they appeal the removal, claiming that doing business "in a court of judicature in the state of Rhode Island is a misfortune to which we are not yet reduced." And they warned that if the Heradons were sent back yet again, they would indeed "call upon you before the Federal Court," now that Rhode Island had finally joined the union and was subject to the federal judicial system. Esther Heradon and her children arrived back in Providence on 25 June.

The Providence officials let the matter rest for a few weeks, while the Heradons were cared for in the workhouse once again. Then, on 12 July, the council decided to send the family back to Windham for the third time, accompanied by a written response to the Windham officials' latest letter. On 16 July the relay began, but this time the Heradons did not make it to Windham. Officials in Voluntown, the first Connecticut town on the way to Windham, refused to transport the family any further into the state. Clearly, the Windham selectmen had put out the word about their dispute with Providence, and Connecticut selectmen closed ranks. On 26 July, the Voluntown selectmen wrote to the Windham selectmen, requesting that they "would grant a warrant" for the Voluntown constables to "remove the said Esther Heradon and children to the town of Foster in the state of Rhode Island," beginning the chain to move the family back to Providence. The warrant was duly provided, and on 28 July, the Heradons were taken from Voluntown to Foster; on 2 August, they arrived back in Providence.

At this point, the Providence officials abandoned their efforts to remove the family. What happened to the Heradons is a mystery. The Providence councilmen would surely have been motivated to send five impoverished people to a town with legal responsibility for them, and the utter silence about them in the Providence record—no indentures of the children, no administration of poor relief to the mother—suggests that they were indeed taken elsewhere. On the other hand, there is no record of the family actually being removed from Providence after the last attempt to deliver them to Windham in July 1790. Perhaps Esther Heradon's husband reappeared and reclaimed his family. Perhaps Esther Heradon married someone else. Or perhaps the Providence officials made some arrangement they did not wish to enter on the permanent record. It is a misfortune that Esther Heradon and her four children, who were spurned by their husband and father and treated with indifference by posturing officials in two towns, should be overlooked again in the written record.

Margaret Fairchild Bowler

Margaret Fairchild Bowler was a former slave who built an independent life for herself in Providence during the Revolutionary War. Her enterprise centered around a house that neighbors considered disorderly for a host of reasons, but primarily because "drinking" and "whoring" went on there. Hers was a typical bawdy house, the eighteenth-century equivalent of a house of prostitution. Such a house was not necessarily a formal establishment, but simply a dwelling house where sexual activity was bought and sold. Although Bowler's house was well known, authorities tolerated it until an irate mob attacked one night in the summer of 1782. The uproar resulted in Bowler being warned out of Providence, but in such a half-hearted way as to indicate that she merited some special consideration on the part of the town council. The mob attack on her house was certainly a misfortune, but it did not derail Bowler's life.

"Negro woman" Margaret Fairchild Bowler grew up as a slave to "Capt. Fairchild," a Newport man of some status. He freed her at the beginning of the Revolutionary War, about the time that the British troops occupied Newport. Fairchild "gave her her freedom without any instrument in writing," perhaps because the family was in haste to vacate the town after the British arrived. Margaret moved to Providence and joined the growing community of free people of color there, drawn by potential jobs associated with both the Continental Army, which was stationed there, and with the booming seaport trade that had moved to Providence when Newport was occupied. She also changed her name from Fairchild to Bowler, perhaps a simple expression of free status, but also perhaps an indication that she had forged a relationship with someone named Bowler. There were several families of that name in Providence—one Medcalf Bowler still had one slave in his household in 1782—and it is possible that a former servant or slave of the Bowler family became the husband or mate of Margaret.

Margaret Bowler established a network of connections in the white community as well, and she built a business of "keeping house," that is providing room and board for others in the town. Neighbors later accused her of allowing "persons of evil name and fame and of dishonest conversation" to live in her house, and soon there was "drinking, tippling, whoring and misbehaving" going on there as well. She "lived in different parts of the town" at first, probably trying to find an agreeable neighborhood where her household would be tolerated, thus building up her finances so she could afford to rent larger and more commodious houses. Finally she settled on "the old jail house" in "the compact part of this town," where shops, warehouses, and dwellings were crowded together near the wharves. She rented this place from Providence man Joshua Burr, and her business apparently thrived. By 1782 she had "lodging" with her in the house both black and white women, all of whom neighbors suspected of engaging in prostitution.

On 22 July 1782, there was a "riot" that "entirely destroyed" Bowler's house. The riot began because neighbors were incensed at the goings-on in the house, which constituted a "great disturbance of the public peace." Bowler, her lodgers, and their clients were scattered and took refuge with neighbors and friends. One woman left town and moved back to Smithfield.

The next day, Rhode Island deputy governor Jabez Bowen wrote an energetic letter to the Providence town council. He sympathized with the motives of the rioters, but found that "however bad the inhabitants of the house might have been," it was "no excuse" for mob actions. He called for the enforcement of the state's "good and wholesome laws," and suggested that if the town's "chosen officers" were "not faithful to do their duty," then they ought to be "displaced with disgrace and others elected in the room who will be more faithful"—a warning, perhaps, to the town councilmen who had tolerated the bawdy house for so long. He "recommended" to the town council that they "break up the wicked nest" of Bowler's household by summoning "all the people that dwelt in the old gaol" and ordering all the transients among them "to leave this town at a short day." He also recommended that "all other bad houses be surprised" and called for a campaign "for the restoration of order and virtue in our town."

The town council immediately convened, gathered information, and issued a warrant, summoning "Margaret Bowler alias Margaret Fairchild, a Negro woman," and all her former lodgers to appear before them two days hence. They also summoned a number of women who plied the same trade in the same neighborhood: "Mrs. McCullough," "[Sarah] Gardner an Indian or mulatto woman," and several women "at the house of Patience Ingraham." (For Sarah Gardner's story, see Chapter 2.) At this hearing, Bowler obligingly named her lodgers: "Phebe Bowen and her daughter Betsey, another white woman in company with the said Phebe Bowen, called Debby, a Negro woman called Black Bets, belonging to Sandwich, and a mulatto girl about eighteen or nineteen years of age,

called Esther." The interracial character of Bowler's and Ingraham's houses probably drew a mixed-race clientele, and this mixing may well have
fueled neighbors' antagonism.

After hearing Bowler's testimony, the council ruled that Newport was
her hometown and ordered that "unless the said Margaret Fairchild shall
depart from the town within ten days not to return here any more to
dwell," they would issue a "warrant for the removal of said Margaret to
said Newport." Her former master still dwelled in Newport, and in 1782
Major Fairchild still had one slave in his household, kin to Margaret perhaps. The generous margin of ten days for her departure from Providence—rather than removal in "a short day," as Deputy Governor Bowen
had directed—suggests that the councilmen sympathized with Bowler's
situation as a victim of mob action and wanted to give her time to recover
any property she could and reorganize her life. There is no evidence in the
record that the council followed up on this order; certainly Bowler was
never forcibly removed.

If Bowler ever did leave Providence, she soon returned and lived there
without incident for many years. She had a baby in Providence within a
year or two of the riot, and the Providence councilmen accepted the child
as a legal inhabitant of their town, binding him out as an indentured servant to Captain Thomas Smart in 1786. At the time of binding, when the
boy was probably three or four years of age, the councilmen called him
Pero Gardner—"Gardner" being in all likelihood the last name of the
boy's father. The contract contained a curious clause: the councilmen stipulated that "the mother of the said Pero shall consent to and sign the said
indenture," which contained generous terms for a "poor Negro child": he
was to be taught "reading, writing, and arithmetic." This education and
the demand for the mother's consent (which she gave) were unusual
requirements for "poor" children and underscored the modicum of
respect accorded Bowler by the town council. Then, in 1796, her son, now
called Pero Fairchild ("Negro boy"), was transferred from Captain Smart
to his son-in-law, Jacob Carpenter, an arrangement approved by the town
council as long as all the stipulations of the original indenture remained in
force. Margaret Bowler's child had indisputably been accepted as an
inhabitant of Providence.

Margaret Bowler herself eventually became a virtual inhabitant of
Providence. In 1800, when yellow fever swept through the town, Bowler
was one of the "sufferers." Perhaps she herself became ill; perhaps someone in her household died. The town council allocated her $5 in cash to

help her recover from the setback, thereby underscoring her accepted status within the community.

Benjamin Champney

Benjamin Champney's testimony, given to the Providence councilmen in 1786, provided basic and unadorned information about his apprenticeship training, his service in the military during the Revolutionary War, and his transient labor afterward. But other existing documents add depth and complexity to his story: his apprenticeship indenture, the censure of town officials when he developed a serious drinking problem, and pieces of his military service record. Taken together, these documents illuminate the troubled course of life of a young man of the "poorer sort" and show how intemperance could prove to be a serious misfortune.

Benjamin Champney was born in Cambridge, Massachusetts, in 1749. His father died or abandoned him when he was a child, and since no remaining family could adequately support him, he was bound out as an apprentice by the Boston overseers of the poor in 1764, when he was fourteen or fifteen. Officials in every New England locality acted in loco parentis when fathers were not capable of supporting their children, and Boston had plenty of children in such circumstances; Champney was one of hundreds of "orphans" placed in servitude contracts by Boston officials in the 1760s. His master was Thomas Emmons, a Boston blockmaker (an artisan who constructed blocks for mounting horses or carriages), who bound himself to provide all necessities of life for Benjamin Champney until the boy turned twenty-one; train him in the craft of blockmaking; teach him to read, write, and do basic arithmetic; and provide him with two new suits of clothing at the end of his indenture. Champney apparently completed his six years of apprenticeship successfully and was freed when he turned twenty-one on 3 September 1770. As evidence that Emmons fulfilled the "writing" stipulation of the contract, Champney later was able to sign his name in a legible hand.

When he became free, Champney moved to Providence, where tradesmen and artisans were much in demand in the 1770s, supplying the households and businesses of the well-to-do. There he labored at his trade for the next ten years, even becoming an independent householder whose name appeared on the Providence tax lists in 1780 and 1781, although his estate was so meager that he was taxed only a bare minimum. He does not appear in the 1782 census, indicating that he had not established an independent household. During this period, he also married, though no children are mentioned. Then a drinking problem complicated his life. In September 1781, the Providence town council was informed by the overseer of the poor that Champney was "frequently intoxicated with liquor" and lived such an "irregular, evil and idle course of life" that officials worried he would soon end up destitute and in need of public poor relief. The councilmen, who had legal authority to take such severe measures with troublesome transient residents, ordered the overseer to "bind the said Benjamin Champney to Capt. James Munro to serve in the cruise now undertaking against the enemies of the United States of America" and ruled that "all profits accruing from his services in said cruise be appropriated to the use of his family" under the overseer's direction. In early 1782, when Champney returned from this "cruise," his earnings, under the council's direction, were paid to Champney's wife and to his creditors.

Instead of returning to blockmaking, Champney, who had apparently developed a taste for seafaring, enlisted for twelve months' further duty with the American navy. He served three months aboard the frigate *Dean*. Then, in September 1782, he enlisted in the Continental Army. The muster master's receipt described him as five feet, six and a half inches high, with a "dark" complexion, "dark" hair, and "dark" eyes. He enlisted for the town of Boston for three years, but he did not finish out his time, since the war would be over in less than three years. At the very end of his time, he was transferred to sea duty again, serving his last military stint aboard the frigate *Hague*.

After leaving the military in 1783, Champney moved around to "several different places," probably laboring at his blockmaking trade to support himself. One of those places was Mistick (now Mendon), Massachusetts, where he purchased some real estate with his wartime earnings, thus making Mistick his place of legal settlement. His wife apparently died or left him, perhaps during his absence at sea, as there is no further mention of her in the records. In 1786, he returned to Providence and tried to resume his life there, but Providence officials spotted and questioned him and were unsympathetic to his residency there. Judging that Champney was "likely to become chargeable," they ordered him removed to his new hometown of Mistick, Massachusetts.

Although he had been trained in a trade and educated to read and write, Benjamin Champney never quite achieved respectability, even after gaining experience and connections in military service. Instead, he was identified by authorities as a drunkard, and he never put down roots in any one place. At age thirty-nine, instead of being settled in a community, heading a household, and raising children, he was being forcibly removed from a place he once called home. Instead of being a welcomed member of a New England community, Champney lived on the margin.

Jacob Burke

Jacob Burke was what neighbors and officials called this man who came from Europe to North America. He signed his name in Gothic script, he called himself a "high Dutchman," he had French associations, and he was eventually sent back to his "homeland," which American officials designated as "Germany." These pieces of evidence suggest that he came to North America from northwest Europe, probably Alsace, where German- and French-speaking people both dwelled in contested territory. A quarter century of toil and trouble in the United States, including a criminal conviction, left him sick at heart and longing for people who spoke his own language. He left Rhode Island in shame and disfavor in 1804, never to return to American soil. For Jacob Burke, America had been a place of misfortune, not of opportunity.

In 1779, Jacob Burke came to Newport, Rhode Island with the French troops that ended the British occupation of that part of New England. Rather than face a serious confrontation with combined French and American forces, the British fleet withdrew to the south. Burke probably came as an ordinary soldier, since he later exhibited no specialized skills, but rather worked as a laborer and a "truckman," loading and unloading ships and carting goods from wharves to warehouses and shops.

Within a few years of his arrival in Newport, Burke met and married widow Rebecca Pariel. Neither Burke nor Pariel appeared on the 1782 census, indicating that neither was an independent householder at that time; she may have been no better off than he in terms of property. The couple remained in Newport for "eight or nine years" and then moved to North Providence in the fall of 1790, perhaps in order for Burke to secure a better job. By that time, three children had been born: Rebecca, Penelope, and a child (never named in the record) who died that winter. In the spring of 1791, the family moved on to Providence, leaving behind a small grave in North Providence.

As soon as Burke, his wife, and his two daughters arrived in Providence, they were noticed by officials, and Burke was summoned to council to be examined on 30 May 1791. He testified that "he never owned a real estate in this country," so the councilmen judged him to belong to Newport, the port where he had first set foot when he came to North America. Burke was permitted to stay in Providence until the end of the summer, probably because he had reliable work and there was no immediate trouble in his household, but the family was warned out to Newport several months later, the charge then being that they were "likely to become chargeable." Given the paucity of Burke's wages as a laborer, it is indeed likely that he, his wife, and his children exhibited some need that neighbors communicated to town officials.

Although the council ordered the preparation of a warrant in September 1791, it was more than two years before the Burkes were actually transported to Newport. Jacob Burke, it seems, had a good enough job that he did not want to leave Providence, and his labor apparently was useful enough that no one pushed to have him removed—at least, not right away. In December 1792, fifteen months after the warning-out order was given, the clerk finally prepared the official warrant for Burke's removal. Then the town sergeant took an unaccountably long time to carry out the order; perhaps Jacob Burke was hard to find or perhaps he had some way of persuading the sergeant to delay the warrant's execution. Whatever the case, the council did not force the issue. Not until November 1793 were Jacob Burke, "his wife Rebeckah, and two children, to wit: Rebeckah and Penelope," removed to Newport. Constable Jesse Whitmore delivered all four to Newport overseer of the poor Edward Thurston on 4 November 1793.

Less than three weeks after he had been delivered to Thurston, Jacob Burke had "returned hither [to Providence] again without leave from this council" and been spotted by authorities. The council ordered the sergeant to take Burke in hand and punish him for this offense by fining him forty shillings or seeing that he was "whipped fifteen stripes upon [his] naked back," and then escorting him "without the limits of this town." If Burke returned, the sergeant was to see "that twenty stripes be inflicted upon him the said second offense," a punishment that was to be repeated "as often as the said offense shall be repeated."

Despite this harsh decree, Burke returned to Providence and somehow persuaded the councilmen to let him stay. In 1799, his name appears on Providence's valuation list for tax assessment; Burke, listed as "truckman," had real estate worth £3, and perhaps this purchase had helped avert a removal. It was a meager estate, hardly worth taxing, but it did allow him to claim identity as "yeoman," and it did demonstrate his desire to make a legal place for himself and his family in the town.

Perhaps Burke should have stayed in Newport. In August 1802, he was tried for "assault and battery" on Sylvester Fuller, another transient then dwelling in Providence. Before Burke could enter his plea, the case was continued from one judicial term (August) to the next (September), leaving Burke in jail in the interim because he could not raise bail money ("two sureties") to guarantee "his appearance at the next court" in order to "answer" the charges. In September, Burke "pleaded guilty" to the charge and was sentenced "to pay a fine of fifty dollars" and to serve two months in jail after "the rising of the court." From his jail cell, he sent a petition to the Rhode Island state legislature, asking that his jail sentence be shortened, since he had already served a substantial portion of the time waiting for the case to be finished and he was still waiting for the court term to be finished, so that his sentence could officially begin. Burke pled that he was "a very poor man" who "supported his family wholly by his labor," and that it was "wholly beyond his power to pay the fine," so that he was doomed to "imprisonment for life." He argued that his forced idleness drove his family into penury and onto poor relief: his wife had already sold "all such property of which he was possessed which any person would purchase," and now she and his children were "destitute" and "must become a charge to the town." He closed his plea with a promise that he would "in future conduct himself a peaceable and orderly citizen."

The state legislature granted his petition. They passed an act that "liberated" him after he had spent two full months in jail, starting from the day of sentencing and continuing no longer. The act also permitted him to give a "note" to the sheriff for the amount of the fine, thus allowing him to pay off the fine—with interest—over a period of time.

Burke seemed to be on a downward slide, unfortunately, and his promise of "peaceable" and "orderly" behavior was soon broken. A year later, in October 1803, he was back in jail—this time awaiting capital punishment. He had been tried and convicted for "a rape on the body of one Elizabeth Stafford," a resident of Coventry, Rhode Island, and he now petitioned that the sentence be commuted to exile. Personal misery imbues his written plea. He acknowledged that he had received "a fair and impartial trial" and expressed gratitude that "his country furnished him with the means of defense [and] gave him a long and patient hearing." He suggested, however, that the court, "governed doubtless by the soundest maxims of law," did not "permit the whole character" of the "principal witness against him"—Stafford herself—to be "given in evidence to the jury." He asked that the state legislature consider this further evidence and then commute his death sentence to one of exile.

Jacob Burke did not want to die an ignominious death. Even though life had offered him "fewer allurements than fall in the ordinary way of man," and even though he was accustomed to "poverty and toilsome labor," still he found that "his frail nature retreats at the awful approach of untimely death." Further, he wanted to spare his "blameless wife and unoffending children" the "painful spectacle and bitter remembrance of his execution." Instead, he asked that the legislature "suffer him forever to leave a country whose hospitality he never merited and whose indignation he would gladly appease by perpetual exile." It was much better for all if he ended his days in his homeland: "Long ago the fortune of war left him destitute and alone on the shores of this country, far from the pleasant fields of his native land and every bosom that beats with kindred blood."

Figure 7. In 1803, German immigrant Jacob Burke petitioned the Rhode Island state legislature to have his death sentence commuted to exile and transportation to Germany. Burke always signed his birth name, Johann Burg, in German gothic script, which English-speaking clerks often transcribed as "Tussiver Luury." Source: Petitions to the Rhode Island General Assembly, 1803–1804, Rhode Island State Archives, C#00165. Courtesy of the Rhode Island State Archives.

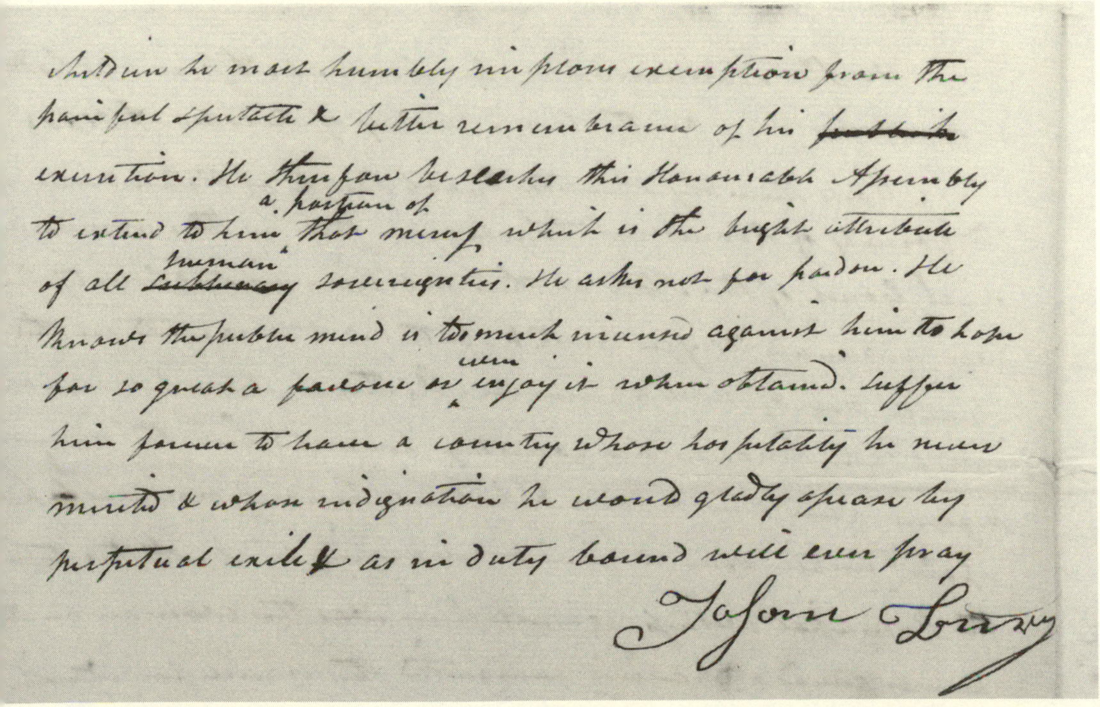
And even he most humbly implores exemption from the painful spectacle & bitter remembrance of his ~~[illegible]~~ execution. He therefore beseeches this Honourable Assembly to extend to him a portion of that mercy which is the bright attribute of all human ~~[illegible]~~ sovereignties. He asks not for pardon. He knows the public mind is too much incensed against him to hope for so great a pardon or even enjoy it when obtained. Suffer him forever to leave a country whose hospitality he never merited & whose indignation he would gladly appease by perpetual exile & as in duty bound will ever pray

Johann Burg

Supporting Jacob Burke's heartbroken appeal were four petitions, each containing the same plea and each signed by a cluster of men, 202 names in all. The signers, all inhabitants of Rhode Island and hailing from all corners of the state, professed not to know Jacob Burke, "who is a stranger to your Memorialists." Nevertheless, they were disturbed at the sentence passed upon him, because the "principal witness" against him, Elizabeth Stafford, was well known to them as someone "infamous for lewdness and disregard to truth, so that her testimony is not entitled to credit." Justice would be "more perfectly administered," they argued, by substituting "voluntary exile or some other punishment" for execution. Stafford, it seems, was well known indeed to some 202 Rhode Island men, and their collective judgment of her was organized to save Burke's life.

The state legislature looked favorably on the petitions of Jacob Burke and his 202 concerned supporters. Within a matter of days, they passed "An Act for the Relief of Jacob Bourke," which postponed his execution for seven months, during which time he could be "transported, free of expense to this State, without the limits of this State, to some part of Germany." The act also required Burke to obtain two bondsmen who would post a total of $10,000 in bonds, the sum to be returned when "evidence" had been produced that Burke had been removed elsewhere. Apparently, Burke had some difficulty finding bondsmen willing to post such an enormous sum, and the following May, as the deadline approached, the state legislature passed a second act, extending the reprieve to November 1804, eliminating the posting of bonds, and amending the original act so that Burke could be transported "to any other part of the world," as long as it was outside the United States. Given these more generous terms, Burke very likely departed before the second deadline; there is no further mention of him in the Rhode Island records.

Jacob Burke was at least in his fifties by the time he was forced to leave the United States, and he wanted to spend his last years at the place he still saw as home. For him, America had not been a good venture. He had begun his sojourn with few resources and few prospects, and he had never risen to prosperity. Culturally, he clung to his identity as a "high Dutchman," retaining his birth name of Johann Burg and signing it on all the official documents, even though he was widely known as Jacob Burke. Certainly his German identity was known to authorities, who labeled him as such in their records and willingly saw him off to Europe. Here was one transient who did not have to be forcibly removed; he begged to be allowed to leave a place he no longer wanted to consider home.

5. Old Age and Death

MANY PEOPLE in early America faced the frailties of old age. While the mortality rate of infants and children was high, those who lived into adulthood had a good chance of seeing "advanced years." About 15 percent of the transient adults in this study were fifty years of age or older, compared to 21 percent of all adults in the 1782 census, a difference that underscores the younger age of most transients. Among those older transients were a number who came to the attention of officials at a ripe old age, such as eighty-year-old John Horn, who for many years had worked as a gardener to two Massachusetts governors, and eighty-three-year-old Michael Field, an Irish immigrant whose labor during the Seven Years' War had been as a "waiter" to an officer.[1]

John Horn and Michael Field would be judged "aged" by virtually any measure used today, but no such label was applied to either man by town officials in the late eighteenth century. Nor were any such terms used to describe two men, one eighty-four and one ninety years old, who "took a couple of scythes from some of the hands then mowing, and each mowed a very good handsome swath." In sharp contrast, fifty-something Daniel Collins and Bristol Rhodes (this chapter) both were described as being "in an advanced age." Town records indicate that officials judged elderliness by mental and physical abilities, and they used such phrases as "old age" to indicate frailty of mind or body. The problem was primarily physical weakness for Stephen Pain, whose "old age and *other* bodily infirmities" made it unlikely that he could "get along with his business without some assistance," and for Hannah Broadfoot, who had "become very old and become almost blind and not able to support herself by her labor." The problem was primarily mental weakness for Deacon William Worden, who was "an aged man, & his natural faculties abated, whereby his estate is likely to be squandered away," and for John Rhodes, who was "far advanced in years," suffering from "shortness of memory," and "much impaired in his Interlectures [sic]," so that he was "easy to be pre-

vailed upon to dispose of his interest different from what he would if he
was in his full strength and understanding, as he had been formerly."[2]

The care of mentally or physically frail old people generally fell to relatives. Town records abound with instances of aged people being put
under the guardianship of younger relatives because they were like Hannah Weaver, who was "far advanced in years and has got very much into
her dotage and hardly capable to manage for herself." Guardianship gave
another adult full control over the "property and person" of the ward and
prevented any "foolish bargains" or "indiscreet management" of worldly
goods. Similarly, younger adults made a place in their households for
aging relatives who could no longer take care of themselves physically.
Exeter man Nathan Codner, for example, supported his aunt and uncle,
who were "much advanced in old age and [the uncle] much unable to help
himself." In 1783, Joseph Bennett began caring for "his father & mother
[who] were far advanced in years, and almost unable to labor any towards
their support"; four years later they were "very infirm" and completely
"unable to labor towards their support."[3]

The younger generation caring for the older was a common and generally expected arrangement, and one rooted in English poor law, but it
did not always occur voluntarily; Rhode Island found it necessary to pass a
law requiring that children and grandchildren—if of ability—support
their parents and grandparents. Those who were slow to perform this duty
were apt to find themselves prodded along by local authorities, who sometimes publicly admonished those who dallied. The Exeter authorities, for
example, once ordered four men to appear at a council meeting and
explain why they neglected to care for their widowed mother, who needed
poor relief. And the Jamestown officials, after learning that Jack Marsh
had "grown old & very decrepit & utterly uncapable of maintaining himself" so that he was likely to "perish in the winter season," bound out
Marsh's "idle" and "dissolute" son Japhet for a year to procure funds to
care for the father because "it is the incumbent duty of all children, to contribute as much as in them lies, toward the support of their aged parents."
In what was perhaps the most blatant case of reluctance to support elders,
William Allen was abandoned on the outskirts of Providence town by his
daughter and grandson. He "had been to see" his family in Scituate and
had stayed about three weeks, but then something went wrong; he was
"brought to this town and left in the road near Capt. John Hoyle's by his
said daughter Eliza Pierce and her son." The Providence councilmen

immediately sent Allen back to his hometown of Branford, Connecticut, where officials presumably could sort out family relations and fold this grandfather into someone's household.[4]

In some cases, the elderly were supported by their churches. When Elizabeth Barker of Middletown became "non compos mentis" in her old age, the Friends meeting to which she belonged took the woman and her small estate under their care. Similarly, the Seventh-Day Baptist Church of Hopkinton took over the primary support of Experience Bassett in her old age; they also paid for her husband's "last sickness and funeral."[5]

If no relatives or church could be found to contribute, then it was up to town officials to care for elderly people who had nothing saved up from their years of labor to carry them through their final days. While destitute children could be bound out as indentured servants and thus pay for their own maintenance, destitute aged people were "past labor" and fully dependent on individual caretakers, as was the case with Daniel Collins and Obadiah Blanding (this chapter) or on the overseer of the poorhouse, as was the case with Latham Clarke (this chapter). In such manner they were supplied with the necessities of life—food, clothing, shelter, firewood, medical care—and, at the last, people to lay out and otherwise tend the corpse, make the coffin, and dig the grave.

Because of the potentially high cost of elder care, town officials were highly reluctant to allow transients to remain within their borders once they were past useful labor. Instead, aged transients were quickly removed, so that the time and cost of arranging poor relief were shifted to officials in the hometown. How long an elderly transient had been resident in the town did not seem to be of concern to officials doing the warning out. Abigail Hull Carr (this chapter) had been living continuously in Providence for thirty years when the councilmen ordered her removed to a place where she had been a slave forty years earlier.

Very occasionally, towns cooperated so that an aged transient could continue to live—and receive poor relief—away from the hometown. This is what happened in the case of widow Elizabeth Stonehouse (this chapter), whose care was shared by Newport and Providence. In another unusual decision, officials refused to remove veteran Bristol Rhodes (this chapter), when neighbors complained about him; instead, Rhodes and his family were permitted to live as transients in Providence, and there Rhodes died some years later, acclaimed as a war hero. In the cases of Stonehouse and Rhodes, officials demonstrated responsibility for people who had contributed to the community—Stonehouse through her husband's taxes and Rhodes through his military service. Because they had been enfolded by the "respectable" community, officials set aside the laws of legal settlement and allowed transients to spend their last days in the place they had come to call home.

Daniel Collins

Daniel Collins lived in and around the Providence area all his life and made the city his home for the last quarter of the eighteenth century. Although he was a poor man, had never acquired a legal settlement, and had never even paid taxes in the town, the town leaders looked with sympathy upon "corporal debility" when he asked for monetary assistance and arranged for his regular care. Officials' generosity with Collins stands in surprising contrast to their refusal to assist Abigail Hull Carr. Did Collins merit special concern simply because he was white?

Daniel Collins was trained to farming and coopering. His mother arranged an apprenticeship contract for him when he was a youngster, probably around the age of eleven of twelve years in the late 1750s, binding him to Thomas Waterman in Coventry, a rural, agrarian community adjoining Collins's hometown of Warwick. There, in all likelihood, the boy learned the work of a farmer: cultivating the land to produce harvests of corn, wheat, oats and barley; nurturing apple orchards and potato fields; breeding, raising, and butchering sheep and cattle; and building and mending barns, sheds, and fences.

Collins's apprenticeship should have lasted "until he was twenty-one years of age," but he became restless long before then. He may have found farm labor tedious, difficult, and not to his liking, since he later gravitated to other kinds of work. He may have clashed with his master over any number of issues. In any case, he demonstrated his unhappiness: "I run away from him and he pursued me and caught me and brought me back." Daniel Collins was eighteen years old, and the year was 1764.

To solve the difficulty between servant and master, Collins's mother "bought my time of said Waterman," paying him "about twenty-five dollars." This sum, the equivalent of two months' wages for a common laborer, reimbursed the master for the loss of Collins's labor over the last three years of the contract, just when his apprentice would have been the most productive. Collins's mother, probably at her son's urging, then bound him to Thomas Biddlecome, also of Coventry, "to learn the trade of a cooper," labor that apparently suited him, for he completed this apprenticeship without incident. In 1767, at twenty-one years of age, he was free to make his way in the world, equipped with general knowledge of farming and some specialized knowledge of coopering, the craft of making wooden barrels. His preparation for adulthood did not include literacy, for Collins later signed his testimony with an "x." If his apprenticeship contract had obligated the master to educate Collins in this regard, then either the master had failed to live up to his word, or else Collins had been an "unlikely" pupil.

For the first four months of independent living, Collins worked as a cooper with fisherman Rufus Greene in East Greenwich. He then moved to Warwick and continued his cooper work for another two months with merchant Silas Casey in Warwick. His work making barrels for shipment put him in steady contact with seafaring people, and he began to eye this new opportunity. Six months after finishing his apprenticeship, he "went to sea in a vessel" owned by Casey, his employer. After his return from that expedition, he "went one voyage a-fishing" in a ship owned by former employer Rufus Greene.

After that voyage, Daniel Collins decided to stay on land and stick to coopering. In 1769 he moved to Providence, where coopers were much in demand for the shipping trades headquartered in the town. For five years he pursued his trade without drawing official attention, but then he fell on hard times. In the deep winter of 1773–74, he may have had a hard time finding work, or perhaps he had fallen ill and could not support himself. In January 1774, the Providence council questioned him, heard his story, and ruled that his hometown was in Coventry, where his apprenticeship master Thomas Biddlecome lived. They sent him away.

Daniel Collins soon returned to Providence, but he avoided any further trouble with authorities. After a bumpy youth, he spent the next twenty-six years without incident in Providence, and he even became accepted as an inhabitant of the town. How he accomplished that is not clear. He does not appear on any Providence tax lists, suggesting that any property he owned was meager; nor does he appear on the census lists, indicating that he did not establish himself as an independent householder and lived instead within someone else's household.[6] Nevertheless, in 1800, when he petitioned the Providence council for poor relief, they accepted his plea that "advanced age" and "corporal debility" had left him "unable to obtain a competent support." The councilmen treated him as an inhabitant of the town and ordered the overseers of the poor to pay $1 a week to Thomas Spooner for as long as Spooner "shall provide for & support the said Daniel."

The record does not indicate how long Spooner served as caretaker for the ailing Daniel Collins. Perhaps it was a short-lived rescue that overseers of the poor chalked up to "common charity," or perhaps Collins was so ill that officials did not expect him to live long. In any case, he had made a successful appeal to town leaders and consequently had some expectation of staying in Providence through his last years. If only every aged and ailing resident could have found the same charity.

Obadiah Blanding

Obadiah Blanding did not come from wealth, and his limited skills did not permit him to rise to wealth. He lived on the lower margin of respectability most of his life, then slipped into poverty in old age and died a pauper's death. As long as he could labor, he kept poverty from his household, but when his strength dwindled his efforts to maintain independence also failed. In the last five years of his life, he declined steadily: unable to pay taxes, then in obvious need, then dislocated by warning out, then one of the poor in his hometown, and finally buried at public expense.

Obadiah Blanding was born in Cumberland in 1725. His father "owned a real estate" in Cumberland, but it was apparently not a large or valuable one. When Obadiah was just "8 years of age," he was sent to Rehoboth, Massachusetts, "where he lived at several places till he was a man grown." This sounds as though his father placed him or bound him out with relatives or friends; the early age of separation suggests that the senior Blanding did not have the wherewithal to raise his son in his own household.

The training Obadiah Blanding received as a child in those "several places" did not set him up for a prosperous adulthood. He did not sign his examination, indicating he was not literate, and his jobs as an adult involved unskilled labor. He first "went to sea," where he labored as a sailor; later, on land, he "tended ferry." Around 1758, when he was in his early thirties, he moved to Providence and probably continued some kind of manual labor connected to shipping, perhaps as a dockhand. At some point, he married, and he and his wife Jane continued to reside in Providence.

In the early 1770s, Blanding was doing well enough to appear on the Providence tax lists for six years. He was always assessed minimal poll taxes, far less than the average of the town's many taxpayers, and his name disappears from the lists after 1776. In September 1775, when Providence was readying itself for invasion by British soldiers, Blanding's name appeared on the "List of Men and Arms in Providence," but he was poorly equipped. He had only a gun, a cartridge box, seventeen cartridges, and five flints—no bayonet, powder, balls, sword, or pistol. By the time hostilities commenced, he was over fifty years old, and there is no evidence that he enlisted in the military at any point.

In 1788, Obadiah Blanding claimed that he "has lived about 30 years last past" in Providence. If this is so, then he must have also retained property in Cumberland, even while he resided in Providence, for he was taxed by Cumberland in 1785. Or perhaps his "30 years last past" was not continuous, and he returned to Cumberland for a brief time. He is listed in neither town on the 1782 census; in fact, he is listed nowhere in Rhode Island, indicating that he did not head his own household, but boarded or roomed with someone else. If he had moved back to Cumberland for a time, he may have lived with a kinsman such as Ephraim Blanding, a man of Obadiah's age (perhaps his brother); the 1782 census shows Ephraim Blanding heading a household that included his wife and a girl less than fifteen years old—a granddaughter, perhaps, or a late-born daughter, or a young servant tending two aging people.

Wherever Blanding was living in the mid-1780s, he was not prospering. He was unable to pay his tax bill in Cumberland, and the town meeting voted to cover the delinquent amount from the town treasury, apparently understanding that he was genuinely unable to produce the money. He was sixty years old at that point and it must have been apparent to his neighbors that his strength was waning.

In 1788, Blanding was clearly resident in Providence, and the overseers of the poor became aware of the diminished abilities and the material needs of this sixty-three-year-old man ("in the 64th year of his age"). He was summoned before the town council and questioned. Having had a good look at him and having heard his story, the councilmen immediately ordered that both Obadiah and Jane Blanding be removed to Cumberland. The Providence councilmen ruled that Cumberland was Blanding's hometown by virtue of his father having owned some real estate there years before; they were apparently unaware of his status as a taxpayer in that town. The Providence town sergeant delivered Blanding and his wife Jane, along with "some household furniture," to Asa Aldrich, Cumberland overseer of the poor, on 25 February 1788, just fifteen days after the removal had been ordered.

Obadiah Blanding qualified as "the poor of the town" of Cumberland, and the overseers of the poor arranged for him and his wife to be boarded and tended at the town's expense. For two years they lived on that meager charity as Blanding's strength continued to decline. In February 1790, in the midst of winter cold, he died. His few personal possessions were not enough to cover the last few expenses of his life, so Cumberland authorities paid Ibrook Whipple three shillings "for digging a grave for Obadiah Blanding."

Blanding had labored steadily for at least fifty-five of his sixty-five years, but he had never been able to achieve economic independence. He had not fallen from a high estate, for he had not inherited wealth or been trained in a lucrative trade. He had simply failed to rise from a low estate, and the poorly compensated manual labor that he performed all his life was insufficient to insulate him from the economic disaster of old age.

Latham Clarke

Latham Clarke started out in Newport, and although he lived in other places for nearly forty years, he wound up back in Newport when he was an elderly man no longer able to support himself. After decades of economic independence as a blacksmith, land owner, and home owner, he was reduced to living with his son, scraping to "get something for a maintenance." At the last, he spent his final days in the Newport almshouse. Clarke's sad demise underscores the vulnerability of aging adults before pensions and Social Security provided a safety net.

Latham Clarke was born around 1700 in Newport, "in a house that was formerly Governor Cranston's." His parents appear to have been people of some means, since they lived in a substantial house and gave their son substantial property. Clarke received literacy training—he signed all his examinations and a petition as well—and practical training as a blacksmith, a trade he pursued for his lifetime.

In 1723 Clarke left Newport and moved to "a freehold at South Kingstown" given to him by his father. After three years there, he moved to

Westerly, but retained his land and house in South Kingstown for a time; eventually he sold that freehold for £50. In Westerly, he "kept house & had a living at the blacksmith's trade" for "about fifteen years." While living in Westerly, he joined with a number of neighbors in a petition to the colonial legislature, asking that the assembly create a fourth militia company for the town to prevent traveling "nine miles to a training or pay a fine of five shillings"; the petitioners presented themselves as "poor" men who were "not very well able to furnish ourselves with horses to ride" and who found it "great hardship" to "go on foot so far."

Despite this plea of "poor" circumstances, Clarke seemed to be at the peak of his powers during these years in Westerly: supporting himself and his family with his blacksmith business, heading his own household, attending training days with his neighbors. Then adventure seemed to beckon to him. In 1740 he left Westerly for Stonington, Connecticut, and lived there "about two years," perhaps trying to establish a blacksmith business in the town. If that was his intent, it was an unsuccessful venture, for he left Stonington, returned to Westerly briefly, and then moved to Shrewsbury, New Jersey in 1742. There he seemed to fare better, owning "twenty-one acres of land and a house on it"; he probably supported his family with a combination of farming and smithing. After twelve years in "the Jerseys," he apparently began to long for Rhode Island again; now in his fifties, he may have wanted to be near kin in his elder years, and he may have viewed his return to New England as a kind of retirement. At the end of 1754, he "sold his possession" in New Jersey and moved back to Hopkinton, which in his absence had been incorporated as a separate town out of the northern part of Westerly. By New Jersey law, he "lost all right of residency" in Shrewsbury "by being absent more than a year and a day" after selling his property. He was a Rhode Islander again by Christmas 1755.

In Hopkinton, Clarke moved in with his son Stephen for two years, but this retirement did not go well. Eventually, the money from the sale of the New Jersey property sale ran out, and Clarke became "desirous to get something for a maintenance." He wanted to return to blacksmithing, but since he had sold all his tools before leaving New Jersey, he needed to reequip himself. He tried to "raise a sum of money in order to buy some tools" by means of a "subscription," a fund-raising effort endorsed by several of his former neighbors, which would have put him back in business. But "few persons [were] signers of the subscription," and the effort failed. Four years after returning "home," Latham Clarke was broke and had no prospects for independent living.

At this point, the Hopkinton councilmen questioned Clarke, determined that he "belonged" to his birthplace of Newport and ordered the town sergeant "to carry said Latham Clarke over to Newport and deliver him to the overseer of the poor for the town." The Hopkinton councilmen did not try to hold Stephen Clarke responsible for his father—it was up to Newport (hometown) authorities to do that. But Stephen Clarke had little to spare, in any case. The year after the elder Clarke was removed to Newport, Stephen and family left Hopkinton in search of better opportunities. They were not successful and were sent back to Hopkinton in 1761 as the "poor of the town," because Stephen Clarke's wife had contracted smallpox and the family was in need. Stephen Clarke died in Hopkinton the next year, leaving only a meager estate behind him.

Newport officials disagreed with Hopkinton's judgment of Clarke's hometown. They appealed the removal in court—and lost. Hopkinton spent nearly £50 defending the removal, but it was apparently worth it to not have the ongoing care of this elderly man. As for Clarke himself, he was questioned by Newport authorities and then placed in the town's workhouse, a fate he deplored. "I now am in the almshouse at the charge of the town of Newport," he testified later, "and I never begged alms in my life in any town whatever." To the place where he had flourished as a young man he had now returned as an aged and destitute old man.

Latham Clarke had a deep hunger for economic independence. He was literate and trained in a skill that brought him a competent living for a time. He achieved freeman status in South Kingstown and in New Jersey through his ownership of land. Even as an elderly man, he was "desirous to get something for a maintenance." But autonomy proved impossible as he aged, and his son's family were themselves in such want that they could not help him out. Over his lifetime, Latham Clarke had watched the family "fortune" dwindle from his father's prosperity to his grandchildren's penury. It must have been a great grief to him to spin out his last days in the almshouse of the town where he had grown up in hope and plenty fifty years before.

Abigail Hull Carr

Abigail Hull Carr had been living in Providence for three decades when she fell into need and came to the attention of town officials. Although she had built a life for herself in her long years of labor in the town, she had not acquired a legal settlement there and so was vulnerable to being removed from the place she called home in the twilight of her life. Although she had escaped slavery as a young woman, she was thrust back into it in her last days, sent back to the place where she had been enslaved a lifetime before.

Abigail Hull was born about the year 1725, the child of a slave and herself a slave in the household of Joseph Hull of South Kingstown. That township was the center of agricultural slavery in eighteenth-century Rhode Island. There Anglo-American colonists with visions of aristocratic living settled down to a way of life that closely resembled plantation systems farther south. They acquired slaves and indentured servants and set them to work planting English grasses, cultivating grain, fencing fields, building barns and houses, tending cattle and horses, and turning out cheese, grain, and other staples for the seagoing trade with the West Indies. The census of 1748 counted 380 "Negroes" and 193 "Indians" (most of them slaves or servants) as well as 1,405 whites in South Kingstown, the largest concentration of "Negroes" anywhere in the colony and a considerably higher proportion of nonwhites than was typical of Rhode Island towns.[7]

Abigail Hull may have been trained to field work, as were so many other slaves in South Kingstown, or she may have been a domestic servant in Joseph Hull's household. In either case, she was freed from slavery in 1745, when she was twenty years old. Her master, apparently a man of liberal sentiments, permitted her to purchase her freedom for £30. She continued to work for her master until 1749, a situation that suggests she paid for her manumission with her first four years of "free" labor.

In 1749, at age twenty-four, Abigail Hull moved the short distance from South Kingstown to Newport, a bustling seaport where she probably found work as a washerwoman or domestic servant in the homes of the prosperous mercantile families of the fifth largest town in the British North American colonies. In Newport she met Jack Carr, a free man of color, and married him in 1753. The couple then moved to Rehoboth, Massachusetts, across the border from Providence. Perhaps they sought better work opportunities or a more congenial community in which to live as free people of color. In October 1757, they moved into Providence, and within a matter of weeks, they came to the attention of town officials, who summoned Jack Carr to council and questioned him. Carr reported he had no children, "only himself and wife in family." The councilmen ordered him to produce a settlement certificate from his hometown of Newport, but they did not pursue the matter for another eight months. Not until August 1758 did authorities warn both Jack and Abigail Carr out of town because Jack had still not produced the certificate. If the Carrs ever actually moved away, they very soon returned and settled down to live and work in Providence. They never purchased any land and apparently supported themselves by their labor in the households or businesses of Providence. In all likelihood, that labor proved useful to the community, for there is no evidence that the couple were questioned or warned out by authorities over the next thirty years.

Then, in 1787, Abigail Carr came to official attention. She was sixty-two years old and a widow by that time, and perhaps it was Jack's death that had brought her to a point of need. But it was the wrong time to be black, needy, and transient in Providence. In 1787, Providence leaders were being inundated by scores of New England transients migrating to their community in search of work; the free black population was expanding rapidly following a wave of manumissions during the Revolutionary War; and this increase in manumissions raised questions about who was responsible for the material welfare of former slaves. Apparently uneasy about Abigail Carr's status, the Providence councilmen demanded proof that she had been freed forty years before. Carr answered that her master had emancipated her "in writing" in 1745, but that she "cannot at present find it"—a not surprising answer after forty years, even when such a highly prized document was at issue.

Despite Abigail Carr's three decades of continuous residence without being warned out (which surely qualified as "uncontested presence" under settlement law), the councilmen judged that she was not a legal inhabitant of Providence. Further, they ignored her marriage to Jack Carr, which had transferred her legal settlement to Newport, Jack's hometown. Instead, they declared her hometown to be South Kingstown, where she had been a slave some forty years before. For the Providence councilmen, Abigail Carr's identity as "former slave" eclipsed her identity as "widow." They gave her one month to leave Providence.

There is no further mention of Abigail Hull Carr in either Providence or South Kingstown records. Already aged and ailing, she may well have died soon after being warned out. A more optimistic scenario is that she spent her last years out of sight of town officials, cared for by other members of Providence's free black community. One thing is sure: her years of labor did not entitle her to even modest support in her last days in the town where she had lived for nearly half her life.

Elizabeth Stonehouse

Elizabeth Stonehouse was "advanced in life" and had been a widow for many years when she became a problem for Providence officials, who learned that she was "poor and indigent and in need of assistance for her support." But rather than sending her back to her hometown, which was the usual procedure, the councilmen elected to care for her there in Providence, as long as support money from her hometown was forthcoming. This arrangement was unprecedented in the Providence records of warning out, and it said a great deal about official sensibilities about her "genteel" background. The way town leaders were willing to bend the settlement rules for Elizabeth Stonehouse reveals the essentially discretionary nature of warning out: that it could be applied or not, as officials saw fit.

Elizabeth Stonehouse was born sometime before 1730 in Newport, the daughter of John Chace, "who owned a valuable estate in that town." This lineage made a difference to the Providence authorities, for she was named "Mrs." Stonehouse or "Missus" Stonehouse repeatedly in the records, a title they rarely gave to poor, transient women, no matter how clear the evidence of their married state. And nowhere is there any indication that she had labored to support herself; her financial legacy from her father may have sustained her for many years. No doubt her manners, speech, and carriage all indicated the authenticity of her upper-class beginnings, and she was literate enough to sign her name in a very legible hand.

Elizabeth Stonehouse lived in Newport in her father's household until she was "about forty years old," an unusually long time for a propertied woman to remain unmarried. But whatever the hindrances to her marriage, they disappeared when she moved to Providence, for "soon after [she] married Capt. Robert Stonehouse." There were apparently no children from the marriage, and following her husband's death, Elizabeth relied only on her own resources to maintain herself.

Robert Stonehouse was apparently also a man of some status, per-

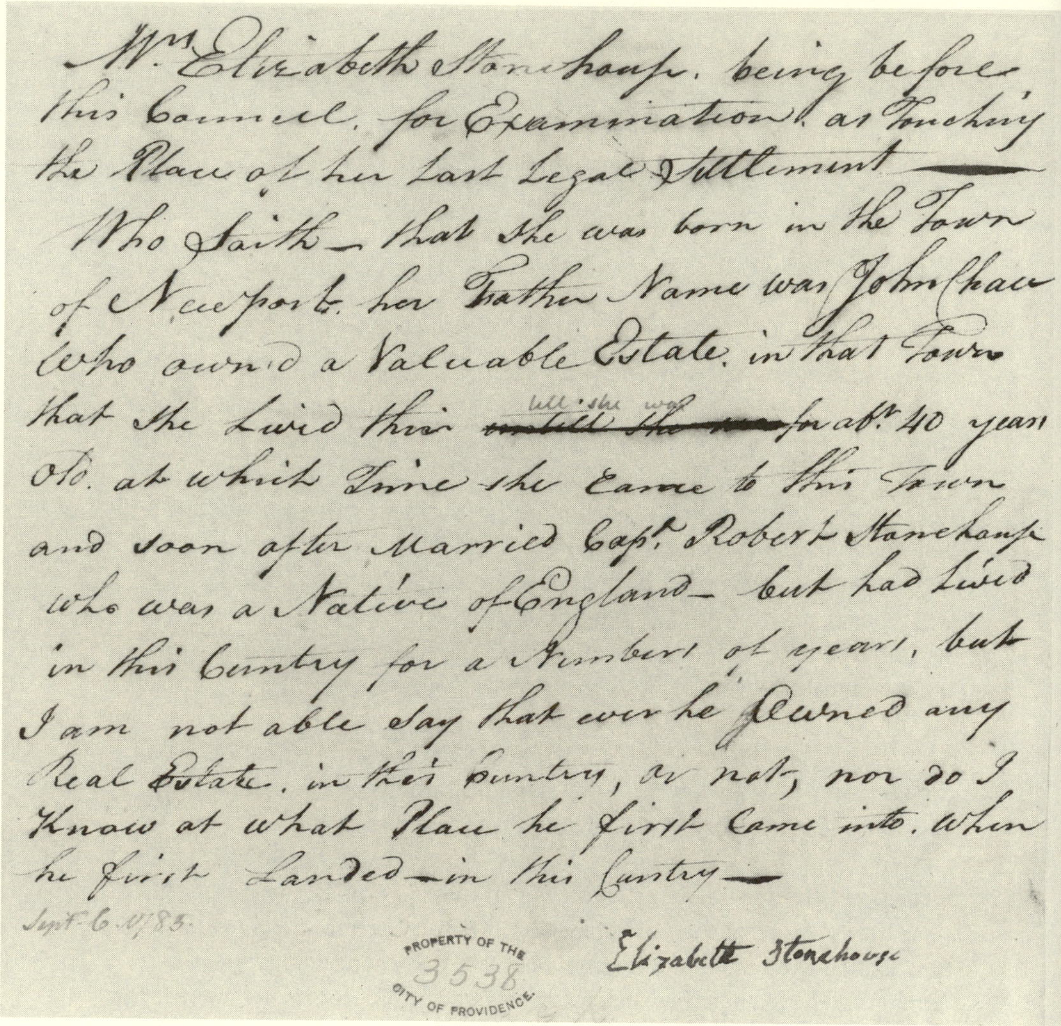

Mrs Elizabeth Stonehouse. being before this Council. for Examination. as Touching the Place of her Last Legal Settlement —

Who Saith — that She was born in the Town of Newport. her Father Name was John Chace Who own'd a Valuable Estate. in that Town that She Lived there ~~untill she was~~ for abt. 40 years Old. at which Time she Came to this Town and soon after Married Capt. Robert Stonehouse who was a Native of England — but had Lived in this Country for a Number of years, but I am not able say that ever he Owned any Real Estate. in this Country, or not, nor do I know at what Place he first Came into. When he first Landed — in this Country —

Sept 6. 1785.

Elizabeth Stonehouse

Figure 8. Elderly widow Elizabeth Stonehouse left this signature when she was questioned by Providence town authorities on 6 September 1785. Source: PTP 8:146, neg. no. RHi (x3) 9399. Courtesy of the Rhode Island Historical Society.

haps an officer in the military during the Seven Years' War. He was "a native of England," but he had migrated to New England "a number of years" before Elizabeth Stonehouse met and married him. When questioned by the town councilmen, she could not tell "whether he ever owned any real estate in this country," although clearly he had never possessed a freehold as long as she was married to him. Nor could she tell "at what place he first landed at in this country," suggesting that his first arrival was such old history that it had never become a topic of conversation between husband and wife. If Robert Stonehouse had ever acquired a legal settlement anywhere in North America, the councilmen could not discover it.

Whatever Robert Stonehouse's status, he was not a wealthy man, and whatever dowry his wife brought to the marriage did not substantially improve his estate, for Robert Stonehouse paid only a minimal poll tax throughout the 1760s, when his name appears on several Providence rate lists. The last mention of him is in 1770, and then he disappears, apparently having died. After that, Elizabeth Stonehouse must have been folded into another family—boarding with neighbors or relatives, perhaps—for she is not listed on the 1782 census as having her own household. Whatever estate she brought to the marriage dwindled away as she used it to support herself in her widowhood. By 1785, she had no more resources to maintain herself, and the overseers of the poor became aware of her need.

In September 1785, the Providence councilmen questioned Stonehouse and formally "rejected" her as a legal inhabitant of their town. Nevertheless, they were greatly moved by her situation: a gentlewoman who had come down in life, now aged and at the point of needing poor relief from the town treasury. They decided to write the Newport council, "informing" them of Stonehouse's "circumstances" and "requesting them to contribute to her relief without her being sent to that city." The Newport councilmen agreed, and Elizabeth Stonehouse was maintained in Providence for at least five years.

Providence officials chose their language carefully when they asked Newport to "contribute to her relief" rather than "pay for her relief." Both towns, it seems, pitched in to maintain this elderly genteel widow. From 1785 to 1790, Providence officials periodically ordered that money be paid out of the Providence town treasury to cover the cost of "wood &c in this inclement season"; in 1790, the town also paid for "the rent of a room for Mrs. Elizabeth Stonehouse" at Charles Holden's house. It is possible that Newport was paying into Providence's treasury; more likely, Newport was paying Stonehouse's caretakers directly to cover the costs of room, board, clothing, and medical care, and Providence was chipping in by supplying firewood. Whatever the arrangement, it was an unusual cooperative effort between two towns on behalf of someone acknowledged indirectly as "belonging" in some sense to both communities.

In the winter of 1788–89, Elizabeth Stonehouse and a "Missis Griffith," who also "belonged" to Newport, were being supported together in Providence. The overseer of the poor described the two women as "now in the decline of life and circumstances and sojourning amongst us for the present"; in an effort to explain the unusual finances to the town treasurer, he added that "although they are inhabitants of Newport, they have lived a great while amongst us."

The incomplete overseer records do not allow us to see beyond 1790 to discover how Elizabeth Stonehouse and her housemate fared at the very end of their lives. It may be that they were sent back to Newport to be tended in their final illnesses. But given Providence authority's unusual care of and courtesy toward these women, it seems more likely they were permitted to finish their days in familiar surroundings.

Bristol Rhodes

Bristol Rhodes's examination, recorded by the Providence clerk in 1794, tells very little about this remarkable man. It summarizes his life in minimal terms: "he was born in Cranston, a slave to Capt. William Rhodes; that he resided in said Cranston until he was about the age of twenty years, at which time he enlisted into the Continental Army; and has since resided in this town for the space of about five years." Other records, however, give us a much fuller picture of Bristol Rhodes the soldier, the veteran, the invalid, and the neighbor.

Bristol Rhodes was born sometime in 1755. The day he became free is known more precisely: 29 May 1778, when he joined the army. In February 1778 Rhode Island's General Assembly passed a law proclaiming "that every able-bodied negro, mulatto, or Indian man slave, in this state, may enlist" in the Rhode Island Regiment. Upon passing muster, every enlisted slave would "be immediately discharged from the service of his master or mistress, and be absolutely FREE, as though he had never been encumbered with any kind of servitude or slavery." The first three slaves enlisted on 25 February; Rhodes enlisted three months later, perhaps because it took that long to persuade his master to free him for the revolutionary cause. He enlisted for the duration of the war, which continued another five years.

Bristol Rhodes's military service took him into battle against the British in Rhode Island and then in New Jersey, New York, and Virginia. At the siege of Yorktown on 17 October 1781, Rhodes was badly injured: his commanding officer reported the "loss of the left leg and hand by a cannon shot." He was tended in hospital for nearly a year, and then was "discharged by his Excellency General Washington" on 1 September 1782. On 23 September, a board of officers awarded him an honorary badge for "long and faithful service."

When he was released from the military, twenty-seven-year-old Rhodes was owed £39 in back wages. Fortunately, influential persons, including his former commanding officer, Jeremiah Olney, took up his cause and the cause of other invalid veterans in the state. A month later, in October 1782, a committee of the Rhode Island state legislature investigated, discovered how much Rhodes and others were due in back pay, and pushed through an act to reimburse the men out of the state treasury. No doubt many legislators wanted to honor the implicit contract they had made with these soldiers when they had offered them freedom in exchange for military service. In May 1783, the state legislature authorized another payment of £12, which brought his back wages up to date. In 1784, he was paid $53.50 directly by the army, an amount that officially represented "a final settlement of accounts." Finally, permanent relief came in sight in June 1785, when the United States Congress passed an act to grant life pensions to invalid soldiers; a committee of the Rhode Island legislature "inspected" forty-six invalids, one of them Bristol Rhodes, who was medically examined on 10 February 1786. Later that month, the state legislature passed an act that granted Rhodes a monthly pension of £1 10s. ($5.31), to be paid by Congress in quarterly installments each year. When Congress got nine months behind in its pension payments, the Rhode Island state legislature stepped in once again in February 1788 and brought pension accounts up to date for a number of invalid veterans, including Rhodes, who received £40 in paper money, equivalent to £13 10s in "real" silver money. The state legislature continued to pay Rhodes periodically out of the state treasury, keeping careful accounts of what he was due from his congressional pension; by April 1790, Congress was about £26 in arrears.

Official activity related to his pension must have bound together Bristol Rhodes and those influential men who championed his case at the state level. When he moved from Cranston to Providence in 1789, Providence authorities did not cite or examine him as a transient, although he must have been highly visible, as markedly disabled as he was. His military service and his invalid status seem to have entitled him to the unofficial protection of authorities, many of whom had been military officers during the Revolutionary War and were bound by honor to care for "mutilated and infirm persons, who have lost their limbs and health in the service of their country." With his (intermittent) pension as income, Rhodes lived peaceably in Providence and built a network of acquaintances. His home, apparently, became a gathering place for other free people of color.

Then, in 1794, trouble erupted between Rhodes and his white neighbors. On 1 September, the Providence council received a petition from eighteen "sundry inhabitants" of Providence, complaining about "a certain Negro family . . . by the name of Bristol Rhodes." The issue was Sunday gatherings at Rhodes's home that his irritated neighbors did not dignify with the label "church." These white neighbors, who identified themselves as "living in the vicinity of the neighborhood near the Congregational church," objected to the "noise and confusion" of these meetings at Rhodes's house "on the sabbath." The "large number" of people who attended the meetings were prone to "behaving in such a manner that it greatly corrupts the morals of children which is [sic] obliged to be in hearing of the ridiculous language, &c." The white neighbors requested that the councilmen "order their remove" or in some other way "accommodate" the offended neighbors.

This complaint suggests that Bristol Rhodes was hosting an informal house church, marking the beginnings of an African American congregation that could not yet afford to construct its own building. The "ridiculous language" wafting over the neighborhood might have been a local black dialect of English, a kind of street language intended to baffle the ears of whites. Or it might have been prayers and hymns spoken and sung in English, but in such a fervent and emotional manner as to sound "ridiculous" to staid Congregational worshipers. Complicating the situation was the state of race relations in the early 1790s, when refugees from slave uprisings on St. Domingue (later Haiti) arrived in Providence, telling blood-curdling tales of murder and pillage. No doubt many whites feared similar rebellions in the United States and looked nervously on any "large" gathering of people of color.

The Providence town councilmen, however, seemed unperturbed. They carefully recorded the petition and they obligingly examined Bristol Rhodes, officially noting that his hometown was in Cranston. But they did not order the "remove" of the Rhodes family, as the petitioners asked. The reason seems clear: Bristol Rhodes was a special case. He had a guaranteed income in his invalid pension, so that economic need was not an issue. More importantly, he was a visible representation of the sacrifices of the Revolutionary War. Bristol Rhodes was a transient, but he was also a local hero, and so town leaders considered him to "belong" in some sense to their community. Perhaps they unofficially urged Rhodes, as "colonel" to "private," to keep down the noise of his Sunday meetings; perhaps they had a quiet word with the chief complainers. In any case, the matter never surfaced again in the town records.

Bristol Rhodes continued to live in Providence, and presumably his house continued to be a focal point for the free African American community there. He regularly visited Dr. Comfort Carpenter for medical care related to his war injury and kept a running account with this physician. Then, on 3 July 1810, at fifty-five years of age, Bristol Rhodes died. The two major Rhode Island newspapers each carried an obituary, a remarkable tribute to the way Bristol Rhodes and other black veterans had won the respect and appreciation of influential people in the community. The *Providence Gazette* eulogized him thus: "Bristol Rhodes, a black man, of the late revolutionary army, in which he served with deserved reputation. At the siege of York-Town he was severely wounded, having unfortunately lost a leg and an arm, and has since subsisted on a pension." The *Rhode Island Republican* which credited him with dying "in an advanced age," described him simply: "A black man of the Revolution."

and the intercourse continued as usual. So much for an affront from Gen. Turreau. The reader is well acquainted with the treatment Mr. Jackson received for an insult which has not yet been found. But here the case was altered. Gen. Turreau is a Frenchman—Mr. Jackson is an Englishman.
N. Y. Ev. Post.

Married.

On Sunday evening last, by the Rev. Mr. Gano, Mr. *JOHN GREENE*, to Miss *MARY WHITE*, both of this town.

On Tuesday evening last, Mr. *HORATIO G. BATES*, to Miss *MARY MUNRO*, second daughter of Mr. John L. Munro.

Died.

In this town, on Tuesday last, in an advanced age, *BRISTOL RHODES*, a black man, of the late revolutionary army, in which he long served with deserved reputation. At the siege of York-Town he was severely wounded, having unfortunately lost a leg and an arm, and has since subsisted on a pension.

"At Attleborough, on Tuesday last, Mrs. *SARAH PIKE*, wife of Mr. Moses Pike, in the 76th year of her age, after a long illness, during which a large share of bodily

---

PIG IRON *now landing.*

20 Tons of Salisbury } Soft grey Pigs,
20 do. of Weymouth } Suitable for Castings, will be sold in Lots to suit Purchasers. Apply to
ISAAC PITMAN.

July 7, 1810.

FOR SALE,

And landing this Day from on board the Sloop Sally, S. Thurber, Master,

50 Hhds. of RUM, of a superior Quality
15 Bbls. of ORANGES and LIMES.

LIKEWISE ON HAND,

Rice, Coffee, Sugars, Teas, Beef, Pork, Butter, Lard, Hams, &c. &c.

Enquire of BENJAMIN T. CHANDLER, ISAAC BOOROM, or JOHN M. GREEN.

July 7, 1810.

TAKE NOTICE.

THE Person who found a WATCH on the 4th of July in Mr. Robinson's Necessary, is requested to leave it at the Bookstore of
J. BREWER.

N. B. The Person's Name is known.

July 7, 1810.

Clarinets and Pitchpipes
Hautboys and Flagelets
Elegant Morocco Stools
Wire Strings for Guitars and Piano Fortes
Strings of all Kinds for Violins, Violoncellos and Harps
Clarinets, Bassoon and Hautboy Reeds, &c.

MUSIC

For all Instruments, and a complete Assortment of Songs, Duets, Rondeaus and Glees.

Boston, July 6, 1810.

Commissioners' Notice.

THE Subscribers having been appointed, by the Honourable Court of Probate of the Town of Providence, Commissioners to receive and examine the Claims against the Estate of Capt. JOHN TILLINGHAST, late of said Providence, deceased, represented insolvent, give Notice, that Six Months from this Date are allowed to the Creditors of said Estate to bring in and prove their Claims.
ABNER DAGGETT,
JOHN HOLROYD.

All Persons indebted to said Estate, are requested to make immediate Payment to
WILLIAM HOLROYD, *Admin.*

July 7, 1810.

Figure 9. When veteran Bristol Rhodes died in 1810, the *Providence Gazette* printed this obituary. Source: *Providence Gazette*, 7 July 1810, neg. no. RHi (x3) 9402. Courtesy of the Rhode Island Historical Society.

Conclusion:
Constructing a Transient's Life

*M*Y GOAL in presenting these narratives has been to recover the experience of people who rarely possessed either the skills or the opportunity to write their own stories. Because of the limitations of the records, all forty tales are fragmentary; none stretch in a satisfactory fashion from cradle to grave, even in those rare cases where we have both birth and death dates. We know, for example, that Jerusha Townsend was sent out of Providence as an infant in 1775 and that she died from yellow fever in Providence in 1797, but we understand little of her life in the intervening twenty-two years. Every narrative contains similar gaps, leaving us to speculate about what happened, and no one account stands as a representative testimony of the life course of warned-out people. Although these stories are incomplete, they are the best information we currently have about the transient poor, and the particular moments of life captured in these narratives do much to illuminate a world formerly hidden from view. The goal of this final chapter is to paint a more complete portrait, to sketch some of the "typical" ingredients of the lives of the transient poor in eighteenth-century New England.

Most people warned out of Rhode Island towns were native-born New Englanders, not immigrants struggling to find a place in a new society. Titus Guinea from West Africa, Jacob Burke from Germany, Thomas Field from Ireland, and Christopher Stocker from England represent that tiny fraction of transients who were foreign-born. The rest had their birth homes in New England. About half were born in or near the commercial centers of Boston (Benjamin Champney, Peter Norton, and others), Providence (Kate Jones, Jerusha Townsend, and others), and Newport (John Treby, Margaret Bowler, and others). The other half came from rural areas in Rhode Island, Massachusetts, or Connecticut: Abner Butler from Martha's Vineyard, Esther Heradon from Canterbury, Connecticut, Judah Hazard from North Kingstown, Rhode Island. These place names claimed by poor, transient people underscore how eighteenth-century New England society and economy did not benefit all its native-born daughters and sons.

Whatever their geographic origins, most transients started out poor. It was the exceptional few who told of prosperous parents like Latham Clarke's, who gave their son a freehold, or like Elizabeth Stonehouse's father, who owned a "valuable estate" and probably devolved a handsome dowry on his daughter when she married. The great majority were born into poor families, indicating that poverty trapped people across generations. Although many people prospered in early New England, it was by no means a society that offered opportunity for all. The transient testimonies provide compelling evidence that a good many New Englanders were never able to rise above the poor circumstances into which they were born. Phebe Perkins and Olive Pero, for example, were born into poverty, and so were their children. Those babies typified the majority of warned-out people in this study, who were born to slaves, indentured servants, or parents too poor to raise their children independently. Seldom were such births written into the vital records, for poor, illiterate parents had neither money for the recording fees nor interest in documentation, and "respectable" citizens routinely overlooked such children when counting the "real" inhabitants of their towns.

As children of the lower sort, transients rarely received significant education in reading and writing or in skills that would enable them to earn even a "decent competency" when they became adults. Nathaniel Bowdish's obvious and extensive literacy training was highly unusual. Instead, the theme of most transient children's early years was practical preparation for an adulthood of manual labor. Judah Hazard Wanton and Cato Freeman grew up as slaves, Mary Carder and Primus Thompson as indentured servants, indicating childhoods of much labor and little book learning. More fortunate were Benjamin Jones and Daniel Collins, whose parents apprenticed them to particular trades, but even these relatively privileged boys received only cursory literacy training.

As children, transients became familiar with disrupted households and the emotional turmoil that likely accompanied them. William and Jerusha Townsend abandoned their four daughters; William Heradon abandoned his wife and their three children. Kate Jones and the sons of Peter Norton were orphaned before the age of seven. Susannah Guinea and the four children of Roseanna Brown were forcibly taken from their mothers and placed in other households. When Sophia Havens's grand-mother died, she was removed from the care of her mother and separated from the rest of her extended family as well. While these transient children may have received more adequate material support in their new homes, they still had to cope with the trauma of splintered birth families.

Adult family relationships of warned-out transients were similarly prone to fracture. Sometimes authorities ignored the bond between couples who had not been married in an official Anglo-American marriage ceremony, either because their masters had prevented it (as suggested by the case of Judah Hazard and Lambo Wanton), or because the couple themselves preferred to follow other wedding customs (as indicated by the case of Mary Cummock and James Fowler). Other times relationship problems stemmed from private grievances: the sham marriage of Christopher Stocker and Abigail Harris; the public brawling of Thomas Field and Mary Justice; the infidelity of Nathaniel Whitaker; Mark Noble's open repudiation of his wife's debts. More typical, if less spectacular, were women who bore and raised children without the visible support of their lovers and husbands: unmarried women like Phebe Perkins, Wait Godfrey, and Elizabeth Springer gave birth to "bastard" children; wives like Esther Heradon and Mrs. Fuller were abandoned outright by their husbands; matriarchs like Patience Havens and Sarah Gardner managed extended households without the help of their mates. It was the exception for warned-out transients to have what authorities called "proper" families, and even those relationships were prone to disruption by illness or accident, as was the case with Patience and Abner Butler. The children of these fractured relationships—unnamed in the record and usually uncounted as well—often reproduced their parents' experience. Since these youngsters seldom possessed (or would inherit) any property, officials treated them as poor orphans, took them from their surviving parents, and bound them out to other masters. There, in a generational repetition, they grew up marginally literate and familiar with hard work.

Labor was thus the common denominator for transients, and with their hands and backs these workers provided the goods and services that eased the lives of their more well-to-do neighbors. Though a few transients identified themselves as skilled artisans (John Treby and William Townsend were goldsmiths, for example), the great majority indicated barely skilled or unskilled labor—the grueling and tedious tasks that sustained household, field, workshop, and wharf. While some transient women labored alongside men in the fields (Phebe Perkins picked fruit and vegetables), most worked in the company of other women, doing such "housekeeping" duties as spinning, washing clothes, preparing food, scrubbing floors, cleaning chamber pots, and nursing the sick. Some transients, Peter Norton among them, worked as general farm laborers, helping with crops, repairing fences, chopping wood, and mending equipment. Those trained in the less lucrative trades of shoemaking, tailoring, and coopering often moved in search of a community that had need of their skills. Others worked as day laborers in towns where a man might earn his keep by carrying loads and sweeping streets. When opportunity arose, some sought the security of a steady maintenance as a soldier or a merchant seaman.

The earnings of these transient workers were meager, sometimes less than three shillings per day, the going rate for unskilled male labor in southeastern New England in the latter part of the eighteenth century.[1] But even six days of such labor rarely covered the weekly cost of essential food, lodging, and clothing to keep a family alive, much less provide extra firewood in the winter or medical treatment in emergencies.[2] And in any case, illness, bad weather, business cycles, and the capriciousness of employers made it highly unlikely that an unskilled transient laborer would work six days of the week. It was nearly impossible, then, for these lower-sort workers to keep their families from disaster.

The seasonal cycles of agricultural work and the unreliable, sporadic market for unskilled labor propelled hungry laborers from their hometowns in search of work. In the latter part of the eighteenth century, many transients gravitated toward Providence, the commercial center of southeastern New England, where jobs were more likely to be found year-round. Providence was in the midst of a major expansion during this period. Its population more than doubled, from 3,159 souls in 1755 to 7,614 in 1800; its rivers, roads, and ocean access made it a transportation center for the region; and its economic base widened to support industrial development as well as maritime business. In Providence and the surrounding towns, unskilled transient women located employment as domestic laborers in upper-class households, and transient men of varying skills found work in the shipping trades or supplying the needs of city dwellers. Mary Carder, Olive Pero, and Phillis Wanton scrubbed the clothes and floors of the better-off; Jacob Burke carted loads from wharf to warehouse and cleared the streets of rubbish; Nathaniel Whitaker labored as a ship caulker, Daniel Collins as a cooper, Benjamin Champney as a blockmaker, and Benjamin Jones as a baker. And in the city transients could try out new job possibilities: Patience Butler took in boarders, Margaret Bowler operated a bawdy house, and Christopher Stocker opened a small tavern in his rented lodgings.

Unskilled transients tended to identify their labor not by the nature of their tasks but by the names of their employers. Their testimonies are thin on specific work routines but dense with specific names of people on whom they depended for a livelihood. While these lists of names reflect the pressure officials put on transients to prove their work history, they also indicate how employers served as important links between transients and their communities. Primus Thompson moved to Jamestown to work for William Wilbur, Phillis Wanton made her employer's house her "home," Bristol Rhodes relied on his former commanding officer to secure his military pension.

Equally powerful magnets were those networks of family and friends that created a refuge for transients in a new community. This is particularly observable in the case of people of color, who relied on such networks to support their transition from bondage to freedom and to soften the social and economic effects of racial prejudice. When newly emancipated Patience Havens joined her three daughters in Providence, she followed a typical course of transient migrations. Further, the extended households that she, Bristol Rhodes, and Sarah Gardner created demonstrate how people of African and Native American ancestry clustered in Providence, and, by their presence, built a haven for people of color in the late eighteenth century. The informal congregation that gathered at Bristol Rhodes's house suggests that religion was sometimes a principal focus of that community, but official records lead more frequently to neighborhood taverns, where black and white transients alike worked and took their leisure. In the 1780s and 1790s, the number of Providence taverns— legal as well as illegal—mushroomed, and transients stimulated that business.[3] Thomas Field very likely met Mary Justice in her tavern; Margaret Bowler and Sarah Gardner appear to have worked as prostitutes in establishments where alcohol was bought and sold. Not jobs only, then, but the potential for support drew transients from one place to another, seeking a community of women to assist during childbirth or illness, a community of men to repair a leaky roof or rebuild a fallen chimney, a community of like-minded people for worship and recreation.

Employers, neighbors, and family were the primary ties that bound transients to their communities. Few had significant political connections, since ownership of land was essential to having a voice in the town meeting; Latham Clarke and Peter West are unusual for having once owned land and voted. The political experience that warned-out transients shared was the humiliation of being summoned and questioned by powerful officials in a manner that exposed and emphasized landless people's political impotence. Those who challenged the politically powerful were likely to find themselves further humiliated by public whipping (Nathaniel Bowdish) or incarceration (Thomas Field).

The material lives of most transients reflected their low status. They lived in rented houses or rooms within other people's homes. Men's possessions were seldom plows, livestock, and other farm goods, and women's were seldom feather beds, silver spoons, and other items of dowries. Instead, warned-out people's goods tended to be the bare essentials, movable and few: a change of clothing that by make and material announced the wearer's low rank; a cup, a bowl, and other household utensils with which to make and eat a small meal; knitting needles or a razor; a knapsack or bag for transporting the whole. When the constable required a cart to move a warned-out family, it was usually because of numerous children, not numerous possessions. The beds and bedding on which poor transients lay, the stools upon which they sat, and the tables at which they ate usually belonged to the more prosperous householders with whom they lodged. Their meals were often thin and unsatisfying, and many would have considered the menu at the Providence workhouse to be almost a banquet. There, every healthy adult inmate was to receive "meat or fish" for the midday meal; for breakfast and the evening meal, "some sort of spoon victuals, such as hasty pudding, broth, water gruel, milk, milk porridge, coffee, [or] chocolate shells boiled"; and with each meal, a pint of beer "stuffed with bread."[4]

Overwork, malnutrition, inferior housing, and inadequate clothing left many transients vulnerable to illness. Poor hygiene and unsanitary living conditions resulted in worms, infections, and infestations of lice, like that of the Fuller children. Transients in crowded housing were also more likely to succumb to contagious diseases such as smallpox, which carried off Peter and Rose Norton, and yellow fever, which killed Patience Havens, Jerusha Townsend, and others. Indeed, the very act of moving from place to place exposed people to greater disease and death. Those who labored in wet and icy weather, exposed to the elements in thin clothing and footwear, were likely to suffer from respiratory ailments, frozen feet, or even broken bones from a fall, as in the case of Primus Thompson. Poor transient women were especially vulnerable during pregnancy and childbirth; Phebe Perkins, Martha Hathaway, and Elizabeth Springer were brought low by childbed fever, and their babies suffered as well.

People already living on the margin possessed few reserves of physical strength or material fortune to cope with illness or accident, which pushed them into a state of dire need. Some solved their difficulties by resorting to petty theft or by putting themselves in debt to neighbors or employers, thus straining community relationships and sparking disputes of the sort that arose between Benjamin Jones and Richard Burke. Others, like Primus Thompson, received charitable assistance from friends and neighbors before they came to official attention. A few, like Olive Pero, voluntarily sought aid from town authorities, while a few others, like Latham Clark, resorted at last to the workhouse.

Finally, old age was cruel to poor transients. A final illness like that of Clarke Pike was all too often followed by the construction of a cheap coffin and the digging of a pauper's grave, like that in which Obadiah Blanding was buried, since most transients could not afford the cost of a funeral or a church burial. No tombstones marked their final resting places, and few (if any) notations in church or town documents recorded their passing. Their widows did not benefit from dower rights, which customarily placed one-third of the husband's estate under the control of the widow. Their children received no bequests of land, houses, or silver; if there was anything to be inherited, it was likely unpaid debts. These transients left no wills; their meager possessions were passed along to friends and kin by informal agreement.

Despite all the grim and depressing elements of these narratives, there are triumphant moments when we can see transients asserting themselves in difficult situations. Mary Fowler insisted that she was married, just not in the manner of "white people." Judah Wanton refused to put her "x" on the written representation of her testimony, because she would not sign what she could not read. Patience Butler eluded the constable and vanished with her children into the streets of Providence rather than be sent back to Martha's Vineyard. Sarah Gardner and her daughters persistently returned to Providence despite being thrown out several times. Benjamin Jones successfully persuaded his taxpaying neighbors to award his crippled son a stipend. Bristol Rhodes earned respectful tributes from powerful and influential people in obituaries that praised him as a "black man of the Revolution."

Such moments suggest that it is important to ask not only how transient people lived, labored, and suffered, but also how they shaped their communities. These stories do more than show us the life course of unwelcome Americans; they tell us how poor people changed the towns where they lived. These were not the homogeneous, harmonious, and prosperous communities of the New England town myth. Rather, they were places of conflict, disorder, and enormous cultural complexity. Recovering the stories of poor transients is essential if we are to understand the eighteenth-century New England town in all its real humanity.

Appendix: Documentary Evidence and Background Information

THIS APPENDIX presents in two forms the information that can be assembled from the raw materials of this study—the warning-out and other documents—to enable readers to participate in the detective work of writing history. The first part provides transcriptions from some of the documents themselves; the second summarizes in graphic form the general characteristics of the transient population reflected in the records.

Documents

From records such as those excerpted below I constructed the narratives in this volume. Here I invite others to do their own reconstructions, using the excerpts below and drawing on the material in the introduction. The narratives are my own interpretations; other students of early America will bring different knowledge and perspectives to the reading of these documents and so may have other insights into these people who lived on the margin.

By providing these transcriptions I also hope to convey to readers the problem of "voice" in the original documents. The town clerks who recorded the examinations and other pertinent data brought their own assumptions and expectations to the business of record keeping. They did not write down everything they heard, and they liberally edited what they did record. One of the most persuasive reasons for *not* presenting the examinations as unmediated transcriptions of the town records is that the clerks' voices interfere considerably with and distort the voices of the transients themselves. The bureaucratic format, legal language, and clerical editing sometimes overwhelm the transients' stories and put the spotlight on the record keeper and the process of warning out rather than on the transient and his or her own story. Since this book is focused on the lives and life courses of poor people, it seemed wise to limit the "static" of the clerks' voices while presenting the stories of those people.

Nevertheless, scrutiny of the record keepers' data is a valuable exercise, and an appendix is the more appropriate place to do it. It is important to understand something of the minds and hands that recorded the words on which we rely to learn about the past. We count on those record keepers to inform us about people who were not literate, not wealthy, and not powerful, and we need to have a measure of their skills and motivations in creating the record.

In the following pages I hope readers will engage the documentary sources in order to discover more about these unwelcome Americans than is provided in their narratives. I also hope readers will learn something about the town clerks who wrote down the fragmentary information we have about transient people. Those clerks did not share a common education, and there is little uniformity in their sentence structure, spelling, and syntax. Thus their written language can frustrate present-day readers. To make the documents most accessible, I have modernized spelling and capitalization and inserted punctuation when it seemed necessary for comprehension.

Documents Relating to Phebe Perkins

Hopkinton Town Council decides to appeal Phebe Perkins's removal—
9 October 1784

Source: Hopkinton TCR 2:144
At a town council held at Hopkinton the 9th day of October AD 1784, at Thompson Wells's, called in order to consider with regard to an order for the removal of one Phebe Perkins from Richmond to this town. . . .

Whereas personally appeared Edward Wells, overseer of the poor, and presented an order which was for the removal of one Phebe Perkins, a transient person, from the town of Richmond to this town of Hopkinton, wherein by the return of the officers and information of said overseer, the said Phebe is removed to said Hopkinton; and after taking the same into consideration and collecting the circumstances attending her last settlement, which are hereafter to be enumerated as reasons of appeal, it is therefore voted that said order be and the same is hereby appealed from.

Council appoints committee to gather evidence for appeal—
3 November 1784

Source: Hopkinton TCR 2:146

Voted that Joseph Witter Jr. and Abel Tanner be and they are hereby appointed to collect the circumstances relating [to] the order for removing Phebe Perkins from Richmond to Hopkinton and to point out the reasons to support the appealing therefrom.

*Council approves payment for Perkins's care—*3 January 1785

Source: Hopkinton TCR 2:214

Voted that Cary Clarke have an order to the treasury for £7-10-0, it being for boarding and nursing, bleeding and assisting Phebe Perkins 12 weeks in her late sickness in lying in;

Voted that Dr. Ross Coon have an order to the treasury for £0-3-0, it being for bleeding and strong drops for Phebe Perkins in her late sickness;

Voted that Joseph Witter Jr. have an order to the treasury for £0-5-6, it being for shoes for Phebe Perkins.

*Examination of Phebe Perkins—*19 January 1785

Source: Hopkinton Town Clerk Papers (draft notes; not entered into the permanent record)

The examination of Phebe Perkins, a transient person who was removed to this town of Hopkinton by an order from the town council of Richmond, concerning her last legal place of residence, who on oath saith that she was born at Newport; that she was bound an apprentice to Abraham Burden, then of Westerly, who carried her to Stephen Perry's in Charlestown, where she lived till said Perry moved to Hopkinton; and went to Hopkinton with said Perry, where she lived till she was of age, which was the 25th day of August 1778; that she knows of no contract between said Burden and said Perry concerning her living with said Perry; that she saw her indentures at Perry's but doth not know whether Perry claimed a right to her time or not; that in about three weeks after her time was out she went to one Avery's in Connecticut to work, where she stayed three weeks and then returned to said Perry's and stayed there till the beginning of the winter following; and then she went to Benjamin

Wilbur's in Richmond, where she lived till the spring following, when people began to pick greens for sauce; that then she went to Thomas Sweet's in Hopkinton, where she worked two weeks; then she went to Timothy Larkin's and worked one week; and then returned to said Sweet's and lived there till strawberries began to be ripe; and then she went to Lebeus Sweet's and lived there till the first of August following; and then returned to said Perry's and stayed there one year; and then went to Amos Collins's in Stonington [Connecticut] and lived there till the next spring; and then went to Sweet Peckham's in Westerly and there lived till the next fall; and then went to Charlestown and lived at different places in said town near 2 years; and then removed to Edward Perry's, Esqr., in Richmond, where she continued more than 2 years.

Council appoints clerk to handle legal appeal—19 January 1785

Source: Hopkinton TCR 2:150
       Voted that the council clerk make out the reasons of appeal in the affair of Phebe Perkins and lodge the same in the clerk's office, agreeable with the laws in that case made and provided, and that he carry on and prosecute the same before the General Sessions of the Peace to final judgment.

Hopkinton Town Meeting confirms and pays clerk as legal agent —14 February 1785

Source: Hopkinton TMR, vol. 1
       Voted that Abel Tanner be and he is hereby appointed overseer of the poor and agent for this town to prosecute the reasons of appeal in the affair of Phebe Perkins to final judgment and execution—and that Ross Coon, [tax] collector, furnish him with £3.0 to defray expenses with, and that he account with the Town for the same.

Council pays agents for expenses of the appeal—14 February 1785

Source: Hopkinton TCR 2:216
       Voted that Abel Tanner have an order to the treasury for 15s., it being for his expenses and services in lodging the reasons of appeal in the affair of Phebe Perkins in the clerk's office.

Voted that Samuel Babcock have an order to the treasury for 3s., it being for going to Richmond in the affair of Phebe Perkins.

Council approves payment for Perkins's care—7 March 1785

Source: Hopkinton TCR 2:218

Voted that Mr. Samuel Witter have an order to the treasury for £1-0-6, it being for supporting Phebe Perkins 6 weeks up to the 17th of February last.

Town Meeting appoints second agent to argue the court case—
7 June 1785

Source: Hopkinton TMR, vol. 1

Voted that Thomas Wells Esqr. prosecute and carry on before the court of General Sessions of the Peace to be held at South Kingstown the second Monday in August next in the case [of] Phebe Perkins, a pauper, being sent by an order from the town of Richmond to this town of Hopkinton and the town of Hopkinton's appealing therefrom, in behalf of Abel Tanner who declines.

Council approves payment for Perkins's care—8 September 1786

Source: Hopkinton TCR 2:259

Voted that Zebulon Weaver have an order to the treasury for £0-12-0, it being for keeping Phebe Perkins and child eleven days and attending council.

DOCUMENTS RELATING TO SARAH GARDNER

Sarah Gardner receives poor relief—19 November 1762

Source: Warwick TCR 2:218

Whereas Sarah Gardner having three small children and is likely to become chargeable to the town unless some house can be procured for her to live in this winter, on consideration this Council doth request the overseers of the poor to hire some suitable house, at the best lay they can, for six months, at the charge of the town, for the term of six months, for the said Sarah Gardner and children to live in.

Gardner's children are bound out—13 December 1762

Source: Warwick TCR 2:221–22

Whereas one Sarah Gardner, an Indian squaw, having three sons and one daughter, which are very likely to become chargeable to the town, one of which boys now lives with Mr. Mitchel, one with Mr. Laurance, and the other with Mr. Sterry of Providence, and the girl now lives with Mr. William Colegrove, and that in case the said Sarah Gardner will not bind out said children apprentices to some suitable persons within one fortnight's time after the rising of this council, that then the clerk is hereby impowered to bind out by indenture to those persons with whom they now live, or to some other suitable person, at the best lay he can.

Warwick Town Council grants Gardner a settlement certificate —19 March 1768

Source: Warwick TCR 2:298

It was moved to this council that one Sarah Gardner, an Indian woman, together with three of her children, have removed from this town into the town of Smithfield to dwell, and as she is an inhabitant of this town and also her children, ordered that the clerk give her a certificate accordingly.

Examination of Sarah Gardner—5 March 1770

Source: Providence TCR 4:299

Sarah Gardner, an Indian woman, being brought before this council and examined concerning her coming to dwell in this town without gaining a legal settlement therein, sayeth that she was born in Warwick in the county of Kent and served her time with David Greene of said Warwick and lived in said Warwick until about three years last past and then came to dwell in this town with six children

Sarah Gardner "x" her mark

Whereupon it is voted that the said Sarah Gardner is rejected from being an inhabitant of this town and that the town of Warwick is the last place of said Sarah and children's legal settlement—it is therefore voted that the clerk of the council grant a warrant to remove the said Sarah and six children to the town of Warwick, the last place of their settlement, provided they do not remove in three weeks from this time.

Providence Town Council orders Gardner whipped for returning to town—17 February 1772

Source: Providence TCR 4:322

Voted that Sarah Gardner, an Indian woman, and her family, being heretofore removed by order of council, and having in direct violation of the law in such cases made and provided returned again to this town; whereupon it is voted that the said Sarah Gardner be publicly whipped eleven stripes on her naked back by the town sergeant, if she be found inhabiting within this town after the tenth day of April next.

Gardner's son William bound out—14 June 1773

Source: Warwick TCR 3:25

Ordered that William Gardner, a mustee boy and son of Sarah Gardner of Warwick, aged about sixteen years, be bound out an apprentice unto Mr. Benjamin Greene of Coventry, until he is twenty-one years of age, and he is to learn him to read and write, etc.

James Gardner runs away from his master—10 October 1778

Source: *Providence Gazette,* 10 October 1778

Absconded from his master's service, James Gardner, an indented Indian servant, about 17 years of age: Had on when he went off, a grey coatee, the sleeves and cape yellow, cloth coloured breeches and a decent beaver hat; he had no shoes or stockings. It is supposed he is gone towards Boston. Whoever will return said servant to his master, the subscriber, shall have Ten Dollars reward, and all necessary charges, paid by William Bowen. N.B. All persons are forbid harboring or carrying off said servant.

Second Examination of Sarah Gardner—20 March 1780

Source: Providence TCR 5:168–69

Sarah Gardner, an Indian woman, on her examination . . . saith that she was fifty years old the 16th day of January last—was born in the town of Warwick, being the daughter of Thomas Gardner—that she has had twelve children—those now living are named Mary, Margaret, Kit, Thomas, William, Sarah, James and Lydia, who were all born in the town of Warwick in the state of Rhode Island, that her father owned a house and land in Warwick, but that she has herself never owned any real estate and was herself never married.

Sarah Gardner "x" her mark

Whereupon the said Sarah Gardner and all her said children are rejected from being inhabitants of the said town of Providence.

Providence Town Council again orders out Gardner and her daughters
—4 April 1780

Source: Providence TCR 5:172

This council taking into consideration the examination of Sarah Gardner before the council on the 20th day of March last, whereby and from other evidence it appears that the place of the last lawful settlement of said Sarah Gardner and her children, viz. Mary, Margaret, Sarah and Lydia, is in the town of Warwick in the county of Kent in this state, and as the said Sarah Gardner and her said daughters Mary, Margaret, Sarah, and Lydia are of bad character and reputation and likely to become chargeable to the said town of Providence, it is ordered that the clerk . . . execute a warrant for their removal to the town of Warwick aforesaid according to law, unless they shall depart from this town before Monday next.

Sarah Gardner involved in a riot—23 July 1782

Source: Letter from Deputy Governor Bowen to the Providence Town Council, PTP 6:150

Gentlemen:

You cannot be uninformed of the riot of last night and that a dwelling house in the compact part of this town was entirely destroyed.

However bad the inhabitants of the said house might have been, that is by no means an excuse for the perpetrators of the act. If *A* can be accused of a crime before the mob, and they decree his house to be pulled down, *B* may be condemned by the same tribunal the next night and so on to C & D. So that this mode of administering in a short time will destroy all the buildings of any town where such proceedings are suffered.

Where is the man of consideration that doesn't shudder even at the thought of these things. We have good and wholesome laws. We have chosen officers to execute them; if they are not faithful to do their duty, they ought to be displaced with disgrace and others elected in their room who will be more faithful.

I recommend the immediate convening of the town council; that they order all the people that dwelt in the old gaol to appear before them, and that they break up the wicked nest by ordering all that are not inhabitants to leave this town at a short day; that all other bad houses be surprised; and in a word that we all exert ourselves for the restoration of order and virtue in our town. So far as interest, influence, or office can be serviceable, you may depend on my support for effecting this good work.

I am, Gentlemen, your most obedient and very humble servant

[signed] Jabez Bowen, Deputy Governor

Gardner ordered to appear before Providence Town Council
—23 July 1782

Source: PTP 6:150

Warrant for sundry persons to appear before the Town Council

To the Town Sergeant and to Mr. Nathaniel Jenckes, one of the constable of the town of Providence—Greeting:

In the name of the Governor and company of the state of Rhode Island, you are hereby commanded to summon and require the following persons, viz. Mrs. McCullough, dwelling at the house of Joseph William, Margaret Bowler alias Margaret Fairchild, a Negro woman, together with all the persons dwelling in the house with her on the 21st day of the present month, and [Sarah] Gardner, an Indian or mulatto woman, to appear before the town council of the town of Providence at the State House at 7 o'clock in the morning of Wednesday the 24th day of July instant, together with the following persons at the house of Patience Ingraham, viz., Nancy Brown alias Nancy Clarkson, Esther Gladding alias Esther Hill, who are also to appear at the same time and place to give information to the said town council of their respective places of lawful settlement.

And you are also required to summon the said Patience Ingraham to appear at the same time and place, to give information respecting the said persons dwelling at her house, and to be examined on a charge of keeping a common ill-governed, and disorderly house, and of permitting to reside there, persons of evil name and fame, and of dishonest conversation, drinking, tippling, whoring, and misbehaving themselves to the damage and nuisance of the town and great disturbance of the public peace.

By order and in behalf of the Town Council at Providence, July 23d 1782,

[signed] Theodore Foster, Council Clerk.

Gardner warned out of Providence again—2 September 1782

Source: Providence TCR 5:215

The warrant heretofore issued for removing Sarah Gardner and her four daughters to Warwick not having been issued, it is ordered that the clerk issue another warrant for their removal, founded on the adjudication of the town council of April 4th, 1780.

Gardner ordered out again—1 October 1787

Source: Providence TCR 6:23, PTP 10:148

Sarah Gardner and three of her children, to wit, Mary Gardner, Margaret Gardner and Lydia Gardner ordered removed to Warwick.

[on reverse of warrant]:

Warwick, Oct. 19th, 1787: Removed Sarah Gardner, the mother, and Mary Gardner and Margaret Gardner, her daughters, to Warwick and delivered them with her grandson Christopher to Jonathan Gorton Esqr., one of the overseers of the poor for said Warwick and left an authentic copy hereof with him.

[signed] Henry Bowen, Town Sergeant

[signed] Jonathan Gorton

Examination of Lydia Gardner—17 December 1796

Source: Providence TCR 7:122

Lydia Gardner, being examined, saith that she was born in Warwick in the county of Kent, and at the age of four or five years came to this town, where she has resided about twenty years but hath gained no legal settlement here.

Lydia Gardner "x" her mark

Whereupon it is voted that the said Lydia Gardner is rejected from being an inhabitant of this town and that the town of Warwick is the last place of said Lydia's legal settlement—it is therefore voted that the clerk of the council grant a warrant to remove the said Lydia to the town of Warwick, the last place of her settlement, provided she does not depart of her own accord in one week.

Documents Relating to Phillis Merritt Wanton

Examination of Phillis Merritt—3 February 1784

Source: Providence TCR 5:256

The examination of Phillis, a Negro woman . . . saith that she was born in the house of Mr. Robert Sanderson in Attleboro; that when she was a child, she came to live at the house of Mr. John Merritt in Providence, as his servant or slave, and lived in his family as such till the time of his death; that the next May after her Master Merritt died, she was sold by Mr. Overring, the executor, to one Mr. John Field of Boston, a leather breeches maker, and in that month went to live in Boston with the said Field as his servant; that some years ago the said Field told her she might go and get her own living; and that he went away out of the country; whereupon she came to Providence about four years ago; since which time she has lived at different places, particularly with Mrs. Goodwin on the west side of the river, whose house she made her home, and used to go out to washing; and that since she lived with Mrs. Goodwin she has lived at the house of Mr. Brown &c.

Removal order for Phillis Merritt—6 February 1784

Source: Providence TCR 5:257

This council having taken into consideration the examination of Phillis, a Negro woman, taken before the town council on the third instant, she is thereon rejected from being an inhabitant of the said town of Providence and as she has become chargeable to the said town it is therefore voted and resolved [that a] warrant [be issued] for the removal of said Phillis to the said town of Boston.

Warrant for removal of Phillis Merritt—24 June 1790

Source: PTP 13:101
   [Warrant for removal of Phillis Merritt, "Negro," to Boston because she is "likely to become chargeable."]

Town Sergeant's account of removal of Phillis Merritt—5 July 1790

Source: PTP 13:101
   [Town sergeant Henry Bowen's account against the town includes "looking after Phillis Merritt near half a day—0-2-0," on 30 June 1790.]

Examination of Jack Wanton—17 December 1792

Source: Providence TCR 6:237
   Jack Wanton, a Negro man . . . saith that he was an African born; that he came to Newport with Capt. John Goddard, who sold him to John Wanton of said Newport, with whom he lived about 15 years; that about a year since his master gave him his freedom; that he has a wife named Phillis and one child named Squire.

Examination of Phillis Wanton—3 October 1800

Source: Providence TCR 7:549
   Phillis Wanton, a black woman being before this council, is examined respecting her place of legal settlement, saith she was born in Attleboro in the County of Bristol, Commonwealth of Massachusetts; that she lived in said Attleboro with a Mr. Sanderson to whom she belonged; that he went for England when she was about five years of age and left her with Mr. John Merritt of Providence, with whom she lived until the time of his death, after which she lived some time in Boston with a Mr. Peck; that she returned from there to this Town and lived in the family of Moses Brown; that she was married to a black man in the Town, by the name of Jack Wanton, who belonged to and is now living in Newport; that her husband is at times insane; saith that she has three children, two of whom, to wit, Squire, a boy about ten years of age, [and] Marianne, a girl about seven years old, both bound out in the Town of Foster, & Vina, a girl about four years of age, is now with her; and the said Phillis further saith that she was

sold by John Overring, executor to the last will and testament of the said
John Merritt, to John Field of Boston, breeches maker, for one hundred
dollars, by whom she was sold to the aforenamed Mr. Peck; and that she
left Boston about the time of the blockade of that place by the British, having been told by the said Peck to seek and provide for herself.

Phillis Wanton "x" her mark

Removal order for Phillis Wanton—4 October 1800

Source: Providence TCR 7:551

Voted and resolved that Phillis Wanton, a black woman now in this
town, and her child, be removed to Newport, the place adjudged by this
council to be the legal settlement of the said Phillis and her child, and that
the clerk be and he is hereby directed to make out a warrant of removal
accordingly for that purpose.

Return of warrant for removal of Phillis Wanton—7 October 1800

Source: PTP 40:33

[Warrant for removal of "a certain black woman, a transient person
by the name of Phillis Wanton," who is "likely to become chargeable", and
her child Vina. Endorsed:]

Newport, October 7th AD 1800

This may certify all whom it may concern that I have received the
within mentioned persons.

[signed] Robert Taylor, one of the Overseers of the Poor.

DOCUMENTS RELATING TO MARY CARDER

Examination of Mary Carder—14 February 1775

Source: PTP 2:127

Mary Carder, a mustee woman, being called before this Council for
coming into this town to dwell, without gaining a legal settlement therein
or producing a certificate of her being legally settled elsewhere, on her
examination saith that she was born in the town of Warwick; and it is said
she was brought to this town when she was about four years old and

bound out by her mother, Abigail Carder, to Manna Burman, a free Negro man, and that she lived with said Manna about 5 years, when her indenture was given up to her mother and she dismissed from his service; that she then went & lived with Jacob Harris, a tenant of David Harris's, and his wife Deborah; she lived there about 2 years and was not bound; from thence went to the town of Warwick and stayed there a few days; & returned with her mother and was left in the care of Mr. Edward Thurber, where she continued about 2 years not bound; she then being like to have a child went back to Warwick and stayed there about a fortnight; and left there and lay in at Cranston and there lived at Col. Waterman's; and at Capt. Samuel Aborn's in Warwick about 3 years; left there and kept house in said Warwick two or three months and had a child born in the time; and has since lived at different places for about 2 years past; and now has two children with her.

Mary Carder "x" her mark

Removal order for Mary Carder and her children—15 February 1775

Source: Providence TCR 5:18

Whereas Mary Carder, a mustee woman being examined before this Council this present day, as by her examination on file may appear touching the last place of her legal settlement, and whereas by her said examination the town of Warwick in the County of Kent was the last place of her legal settlement. Whereupon it is voted that the town of Warwick is the place of her said Mary's last legal settlement and that the clerk issue his warrant and that she be moved to the Town of Warwick as soon as may be together with her two children.

Removal costs for Mary Carder—5 May 1775

Source: Providence TCR 5:20

Providence town sergeant William Compton is paid 15/10 for his expenses in "removing Mary Carder and two children to the town of Warwick."

Settlement certificate issued to Mary Carder—13 March 1775

Source: Warwick TCR 3:39

Whereas an Indian woman named Moll Carder, having a mind to live in the town of Providence, on consideration, the Council doth order the clerk to give her certificate to dwell there, she being an inhabitant of this town, as also two children.

Settlement certificate issued to Mary Carder—14 June 1784

Source: Warwick TCR 3:161

Mary Carder, a "Negro woman," is granted a certificate for herself "and two daughters" to live in Scituate.

DOCUMENTS RELATING TO PATIENCE HAVENS

Examination of Deliverance Havens—7 March 1785

Source: Providence TCR 5:302–3

The examination of Deliverance Havens, a Negro girl . . . saith that she was born in the town of North Kingstown in the county of Washington in the family of Mr. William Havens where she lived until about one year ago, at which time the said William Havens gave her freedom—since which she went to Newport and lived there almost a year, from whence she came to this town and has lived at Mr. Malem's and Col. Sproat's, and that she is now about sixteen years old.

Deliverance Havens "x" her mark

Whereupon the said Deliverance Havens is rejected from being an inhabitant . . . her lawful settlement is North Kingstown and as she is likely to become chargeable, ordered that the clerk issue a warrant for her removal to the said town of North Kingstown according to law.

Examination of Patience Havens—23 October 1793

Source: Providence TCR 6:299

Patience Havens, being before this council for examination, saith that she was born in North Kingstown, a slave to William Havens, who manumitted her about eight years since; that she came from said North Kingston to this town about a week since; that she has three children in this town under the age of twenty-one years, to wit: Deborah, about eighteen years, Ruth, about seventeen, and Simon, about seven; that her said children were born in said North Kingstown; and that she is fifty years of age.

Patience Havens "x" her mark

Whereupon it is voted that the said Patience Havens and her said children . . . are rejected from being inhabitants of this town and that the town of North Kingstown is the last place of said Patience and children's legal settlement.

Examination of Ruth Havens—17 December 1795

Source: Providence TCR 7:69

Ruth Havens, a Negro girl, being before this council for examination, saith that she was born in North Kingstown in the county of Washington, that she has resided in this town about three years, and hath gained no legal settlement.

Ruth Havens "x" her mark

Whereupon it is voted that the said Ruth Havens is rejected from being an inhabitant of this town and that the town of North Kingstown is the last place of her legal settlement; it is therefore voted that the clerk of the council grant a warrant to remove the said Ruth Havens to the town of North Kingstown.

Providence Town Council repays Patience Havens for services to the town—8 October 1796

Source: PTP 25:156

[Patience Havens receives an order on the town treasury for twelve shillings "in order to help support Nero Douglas in his sickness."]

Indenture of Sophia Havens—7 August 1797

Source: Providence TCR 7:155, PTP 28:48

Voted that the clerk be directed to execute an indenture of Sophia Havens, daughter of Deborah Havens, to David Vinton on the usual terms and conditions, till she arrives to the age of twenty-one years.

Second examination of Patience Havens—31 August 1797

Source: Providence TCR 7:167

The examination of Patience Havens, viz: the said Patience says she was born at North Kingstown in the family of William Havens; and that she is now a widow and has five children, all of whom are of age; and that she is fifty-three years old and has resided in this town four years.

Patience Havens "x" her mark

Whereupon it is voted that the said Patience Havens is rejected from being an inhabitant of this town . . . and order her to depart the same for North Kingstown in one week from this date, August [September] 7th, 1797.

Examination of Deborah (Havens) Greene—31 August 1797

Source: Providence TCR 7:167–68

The examination of Deborah Greene, viz.: The said Deborah says she was born at North Kingstown and is a married woman, and that her husband is now at sea, that she was married in this town; but her husband was born and resided in Warwick, and is named Ned Greene; that she is twenty-three years of age; and has two children, one a girl named Sophia and is seven years old; and the other a boy named George, eighteen months old; the first child was born before marriage at North Kingstown.

Deborah Greene "x" her mark

The town council do hereby reject the said Deborah as an inhabitant of this Town, and do hereby order her to depart the same within one week from this date for the town of Warwick.

Examination of Nancy Havens Hazard—31 August 1797

Source: Providence TCR 7:168

The examination of Nancy Hazard, viz: The said Nancy Hazard was born at North Kingstown in the family of William Havens, says that she is thirty years of age, was married to Peter Hazard, but lives with a man now as his wife, whose name is Cesar Greene; she has lived in this town eleven years, has three children, one a boy eight years old named George, one a girl of about six years old named Chloe, and the other about fourteen months old named Phebe.

Nancy Hazard "x" her mark

The council do hereby reject the said Nancy Hazard as an inhabitant of this town; and have deferred their order for her departure from the place for the present, and adjudge the town of North Kingstown as the place of her last legal settlement.

Patience Havens dies of yellow fever—30 September 1797

Source: Providence TCR 7:189; PTP 28:70
Since the last statement, one only sick at the hospital and four in town, all likely to recover; one Negro woman deceased.
[Thomas Pigging is paid $1.50 "for digging grave for Patience Havens who died of the malignant fever."]

Deborah Havens Greene ordered removed—15 December 1797

Source: Providence TCR 7:212
Voted that Deborah Greene be removed by warrant from the clerk, to be issued forthwith.

Nancy Havens Hazard ordered removed—10 February 1798

Source: Providence TCR 7:221
Voted that Nancy Hazard who was heretofore examined before this council be removed from this town by warrant as soon as may be.

Removal of Nancy Havens Hazard from Providence—4 March 1799

Source: PTP 31:136
[Warrant for removal of "Nancy Hazard, wife of Peter Hazard, a black or mulatto, and her three children, namely George, Chloe and Phebe" to North Kingstown.]
[Endorsed on reverse by George Gordon, constable, who delivered them to Joseph Eldred overseer of the poor for North Kingstown, and by Joseph Eldred, who received them on 7 March 1799.]

DOCUMENTS RELATING TO BRISTOL RHODES

Bristol Rhodes discharged from the Continental Army—1 September 1782

Source: Casualty Book, Rhode Island Regiment, p. 82
[Pvt Bristol Rhodes discharged 1 September 1782 "for invaliding, lost one leg and one arm in the siege of Yorktown in October 1781 and entitled to a pension."]

Rhode Island State Legislature awards Bristol Rhodes back pay—
October 1782

Source: Bartlett 9:605–6
[Report of legislative committee:] It also appears that Bristol Rhodes, a soldier, was discharged in like manner, on the 1st day of September last, from this state's Continental regiment, as unfit for field or garrison duty, he having lost a leg and an arm at the siege of Yorktown; and that there was due to the said Bristol Rhodes, at the time of his discharge, for wages in arrear, the sum of thirty-nine pounds, silver money, twenty-three pounds of which was due before the 1st day of January last, and sixteen pounds became due since. . . .
Voted and resolved . . . that the sums found due to the said persons be paid . . .

Rhode Island State Legislature awards Bristol Rhodes a veteran's pension—
February 1786

Source: Bartlett 10:163
Bristol Rhodes, private in the Rhode Island regiment commanded by Col. Jeremiah Olney, now aged 31, inspected 10 February 1785, to receive $5.00 per month for loss of left leg and left hand by a cannon shot in the memorable siege of Yorktown, in Virginia, in October, 1781.

*Rhode Island State Legislature pays Bristol Rhodes's pension during interim—*February 1788

Source: Bartlett 10:269–70
It is voted and resolved, that the general treasurer be, and he is, hereby directed to pay unto Bristol Rhodes, an invalid, late a soldier in the Continental army, and who is entitled to a pension agreeably to a resolution of Congress, the sum of forty pounds, lawful money, to be accounted for by him towards his pension as an invalid.

*Bristol Rhodes's medical care—*23 May 1789

Source: Petition of Comfort A. Carpenter, *Petitions* 34 (1802–3):43
[In 1802, Bristol Rhodes listed as owing Dr. Comfort Carpenter $8.67 for medical care received initially in 1789.]

Petition against Bristol Rhodes—1 September 1794

Source: PTP 20:101

Petition against Bristol Rhodes from Sundry Inhabitants:

We the subscribers, inhabitants of the town of Providence and living in the vicinity of the neighborhood near the Congregational Church, beg leave to present to the honourable town council that a certain Negro family resides near them by the name of Bristol Rhodes, which by their noise and confusion trouble the peaceable inhabitants in such a degree 'tis not possible for them to enjoy themselves and families, and more especially on the Sabbath, by convening a large number together and behaving in such a manner that it greatly corrupts the morals of children which are obliged to be in hearing of the ridiculous language, etc., and they pray the honorable council in their wise deliberations will order their remove or some other way that they shall think most advisable for the better accommodation of the aforesaid neighborhood and the town in general; and your petitioners in duty bound will ever pray.

[Signed by] Samuel Proud, Solomon Searll Jr., Solomon Searll, Samuel Gorton, Esek Eddy, J. Grummond, Peter Penno, William Field, Nathan Warner, Jona. French, Stephen Ward, N. Frothingham, Francis Magwire, William Potter, Arthur Fenner Jr., Peleg Eddy, Daniel Proud, James Snow Jr.

Examination of Bristol Rhodes—1 September 1794

Source: Providence TCR 6:354–45

Bristol Rhodes, being before this council for examination, saith that he was born in Cranston, a slave to Capt. William Rhodes; that he resided in said Cranston until he was about the age of twenty years, at which time he enlisted into the Continental Army; and has since resided in this town for the space of about five years.

Bristol Rhodes "x" his mark

Obituary of Bristol Rhodes—8 July 1810

Source: *Providence Gazette*

Died. In this town, on Tuesday last, in an advanced age, Bristol Rhodes, a black man, of the late revolutionary army, in which he long served with deserved reputation. At the siege of York-Town he was severely wounded, having unfortunately lost a leg and an arm, and has since subsisted on a pension.

Characteristics of the Transient Population

The five figures and table that follow present the general patterns of warning out in Rhode Island in the period of study, 1751–1800, and the demographic characteristics of the transient population in that period. They illustrate as well the kinds of information that can be drawn from such records.

Figure A1. Seasonal pattern of warn-outs, all towns, all households, 1751–1800 ($n = 1924$).

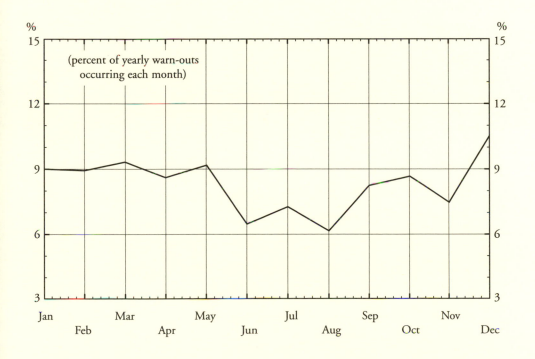

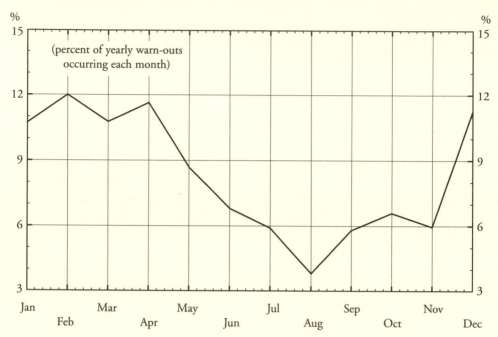

Figure A2. Seasonal pattern of warn-outs, agrarian towns, male household heads, 1751–1800 ($n = 475$).

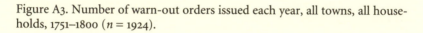

Figure A3. Number of warn-out orders issued each year, all towns, all households, 1751–1800 ($n = 1924$).

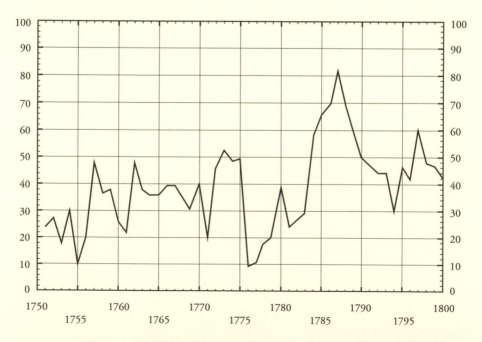

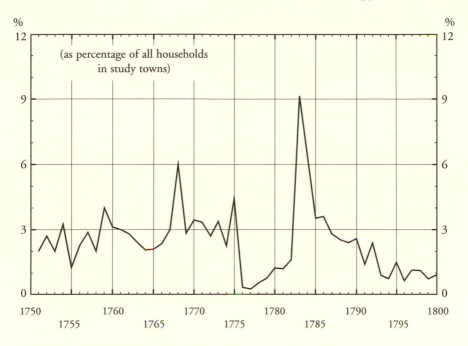

%
12
(as percentage of all households
in study towns)

9

6

3

0

1750   1755   1760   1765   1770   1775   1780   1785   1790   1795   1800

Figure A4. Transient families warned out, all towns, 1751–1800.

Figure A5. Race and sex of transient household heads.

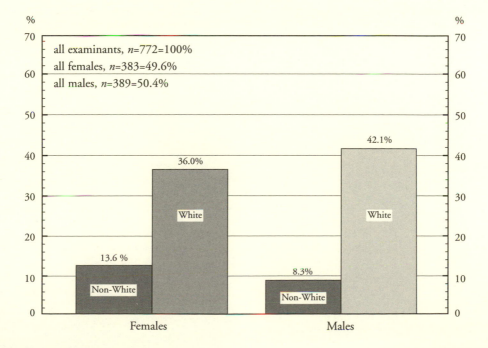

%
70   all examinants, *n*=772=100%
60   all females, *n*=383=49.6%
      all males, *n*=389=50.4%
50

40   42.1%

36.0%
30   White   White

20

13.6 %
10   8.3%
      Non-White   Non-White
0
        Females   Males

Table A1. Characteristics of Transient Household Heads

	White	Women of color	White men	Men of color
Average age (years)	27.3 (*n*=92)	28.5 (*n*=59)	41.7 (*n*=70)	34.5 (*n*=18)
Name-signing literacy	28.5% (*n*=179)	6.3% (*n*=79)	77.1% (*n*=214)	20.8% (*n*=48)
Former indentured servant (*n*=134)	34.3%	19.4%	41.0%	5.2%
Former slave (*n*=80)	0	24.1%	0	46.2%
Average length of residence (years)	4.5 (*n*=101)	7.1 (*n*=68)	4.0 (*n*=145)	4.9 (*n*=38)
Living with spouse (*n*=1924)*	5.2%	1.5%	94.1%	83.3%
Household with children (*n*=772)	38.5%	49.5%	53.8%	65.6%
Average number of children (*n*=339)**	2.2	2.75	2.8	1.8

*92.8% of men, 0.5% of white women, 9.1% of black women. **Where warning-out orders specified the number of children, the mean was 2.4; I estimated 2.0 for "families" without a specified number.

Documentary Sources
for the Narrative Chapters

Chapter 1: Birth, Infancy, and Childhood

PHEBE PERKINS

Examination of Phebe Perkins: The only official examination exists solely in a rough draft version of the TCM 19 Jan. 1785; it was never entered into the permanent record by the town clerk, and it is filed with miscellaneous eighteenth-century town clerks' papers at the Hopkinton town clerk's office.

Other sources: TCM 9 Oct. and 3 Nov. 1784, 3 Jan., 19 Jan., 14 Feb. and 7 Mar. 1785, 9 Sept. 1786, Hopkinton TCR 2:144, 146, 150, 213–14, 216, 218, 259; TM 14 Feb. and 7 June 1785, Hopkinton TMR vol. 1; TCM 6 Sept. 1784, Newport TCR (1784–1794).

Sources about Edward Perry: Edward Perry was elected to the position of town council president every year from 1780 through 1789; the record of his election to that and other offices in the 1760s, 1770s, and 1780s can be found in Richmond TMR, vols. 2 and 3. His wealth I have deduced from his position in the tax and estate valuation records. In 1782, for example, his real estate was estimated by the tax assessors as £950, putting him at the very top of the economic scale, which ranged from a low of £10 to a high of £1050. Only five men had property of greater value in this town of 243 tax-payers ("Estimate of Rateable Property for Richmond, Rhode Island," 1 Aug. 1782, Richmond town clerk's office).

ANTHONY HATHAWAY

Examination of Martha Hathaway: TCM 6 Aug. 1783, Providence TCR 5:239–40.

Other sources: Overseer of the poor account, 7 Aug. 1783, PTP 7:140; TCM 26 June 1784 and 11 Jan. 1786, East Greenwich TCR 4:3, 4:32; TCM 13 Oct. 1788 and 31 Aug. 1790, Warwick TCR 3:233, 3:382; TM 31 Aug. 1790, Warwick TMR 3:382; Indenture of Anthony Hathaway, TCM 29 Nov. 1788, East Greenwich TCR 4:88; Indenture of Mahala Hathaway, TCM 21 Apr. 1792, Warwick TCR 4:311.

Sources about Silvester Sweet: Numerous references to Silvester Sweet in the East Greenwich town records indicate that he had both significant property and powerful influence in the community. He consistently ranked among the very wealthiest taxpayers in the town; see, for example, the East Greenwich town tax lists for 1 Aug. 1763 and 17 Dec. 1796, both at the Rhode Island Historical Society Library. On his good reputation in the community throughout his adult life, see his selection as guardian to an orphaned young man in TCM 31 Mar. 1759, his appointment to committees to oversee the construction of a workhouse during TM 15 Apr. 1761 and TM 21 Apr. 1773, and his appointment as guardian to a "old" and "infirm" widow in TCM 26 Dec. 1795, East Greenwich TCR 3:53 and 4:236 and TMR, vol. 2. On his public service see, for example, his election as town councilman in 1759, 1761, 1763, and 1764, his election as deputy to General Assembly in TM 17 Apr. 1771, 27 Aug. 1771, 15 Apr. 1772, and 25 Aug. 1772, and his election as overseer of the poor in TM 26 May 1795, all in East Greenwich TMR, vols. 2, 4. Later, his son James was elected as deputy (1789–92), and Silvester Sweet himself was frequently appointed to committees who would "instruct" the deputies on various matters; see, for example, TM 22 Nov. 1788, East Greenwich TCR vol. 2. On his skill as a bonesetter, see his bill "for the setting of Robert Nichols' bones" in TCM 30 June 1764, and his bill "for setting the shoulder of Thomas Langrod" in TCM 28 Aug. 1773, East Greenwich TCR 3:94, 3:144. The "Bonesetter" Sweets were a locally famous extended family in Rhode Island in the eighteenth and nineteenth centuries. On his business of providing room and board for people see, for example, his caretaking of widow Abigail Sweet (probably a relative), discussed in TCM 28 June 1766 and 29 Oct. 1768, East Greenwich TCR 3:104, 3:116; and his boarding of "Bridget Hill and family," reported in TCM 2 Apr. 1774, East Greenwich TCR 3:152. For indenture of Simon Talbury, see TCM 27 Mar. 1773, East Greenwich TCR 3:142.

KATE JONES
Sources: TM 24 Mar. 1786 and 13 Aug. 1787, Providence TCR 5:372, 6:15; Letter to Johnston Town Council, 27 Apr. 1787, Providence TCR 6:2–3; Examination of Margaret Abbee Harris: TCM 4 June 1787, Providence TCR 6:7; Warrant for the removal of Katherine Jones, 13 Aug. 1787, PTP 12:60.

Sources on Nathaniel Jones: Jones's service in various companies of Lt. Col. Jeremiah Olney's Rhode Island Regiment is documented in the Revolutionary War Index, Rhode Island State Archives. For a record of his death, see "Regimental Book, Rhode Island Regiment, 1781–82," 66, Rhode Island State Archives.

SUSANNAH GUINEA

Examination of Binah Pearce concerning Susannah Guinea: TCM 15 Mar. 1788, Providence TCR 6:40; Examinations of Titus Guinea, 6 Oct. 1770, PTP 2:38, and TCM 15 Mar. 1788, Providence TCR 6:39–40; [nd] Oct. 1789, Providence TCR 6:97; Warrant for removal of Titus Guinea, 4 Dec. 1789, PTP 12:132; Warrant for removal of Susannah Guinea, 15 Mar. 1788, PTP 11:102; Indenture of Samuel Pearce, TCM 3 July 1797, Providence TCM 7:153; Holbrook, *Rhode Island 1782 Census*, 1.

Source of information about Rhode Island apprenticeship indentures: Herndon, "Indentured Servitude of Children as a Community Strategy."

JERUSHA TOWNSEND

Examination of Jerusha Townsend: 6 June 1796, Providence TCR 7:97.

Other sources: Warrant for removal of Townsend children, 9 Aug. 1775, PTP 2:155; Town constable account, 17 Apr. 1775, PTP 3:17; TCM 9 Aug. 1775, Providence TCR 5:26–27; Warrant for removal of Jerusha Townsend, 6 June 1796, PTP 25:69; TCM 15 Sept. 1797, Providence TCR 7:174.

SUSANNAH, JAMES, JOHN, AND ISABEL BROWN

Examination of Prince Brown: TCM 7 June 1797, Exeter TCR 6:104.

Examination of Roseanna Brown: TCM 12 June 1797, South Kingstown TCR 6:245–46.

Other sources: TM 7 Aug. 1797, Exeter TMR, vol. 3; TCM 13 May 1799, 11 July 1808, South Kingstown TCR 6:275, 7:53; Indenture of Susannah Brown, TCM 2 Oct. 1797, Exeter TCR 6:115; Guardianship of James Brown, TCM 2 June 1800, Exeter TCR 6:198; Indentures of John Brown and Isabel Brown, TCM 4 July 1800, Exeter TCR 6:200–201.

Chapter 2: Family Life

CLARKE, WILLIAM, AND SANFORD PIKE

Examination of William Pike Jr.: TCM 6 May 1793, Providence TCR 6:262–63 and PTP 18:60.

Examination of Sanford Pike: TCM 6 May 1793, Providence TCR 6:263 and PTP 18:60.

Other sources: Holbrook, *Rhode Island 1782 Census*, 96; TCM 23 Aug. 1790, Providence TCR 6:123–24; Overseer of the poor accounts, 24 Aug. 1790, 13 Apr. 1793, 29 Apr. 1793, 17 Jan. 1798, PTP 13:138, 18:50, 18:57, 29:13; Indenture of Robert Howard to Jonathan Pike, TCM 11 May 1785, Johnston TCR 2:219; Jonathan Pike named joint guardian of Gaius Davis, 21 Mar. 1786, Providence TCR 5:371.

PATIENCE AND ABNER BUTLER

Examination of Patience and Abner Butler: TCM 22 Apr. 1793, Providence TCR 6:259–60.

Other sources: TCM 9 June 1790, 6 May 1793, 4 Aug. 1794, and 3 Nov. 1794, Providence TCR 6:118, 6:262, 6:349, 7:5; Receipt from Edgartown selectmen, 12 Aug. 1794, PTP 20:88; Town sergeant's account, 1 Sept. 1794, PTP 20:101; Holbrook, *Rhode Island 1782 Census*, 24; Providence Rate Streak, November 1790, p. 6, Rhode Island Historical Society Library; *Rhode Island 1790 Census*, 33.

JUDAH HAZARD WANTON

Examination of Judah Wanton Hazard and Urania Barker Hazard: TCM 20 Mar. 1780, Providence TCR 5:169–70 and PTP 5:39.

Other sources: TCM 8 Jan., 13 Mar., 16 Mar., and 20 Mar. 1780, and 7 Mar. 1782; Providence TCR 5:157, 5:163, 5:166, 5:171, 5:204.

Sources on the Hazard family: Jeremiah Hazard admitted as a voter, TM 15 Apr. 1747, North Kingstown TMR 1:331; Jeremiah Hazard will, North Kingstown Probate 9:335; Jeffrey Hazard elected councilman, TM 3 June 1729, North Kingstown TMR 1:99.

MARY CUMMOCK FOWLER AND MARY FOWLER CHAMPLIN

Examinations of Mary Cummock Fowler and Mary Fowler Champlin: TCM 14 May 1796, South Kingstown TCR 6:229–30.

Other sources: TCM 11 Apr., 9 May, 14 May 1796, 10 Apr. 1797, 9 Feb. 1801, 11 Sept. 1837, 10 Sept. 1838, South Kingstown TCR 6:227, 6:229, 6:230, 6:243, 7:2, 7:325, 7:331; *Rhode Island 1790 Census*, 48.

SARAH GARDNER AND HER DAUGHTERS

Examinations of Sarah Gardner: TCM 5 Mar. 1770 and 20 Mar. 1780, Providence TCR 4:299, 5:168–69, PTP 5:40.

Examination of Lydia Gardner: TCM 17 Dec. 1796, Providence TCR 7:122.

Other sources: TCM 14 June 1762, 19 Nov. 1762, 13 Dec. 1762, 19 Mar. 1768, and 14 June 1773, Warwick TCR 2:211, 218, 221–22, 298, 3:25; TCM 17 Feb. 1772, 4 Apr. 1780; 2 Sep. 1782, 1 Oct. 1787, Providence TCR 4:322, 5:172, 5:215, 6:23; Letter from Deputy Governor Jabez Bowen to the Providence Town Council, 23 July 1782, PTP 6:150; Warrant to appear before the Providence Town Council, 23 July 1782, PTP 6:150 (the group warrant includes "Indian" woman "Elizabeth Gardner," but I believe this is the clerk's slip, because all other documents of the incident indicate the clerk meant Sarah Gardner); Warrant for removal of Sarah Gardner, 1 Oct. 1787, PTP 10:148; Taylor, *Runaways*, 97.

WAIT GODFREY ALIAS WHITNEY ALIAS GRAFFT

Examinations: TCM 20 Mar. 1780, Providence TCR 5:166–67 and PTP 5:40; TCM 25 Jan. 1783, East Greenwich TCR 3:222; TCM 30 May 1783, Providence TCR 5:233.

Other sources: TCM 8 June 1782, 26 Apr. 1783, 17 June 1783, East Greenwich TCR 3:218, 3:223, 3:225; TCM 9 Aug. 1784, 1 Nov. 1784, 3 Jan. 1785, 10 June 1786, Providence TCR 5:282, 5:294–95, 5:297, 5:385–86; Warrant to summon Wait Godfrey, 9 Aug. 1784, PTP 7:159, Warrant for removal of Wait Godfrey, 9 Aug. 1784, PTP 7:160; TCM 8 Sept. 1766, 31 Dec. 1798, Warwick TCR 2:276, 4:455; Indenture of Susanna Godfrey, 31 Aug. 1771, East Greenwich TCR 3:130; Indenture of George Parker and Lemuel Whitney, 7 July 1783, Providence TCR 5:235; Indenture of John Godfrey, 26 May 1787, East Greenwich TCR 4:60; Indenture of Sophia Grafft alias Godfrey, 9 Mar. 1789, Warwick TCR 3:248 and see also TCM 6 Apr. And 18 Apr. 1789, Warwick TCR 3:251–52 and 3:258; Indenture of Elisabeth Grafft alias Godfrey, 30 Nov. 1790, Warwick TCR 4:294.

CHRISTOPHER STOCKER AND ABIGAIL HARRIS

Examinations of Abigail [Harris] Foster and Christopher Stocker: TCM 7 Aug. 1786, Providence TCR 5:390–92.

Other sources: Petition of Christopher Stocker to the Providence Town Council, 1 Oct. 1787, PTP 10:134; TCM 6 Aug. 1787 and 5 Apr. 1790, Providence TCR 6:14–15 and 6:112; Providence Valuation of Estates, July 1785, Rhode Island Historical Society Library; *Rhode Island 1790 Census*, 34; *Massachusetts Soldiers and Sailors*, 15:42; Neagles, *Summer Soldiers*, 252;

Genealogical Abstracts of Revolutionary War Pension Files, 3:3348.

NATHANIEL WHITAKER

Examinations of Nathaniel Whitaker: TCM 3 Jan. 1791, 2 Feb. 1795, 28 Sept. 1801, Providence TCR 6:144, 7:20, 8:102.
Examination of Martha Spears: TCM 2 Feb. 1795, Providence TCR 7:20.
Examination of Peggy Mason: TCM 28 Sept. 1801, Providence TCR 8:102–3.
Other sources: Overseer of the poor account, 29 Dec. 1790, PTP 14:48; Warrant for removal of Nathaniel Whitaker, 7 Apr. 1795, PTP 22:65; Warrant for removal of Martha Spears, 6 Apr. 1795, PTP 22:64; TCM 17 Oct. 1801, Providence TCR 8:109–10; Warrant against Timothy Brownell, 6 Oct. 1783, PTP 7:70.
Source of information on banned interracial marriages: *Public Laws* (1798), 483.

ROBERT FULLER'S FAMILY

Examination of Robert Fuller: TCM 13 Sept. 1796, Providence TCR 7:111.
Other sources: TCM 16 Nov. 1796, 8 Aug. 1797, 15 Sept. 1797, Providence TCR 7:119; Town sergeant's account, 23 Nov. 1796, PTP 26:37; Letter from Attleboro overseers of the poor to Providence council, 13 Dec. 1796, PTP 26:74; Attleboro account for care of Fuller family, 27 Dec. 1796, PTP 26:125; Overseer of the poor account, 9 Jan. 1797, PTP 26:125; *Rhode Island 1790 Census*, 33.

THOMAS FIELD

Examination of Thomas Field: TCM 9 Apr. 1789, Providence TCR 6:75–76.
Other sources: TCM 10 Apr., 13 Apr., 1 May, 14 May, 9 July, 13 July, and 3 Aug. 1789, Providence TCR 6:76, 6:77, 6:79–80; 6:83; 6:84; 6:89 and PTP 12:106; Council orders to the town sergeant, 31 Aug. and 7 Sept. 1789, PTP 12:114, 12:116; Tavern license granted to Mary Justice, TCM 6 Oct. 1788, Providence TCR 6:62.

Chapter 3: Work Life

PHILLIS MERRITT WANTON

Examinations of Phillis Merritt Wanton: TCM 3 Feb. 1784, Providence TCR 5:256; 3 Oct. 1800, Providence TCR 7:549.

Examination of Jack Wanton: 17 Dec. 1792, Providence TCR 6:237.
Other sources: Warrants for removal, TCM 6 Feb. 1784, Providence TCR 5:257, 24 June 1790, PTP 13:101, and 4 Oct. 1800, Providence TCR 7:551; Town sergeant's account, 5 July 1790 PTP 13:101; Return of removal order, 4 Oct. 1800, PTP 40:33.

MARY CARDER

Examination of Mary Carder: 14 Feb. 1775, PTP 2:127.
Other sources: TCM 14 Feb. and 5 May 1775, Providence TCR 5:18, 5:20; TCM 13 Mar. 1775 and 14 June 1784, Warwick TCR 3:39, 3:161.

OLIVE PERO

Examination of Olive Pero: 30 Jan. 1767, PTP 2:22.
Other sources: TCM 30 Jan. 1767, Providence TCR 4:264; Warrant for removal of Olive Pero, 31 Jan. 1767, PTP 2:22.

ELISABETH AND MOLLY HODGES

Examination of Elisabeth Hodges: 5 Nov. 1763, PTP 2:14.
Other sources: TCM 26 Nov. 1763 and 28 Dec. 1763, Providence TCR 4:245–46; TCM 3 Mar. 1766 and 13 May 1766, North Providence TCR A:18.

CATO FREEMAN

Examination of Cato Freeman: TCM [nd] Feb. 1787, Providence TCR 5:415–16.
Other sources: Letter from Cambridge, Massachusetts clerk to Cranston TC, 11 Dec. 1787, PTP 11:25; Town sergeant account, 31 May 1790, PTP 13:91; TCM 5 July 1790, Providence TCR 6:121; Warrant for removal of Cato Freeman, 12 July 1790, PTP 13:104; *Massachusetts Soldiers and Sailors*, 6:33–34; Neagles, *Summer Soldiers*, 138; Warrant Number 4158, "Land Warrants Issued Prior to 1800," National Archives; *Rhode Island 1790 Census*, 35.

MARK NOBLE

Examinations of Mark Noble: TCM 1 Jan. 1787, Providence TCR 5:407–8; TCM 3 Dec. 1792, Providence TCR 6:233–34; TCM 12 Jan. 1799, Providence TCR 7:323.
Other sources: TCM 4 Dec. 1787, Providence TCR 6:31; TCM 14 Jan. 1793, Providence TCR 6:238; *Rhode Island Colony Records* 5:484 and 6:26; Chapin, *Rhode Island Soldiers and Sailors*, 106; Petition for increase in offi-

cer pay, March 1757, *Petitions* 9:154, Rhode Island State Archives; *Indentures of Poor Children of Boston*, 2:142; *Massachusetts Soldiers and Sailors*, 11:493–94; Revolutionary War Index, Rhode Island State Archives; "Register of Casualties in the Rhode Island Regiment Since January 1781," 70, Rhode Island State Archives; *Rhode Island 1790 Census*, 36; Neagles, *Summer Soldiers*, 212; Warrant Number 4750, "Land Warrants Issued Prior to 1800," National Archives; Taylor, *Runaways*, 165.

PETER NORTON

Examination of Peter Norton: 26 Nov. 1763, PTP 3:64.

Other sources: TCM 29 Sept. 1763 and 26 Nov. 1763, Providence TCR 4:244, 4:245; TCM 7 Oct. 1765, North Providence TCR A:6–7; Overseer of the poor records, 28 Aug. 1776, 17 Feb. 1777, 28 Feb. 1777, PTP 3:64, 3:95, 3:99; Indenture of Richmond Norton, TCM 29 Sept. 1777, Providence TCR 5:92 and PTP 3:155; Indenture of Peter Norton, TCM 16 Mar. 1780, Providence TCR 5:163–64 and PTP 5:38.

JOHN TREBY

Examination of John Treby: TCM 22 July 1775, Providence TCR 5:25.

Other sources: Warrant for the removal of John Treby to Newport, 22 July 1775, PTP 2:151; TCM 9 July 1781, PTP 6:48; Petition to raise a lottery, *Petitions* 10:175; William Richardson's Petition to declare bankruptcy, *Petitions* 13:96; Holbrook, *Rhode Island 1782 Census*, 126.

NATHANIEL BOWDISH

Examination of Nathaniel Bowdish: TCM 12 Mar. 1771, Charlestown TCR 2:196.

Other sources: Glocester Births, Deaths, Marriages 1:118, 126, 147; Glocester Land Evidence 5:20, 5:176, 5:214, 6:542; TCM 30 May 1752, Smithfield TCR 1:52; TCM 16 Oct. 1771, 2 Dec 1771, 1 Apr. 1772, 15 Apr. 1772, Charlestown TCR 2:199, 2:200, 2:203, 2:204; TCM 30 Jan. 1772, Jamestown TCR 2:84; TM 7 June 1779, 30 Aug. 1785 and 1 June 1789, Glocester TMR 1:135, 1:181 and 2:14; TCM 29 June 1799, Glocester TCR 2:205; Town meeting admission recorded in colonial records in May 1759, Bartlett 6:203 and in TM 18 Apr. 1759, Glocester TMR 1:53; Tavern license renewals in TCM 10 Dec. 1781 and subsequent December TCM through 1795, and TCM 5 Apr. 1798, Glocester TCR, vols. 1, 2; Glocester Estate Valuation, October 1778, Glocester town clerk's office; TCM 4 Apr. 1796, Providence TCR 7:85; Agreement of Glocester Alarm Company, 9 Jan. 1777, *Revolutionary War Military Papers* 9:183; Petition of Nathaniel Bowdish, 27 Feb. 1760, Petition of Rufus Peck, Feb. 1797, and Petition of Nathaniel Bowdish, 26 Oct 1797, *Petitions* 11-2, 30:95, 31:55; Military records in Chapin, *Rhode Island Soldiers and Sailors*, 38, Bartlett 6:134, *Rhode Island 1777 Census*, 45, "List of the names of the officers and privates belonging to Topham, Elliot, and Crary's regiments," unbound manuscript, Revolutionary War records, Rhode Island State Archives, and pension records of Benjamin Paine, *Genealogical Abstracts of Revolutionary War Pension Files*, 268; *Rhode Island 1790 Census*, 31.

Chapter 4: Reversal of Fortune

PATIENCE HAVENS AND DAUGHTERS
Examinations of Patience Havens: TCM 23 Oct. 1793 and 31 Aug. 1797, Providence TCR 6:299, 7:167.
Examination of Deliverance Havens: TCM 7 Mar. 1785, Providence TCR 5:302–3.
Examination of Ruth Havens: TCM 17 Dec. 1795, Providence TCR 7:69.
Examination of Deborah Havens Greene: TCM 31 Aug. 1797, Providence TCR 7:167–68.
Examination of Nancy Havens Hazard: TCM 31 Aug. 1797, Providence TCR 7:168.
Other sources: William Havens will (1786) and estate inventory (1787), North Kingstown Probate Records 12:66–72; *Rhode Island 1790 Census*, 45; TCM 7 Aug. 1797, 30 Sept. 1797, 15 Dec. 1797 and 10 Feb. 1798, Providence TCR 7:155, 7:189, 7:212 and 7:221; Indenture of Sophia Havens, PTP 28:48; Overseer of the poor accounts, 8 Oct. 1796 and 25 Oct. 1797, PTP 25:156, 28:70; Warrant for removal of Nancy Hazard and children, 4 March 1799, PTP 31:136.

ELIZABETH SPRINGER
Examination of Elizabeth Springer: TCM 17 Dec. 1792, Providence TCR 6:237.
Other sources: Warrant for removal of Elizabeth Springer, 17 Dec. 1792, PTP 17:71; Overseer of the poor accounts, 22 Dec. 1792, 5 Jan., 6 Jan., 22 Jan., 30 Jan., and 6 June 1793, PTP 17:80, 17:134, 17:137, 17:156, 18:86, 18:79; Birth record of Lawrence Springer, Tiverton Vital Records 1:31; Poor relief

account of Thomas and Elizabeth Springer, TCM 1 Oct. 1764 passim to 21 Oct. 1782, Tiverton TCR, vol. 1; Tiverton tax books, 1784 and 1788, Rhode Island Historical Society Library.

PRIMUS THOMPSON
Examination of Primus Thompson: TCM 20 Jan. 1775, Jamestown TCR 2:117–18.
Other sources: TM 19 Apr. 1775, Jamestown TMR 1:209; TCM 30 Jan. 1775, Westerly TCR 4:250; William Wilbur's settlement certificates from Richmond, issued TCM 7 Dec. 1767 and 19 Apr. 1780, Richmond TCR 1:470 and 2:290.

BENJAMIN JONES
Examination of Benjamin Jones: TCM 9 July 1787, Providence TCR 6:12 and PTP 10:99.
Other sources: Benjamin Jones's petitions to General Assembly, February 1763 and February 1800, *Petitions* 11-2:44, 33:35; Benjamin Jones's petitions to Providence town meeting, 6 June 1791 and 29 Aug. 1797, PTP 5:14, 27:155; TM 13 June 1791 and 31 Aug. 1797, Providence TMR 7:207–8, 7:411; Treasurer's account, 19 July 1791 and 31 Aug 1797, PTP 15:38, 28:130; Assize of bread at TCM 27 Oct. 1771 and 14 Sept. 1785, Providence TCR 4:319 and 5:332, and passim; Holbrook, *Rhode Island 1782 Census*, 71; *Rhode Island 1790 Census*, 33.

ANN WEST AND PETER WEST
Examination of Ann West and Seth Eldred: TCM 21 Dec. 1772, South Kingstown TCR 6:9.
Examination of Peter West: TCM 7 Jan. 1773, South Kingstown TCR 6:10–11.
Other sources: TCM 16 Feb. and 3 Mar. 1756, Exeter TCR 1:176–77; TM 3 June 1760, Exeter TMR 1:132; Petition of militia men to elect their own officers, October 1736, *Petitions* 3:76; Petition to create West Greenwich township, October 1740, *Petitions* 4:68; Petition for a third militia company, February 1741/42, *Petitions* 4:92; Exeter Land Evidence, 21 Apr. 1756 and 7 Mar. 1763, 6:444–45 and 9:484–85; *Rhode Island 1790 Census*, 35.

ESTHER HERADON
Examination of Esther Heradon: TCM 13 May 1790, Providence TCR 6:115.
Other sources: TCM 11 June 1790 and 12 July 1790, Providence TCR 6:118,

6:121; Town sergeant accounts, 14 May 1790, 31 May 1790, 5 July 1790, 23 Aug. 1790, PTP 13:84, 13:91, 13:103, 13:119; Workhouse overseer accounts, 28 June 1790, 28 July 1790, 28 Aug. 1790, 28 Sept. 1790, and 28 Oct. 1790, PTP 13:102, 13:108, 14:48, 14:46, 14:47; Letters from Windham selectmen to Providence council, 7 June 1790 and 21 June 1790, PTP 13:94 and 13:99; Letter from Voluntown selectmen to Windham County justices of the peace, 26 July 1790, PTP 13:109; Warrant for removal of Esther Heradon from Windham to Providence, 8 June 1790, PTP 13:95; Warrant for removal of Esther Heradon from Voluntown to Providence, 27 July 1790, PTP 13:109.

MARGARET FAIRCHILD BOWLER
Examination of Margaret Fairchild Bowler: TCM 24 July 1782, Providence TCR 5:215.
Other sources: Letter from Deputy Governor Bowen to Providence council, 23 July 1782, PTP 6:150; Warrant for summons to council, 23 July 1782, PTP 6:150; Indenture of Pero Gardner, 17 Feb. 1786, Providence TCR 5:363; Indenture of Pero Fairchild, 7 Mar. 1796, Providence TCR 7:83; TCM 16 Dec. 1800, Providence TCR 8:115; Holbrook, *Rhode Island 1782 Census*, 16, 47.

BENJAMIN CHAMPNEY
Examination of Benjamin Champney: TCM 7 Aug. 1786, Providence TCR 5:389–90.
Other sources: TCM 29 Sept. 1781 and 7 March 1782, Providence TCR 5:193, 5:204; Providence town valuations 1780 and 1781, Rhode Island Historical Society; Indenture of Benjamin Champney, *Indentures of Poor Children*, 3:30; *Massachusetts Soldiers and Sailors*, 3:278, 3:281.

JACOB BURKE
Examination of Jacob Burke: TCM 30 May 1791, Providence TCR 6:163.
Other sources: TCM 10 Sept. 1791, 3 Dec. 1792, 22 Nov. 1793, Providence TCR 6:177–78, 6:233, 6:305; Warrant for removal of Jacob Burke, 3 Dec. 1792, PTP 18:157; Providence valuation of estates, 1799, 7; Petition of Jacob Burke, *Petitions* 34:64; Petition of Jacob Burke, *Petitions* 35:11; "J. Bourke to be liberated," October 1802, Bartlett [no volume]:4; "An Act for the Relief of Jacob Bourke," October 1803, Bartlett [no volume]:43; "An Act in addition to the Act for the Relief of Jacob Bourke," May 1804, Bartlett [no volume]:13.

Chapter 5: Old Age and Death

DANIEL COLLINS
Examination of Daniel Collins: TCM 15 Jan. 1774, Providence TCR
4:357–58.
Other source: TCM 15 Oct. 1800, Providence TCR 7:560.
Note: A man named Daniel Collins enlisted in the Rhode Island Regiment
in 1780 and again in 1782 ("Regimental Book, Rhode Island Regiment," 5,
32, 57, Rhode Island State Archives), but this cannot be the same person.
Daniel Collins the soldier was nineteen years old in 1780 (when Daniel
Collins the cooper was about thirty-five years old), came from Nova Sco-
tia, and described himself first as a laborer and later as a blacksmith.

OBADIAH BLANDING
Examination of Obadiah Blanding: TCM 10 Jan. 1788, Providence TCR
6:34.
Other sources: Warrant for removal of Obadiah Blanding, 10 Jan. 1788,
PTP 11:79; "List of Men and Arms in Providence, September 6, 1775," and
Providence tax lists for 2 Nov. 1770, 26 Sept. 1771, 29 Sept. 1772, 22 Oct. 1773,
and 7 Jan. 1776, Rhode Island Historical Society Library; Holbrook, *Rhode
Island 1782 Census*, 14; TM 18 Nov. 1785, Cumberland TMR 2:237–38; TCM
22 Feb. 1790, Cumberland TCR 3:225.

LATHAM CLARKE
Examinations of Latham Clarke: TCM 14 May 1759 and 30 July 1759, Hop-
kinton TCR 1:23, 1:26; TCM 6 Oct. 1760, Newport TCR 13:50–51.
Other sources: TCM 12 Feb. 1759, 3 Mar. 1760, 7 July 1760, 10 Nov. 1760, 31
Jan. 1761, Hopkinton TCR 1:21, 1:34, 1:37, 1:41, 1:50; Petition of Edward
Greenman et al., May 1733, *Petitions* 2:132; Inventory of Stephen Clarke's
estate, 1 Nov. 1762, Hopkinton Probate Records, 1:62.

ABIGAIL HULL CARR
Examination of Jack Carr: 31 Dec. 1757, Providence TCR 4:168.
Examination of Abigail Hull Carr: 2 July 1787, Providence TCR 6:10.
Other source: TCM 30 Aug. 1758, Providence TCR 4:181.

ELIZABETH STONEHOUSE
Examination of Elizabeth Stonehouse: TCM 5 Sept. 1785, Providence TCR
5:329, PTP 8:np.

Other sources: Overseer of the poor accounts for 25 Dec. 1788, 10 Feb. 1789, 11 Mar. 1789, 9 Dec. 1789, 15 Jan. 1790, 7 July 1790, PTP 12:44, 12:59, 12:66, 12:145, 13:21, 13:106; Providence tax records (Robert Stonehouse), 12 July 1760 colony tax, 2 Nov. 1761 colony tax, 24 July 1768 town tax, 7 June 1769 town tax, 2 Nov. 1770 colony tax.

Bristol Rhodes

Examination of Bristol Rhodes: TCM 1 Sept. 1794, Providence TCR 6:354–55.

Military records at the Rhode Island State Archives: "Casualty Book, Rhode Island Regiment," 82; "Regimental Book, Rhode Island Regiment, 1781–82," 87; *Certificates of the Rhode Island Line* (1784), 29; "Statement of Invalid Accompts, 8 April 1790," 14; "Return of Invalid- Pensioners in the State of Rhode-Island" (8 April 1790), No. 27.

Other sources: Bartlett 8:358–60, 399, 9:604–5, 697, 10:159–63, 269–70, 297; *RISR* 8:270, 236, 13:195, 440, 526; Petition against Bristol Rhodes's family, 1 Sept. 1794, PTP 20:101; Comfort A. Carpenter vs. Creditors, 29 Jan. 1802, *Petitions* 34:43; *Providence Gazette*, 7 July 1810; *Rhode Island Republican*, 18 July 1810.

Secondary sources on Rhode Island's "Black Regiment": Lorenzo J. Greene, "Some Observations on the Black Regiment of Rhode Island in the American Revolution," *Journal of Negro History* 37 (April 1952), 158; Sidney S. Rider, "The Rhode Island Black 'Regiment' of 1778," in *An Historical Inquiry Concerning the Attempt to Raise a Regiment of Slaves by Rhode Island During the War of the Revolution*, Rhode Island Historical Tracts (Providence: Sidney S. Rider, 1880); Gary Alexander Puckrein, *The Black Regiment in the American Revolution* (Providence: Rhode Island Black Heritage Society, 1978).

Notes

Introduction

1. For Phebe Perkins's narrative, see Chapter 1.

2. The historical literature on warning out begins with Josiah Henry Benton, *Warning Out in New England* (Boston: W.B. Clarke, 1911; reprint Freeport, N.Y.: Books for Libraries Press, 1970). More recent studies include Douglas Lamar Jones, "The Strolling Poor: Transiency in Eighteenth-Century Massachusetts," *Journal of Social History* 8 (1975): 28–54, and *Village and Seaport: Migration and Society in Eighteenth-Century Massachusetts* (Hanover, N.H.: University Press of New England, 1981); Alden M. Rollins, *Vermont Warnings Out* (Camden, Maine: Picton Press, 1995–97), 2 volumes, covering warning out from 1768 to 1818; and Cornelia Dayton and Sharon Salinger, "Mapping Migration into Pre-Revolutionary Boston: An Analysis of Robert Love's Warning Book," paper presented to the McNeil Center for Early American Studies, 10 September 1999.

3. Published collections of warning-out records include Rollins, *Vermont Warnings Out*; Phyllis Hembry, ed., *Calendar of Bradford-on-Avon Settlement Examinations and Removal Orders, 1725–98*, Wiltshire Record Society series (Trowbridge: Wiltshire Record Society, 1990); Francis E. Blake, *Worcester County, Massachusetts Warnings, 1737–1788* (Worcester, Mass.: F. P. Rice, 1899; reprint Camden, Maine: Picton Press, 1992); Ann Theopold Chaplin, "Rindge Warnings Out," *New Hampshire Genealogical Record* 7 (October 1990): 145–53. Settlement and removal laws were on the books in every Anglo-American colony; see Howard Mackey, "The Operation of the English Old Poor Law in Colonial Virginia," *Virginia Magazine of History and Biography* 73 (January 1965): 29–40; Barbara Ulmer, "Benevolence in Colonial Charleston," *Proceedings of the South Carolina Historical Association* (1980): 1–12; and Marshall J. Becker, "Hannah Freeman: An Eighteenth-Century Lenape Living and Working Among Colonial Farmers," *Pennsylvania Magazine of History and Biography* 44, 2 (April 1990): 249–69, which reproduces the official examination of Hannah Freeman taken by the Chester County, Pennsylvania overseers of the poor in 1797. K. D. M. Snell, *Annals of the Labouring Poor: Social Change and Agrarian England, 1660–1900* (Cambridge: Cambridge University Press, 1985) uses thousands of settlement examinations as a database for an analysis of social and economic change, but does not reproduce examinations in a systematic way.

4. Elaine Forman Crane, *Ebb Tide in New England: Women, Seaports, and Social Change, 1630–1800* (Boston: Northeastern University Press, 1998); Robert A. Gross, *The Minutemen and Their World* (New York: Hill and Wang, 1976); Jones,

"The Strolling Poor"; Kenneth A. Lockridge, "Land, Population, and the Evolution of New England Society," *Past and Present* 39 (1968): 62–80; Gary B. Nash, *The Urban Crucible: Social Change, Political Consciousness, and the Origins of the American Revolution* (Cambridge, Mass: Harvard University Press, 1979).

5. Jones, "The Strolling Poor"; Nash, *Urban Crucible*; Robert E. Cray, Jr., *Paupers and Poor Relief in New York City and Its Rural Environs, 1700–1830* (Philadelphia: Temple University Press, 1988). For a useful overview and bibliography of studies of poverty and poor relief in early America, see Walter I. Trattner, *From Poor Law to Welfare State: A History of Social Welfare in America*, 6th ed. (New York: Free Press, 1999), chapters 2 and 3. Recent studies that have reconstructed the lives of the poor by innovative analysis of statistical data and personal documents include Billy G. Smith, *The "Lower Sort": Philadelphia's Laboring People, 1750–1800* (Ithaca, N.Y.: Cornell University Press, 1990); Tim Hitchcock, Peter King, and Pamela Sharpe, eds., *Chronicling Poverty: The Voices and Strategies of the English Poor, 1640–1840* (Basingstoke: Macmillan, 1997); and a rare full biography of an eighteenth-century lower sort artisan by Alfred F. Young, *The Shoemaker and the Tea Party: Memory and the American Revolution* (Boston: Beacon Press, 1999).

6. Richard Burn, *The Justice of the Peace, and Parish Officer*, 12th ed. (London: Strahan and Woodfall, 1772), 3:272–520; William Blackstone, *Commentaries on the Laws of England* (Oxford: Clarendon Press, 1765), 1:347–48; "Poor Laws," *The Dictionary of English History*, rev. ed. (London: Cassell and Company, 1928), 857–59.

7. Legal settlement by means of a freehold meant purchasing real estate worth at least £40 sterling before 1798, $200 after 1798. Such a purchase gave most white men the privilege of voting and holding office in the town. Rhode Island's eighteenth-century suffrage laws excluded white men without freeholds, Jewish and Catholic men, men of color, and all women. A young person who had completed a contractual "apprenticeship" (commonly used to designate indentured servitude of children, which ended when they became legal adults) had the option of acquiring the master's legal settlement or reclaiming his or her own hometown. If a town was lax about enforcing settlement law, a resident could acquire settlement by "uncontested presence"—living unchallenged in the town for a year; other colonies had longer and shorter minimum times for "uncontested presence." For the full text of Rhode Island's eighteenth-century settlement laws, see *Acts and Laws of His Majesty's Colony of Rhode-Island and Providence Plantations* (1745–52), 48–51; *Acts and Laws* (1767), 228–32; *Public Laws* (1798), 345–47.

8. TCM 26 Apr. 1762, Tiverton TCR 2:175; TCM 20 Jan. 1775, Jamestown TCR 2:117–18; TCM 12 June 1788, Glocester TCR 2:24.

9. TCM 25 Jan. 1752, Glocester TCR, vol. 1; TCM 6 Dec. 1762 and 25 Jan. 1763, Providence TCR 4:236; TCM 26 Nov. 1768, East Greenwich TCR 3:116–17; TCM 6 May, 3 June, and 1 July 1793, Hopkinton TCR 3:33–35; TCM 30 Apr. 1792, West Greenwich TCR vol. 4. Rhode Island's warning-out records do not consistently provide the data needed to make an exact determination of the percentage of transients warned out because of objectionable *behavior* rather than impoverished

condition. Town clerks frequently wrote "likely to become chargeable" (meaning "likely to need poor relief") as the rationale for warning out, even when other documents make it clear that someone had complained about the transient's behavior. A sampling of the warning-out orders issued in Providence (where records are especially detailed) shows that between 1780 and 1800 clerks specifically referred to objectionable behavior in 18 percent of the orders (84 of 470). The actual percentage of transients considered troublesome is probably higher.

10. The Exeter councilmen cautioned Marcy Codner and Rachel Robbins that if they were to "throw themselves on the town," they would be forced to labor for their maintenance. TCM 4 July 1791, Exeter TCR 5:115; Thomas Strait to West Greenwich Town Council, 3 July 1798, West Greenwich TCR, vol. 4. On poor relief in Rhode Island, see Ruth Wallis Herndon, "'She died an expence to this town': Poor Relief in Eighteenth-Century Rhode Island," in *Down and Out in Early America*, ed. Billy G. Smith (University Park: Penn State University Press, forthcoming).

11. TCM 29 Mar. 1783, West Greenwich TCR, vol. 3; TCM 2 July 1767, Providence TCR 6:10; TCM 3 Feb. 1800, Cumberland TCR 4:132–33. Rhode Island law—frequently ignored—required householders to notify town leaders of any newcomers they took in for more than a week and also required transients to produce a "settlement certificate" from officials in their hometown (*Acts and Laws* [1767], 228–32; *Public Laws* [1798], 357).

12. Providence overseer of the poor to town treasurer, 27 Dec. 1788, PTP, 12:46; warrant for removal of John Skyrme, June/July 1785, PTP 8:127. Skyrme's route was Eastchester, Pelham, New Rochelle, Mamaroneck, Rye, Greenwich, Stamford, Norwalk, Stratford, Milford, New Haven, East Haven, Branford, Guilford, Killingworth, Saybrook, Lyme, New London, Groton, Stonington, Voluntown, Coventry, Scituate, Cranston, and Providence.

13. TCM 5 May 1788, Tiverton TCR, vol. 1; TCM 19 Mar. 1791, Cumberland TCR 3:257; town sergeant account, 17 Apr. 1775, PTP 3:17; town sergeant account, 29 Apr.–1 May 1788, Exeter TCR 5:42.

14. TCM 23 April 1764 and 12 Jan. 1785, Cumberland TCR 2:43–44, 2:54; TCM 12 Mar., 16 Oct., and 2 Dec. 1771, 1 Apr. and 15 Apr. 1772, Charlestown TCR 2:196, 2:199, 2:200, 2:203, 2:204.

15. Rollins, *Vermont Warnings Out*, 1:1–9; Dayton and Salinger, "Mapping Migration," 9–10; Ann S. Lainhart, "Records of the Poor in Pre-Twentieth-Century New England," *National Genealogical Society Quarterly* 81 (December 1993): 257–69.

16. TCM 25 June 1792, West Greenwich TCR 4:np; letter to Providence town council, 1 Dec. 1794, PTP, 20:157.

17. For a general discussion of the postwar depression, see John J. McCusker and Russell R. Menard, *The Economy of British America, 1607–1789* (Chapel Hill: University of North Carolina Press, 1985), 367–77. For a specific discussion of economic problems in postwar Rhode Island, see Ruth Wallis Herndon, "Governing the Affairs of the Town: Continuity and Change in Rhode Island, 1750–1800"

(Ph.D. dissertation, American University, 1992), chapter 10.

18. Herndon, "'She died an expence to this town'."

19. The Rhode Island General Public Assistance Act of 1942 finally did away with any settlement restrictions on people's eligibility for welfare. See Glen Leet, "Rhode Island Abolishes Settlement," *Social Service Review* 18,3 (September 1944): 281–87. On the persistence of settlement restrictions and removal laws through the nineteenth and early twentieth centuries, and on the creation of state welfare authorities, see Margaret Creech, *Three Centuries of Poor Law Administration: A Study of Legislation in Rhode Island,* Social Service Monograph 24 (Chicago: University of Chicago Press, 1936), 111–63. Creech found scattered instances of warning out still occurring in Rhode Island towns throughout the nineteenth century.

20. On Providence and Newport, see Lynne Withey, *Urban Growth in Colonial Rhode Island: Newport and Providence in the Eighteenth Century* (Albany: State University of New York Press, 1984); Elaine Forman Crane, *A Dependent People: Newport, Rhode Island in the Revolutionary Era* (New York: Fordham University Press, 1985); and Florence Parker Simister, *The Fire's Center: Rhode Island in the Revolutionary Era, 1763–1790* (Providence: Rhode Island Bicentennial Foundation, 1979). No Rhode Island law directly addressed the problem of immigrant transients who had no legal settlement anywhere in North America. The 1798 settlement law eased the problem indirectly, by stipulating that a woman retained her premarriage settlement if she married a man who had no legal settlement anywhere in the United States; thus native-born wives and children of immigrant men could not be sent to the town where their household head had arrived from Europe (*Public Laws* [1798], 346). In some cases, officials did indeed send transient immigrants to their port of entry, but just as often officials sent them to the last town from which they had come or directed the sergeant to escort them to the borders of the town and send them away. There is no evidence that Providence became a dumping ground for transients who had come through their port of entry, or that Providence increased its poor-relief expenses to meet immigrant needs. Providence poor-relief records for the eighteenth century are fragmentary and cannot support sustained analysis of expenditures over the period.

21. The following profile of transient people is based on an analysis of warning-out orders and transient examinations in fourteen of Rhode Island's twenty-seven late eighteenth-century towns: Cumberland, East Greenwich, Exeter, Glocester, Hopkinton, Jamestown, Middletown, New Shoreham, Providence, Richmond, South Kingstown, Tiverton, Warren, and Warwick. A total of 1,924 people (and their households) were warned out of these fourteen towns between 1751 and 1800, and 772 transient examinations are preserved in the records of these towns. Details such as sex, race, and legal settlement of the household head are usually provided in every warning-out order, but only the transient examinations provide information about age, occupation, literacy, family composition, length of residence, and personal history.

22. On meanings of "household" and "family," see Chapter 2. In many cases, the warning-out order indicated each member of the household, including the exact number of children; the mean of these orders was 2.4 children per family. I

rounded down this average and conservatively credited 2.0 children to each transient household described only as a "family," without a specific number of children indicated.

23. 92.8% of the male heads of households were accompanied by their wives. The rest were widowered, never married, or cohabiting with women who were not their wives. For white women, 39.8% were never married, 34.1% were abandoned, divorced, or separated; 20.4% were widowed; and 0.5% were cohabiting with their mates. For women of color, 40.9% were never married, 36.4% were separated from their husbands, 12.1% were widowed, and 9.1% were cohabiting with their mates.

24. TCM 10 May 1771, Providence TCR 4:314; TCM 19 Sept. 1785, Middletown TCR 2:149; TCM 29 Apr. and 16 May 1775, Jamestown TCR 2:125–26; TCM 3 Feb. and 10 Apr. 1769, Cumberland TCR 2:109–10, 2:114. Until 1798, the ambiguity of Rhode Island settlement law meant that an illegitimate child could arguably be considered the legal responsibility of the town where it was born. In 1798, the law was revised so that a legitimate child took the settlement of its father, an illegitimate child took the settlement of its mother, and no child could claim settlement in its birthplace unless one of its parents already had a legal settlement there. *Public Laws* (1798), 346.

25. TCM 31 Dec. 1757, Providence TCR 4:167; TCM 24 July 1782, Providence TCR 5:215; Examinations of Jenny Rose, Isaac Rodman, and James Taylor, TCM 21 Oct. 1799 and 28 Oct. 1800, Providence TCR 7:407, 567, 586.

26. TCM 26 Oct. 1767, Cumberland TCR 2:87; see Chapter 1.

27. In 1755, people of color constituted 11.6% of Rhode Island's population; in 1783, Indians constituted 0.9% and blacks 4.5% (Evarts B. Greene and Virginia D. Harrington, *American Population Before the Federal Census of 1790* [Gloucester, Mass.: Peter Smith, 1966], 67–70). Later counts show blacks representing 6.3% of Rhode Island's population in 1790 and 5.3% in 1800 (U.S. Bureau of the Census, *Negro Population, 1790–1915* [Washington, D.C.: U.S. Government Printing Office, 1918], 51). On gradual emancipation statutes in southern New England, which promised an increase in the number of free people of color in the early nineteenth century, see Joanne Pope Melish, *Disowning Slavery: Gradual Emancipation and "Race" in New England, 1780–1860* (Ithaca, N.Y.: Cornell University Press, 1998). On the use of racial designations in the official record, see Ruth Wallis Herndon and Ella Wilcox Sekatau, "The Right to a Name: Narragansett People and Rhode Island Officials in the Revolutionary Era," *Ethnohistory* 44, 3 (Summer 1997): 433–62.

28. On Providence as a gathering place, see Robert J. Cottrol, *The Afro-Yankees: Providence's Black Community in the Antebellum Era* (Westport, Conn.: Greenwood Press, 1982); see also Gary B. Nash, "Forging Freedom: The Emancipation Experience in Northern Seaport Cities, 1775–1820," in *Slavery and Freedom in the Age of the American Revolution*, ed. Ira Berlin and Ronald Hoffman (Urbana: University of Illinois Press, 1986), 3–48.

29. TCM 26 Feb. 1780, East Greenwich TCR 3:201; TM 6 Mar. 1786, Tiverton TCR 1:np; TCM 8 Nov. 1800, Providence TCR 7:576.

30. Ruth Wallis Herndon, "Literacy Among New England's Transient Poor, 1750–1800," *Journal of Social History* 29,4 (June 1996): 963–65.

31. "An Act providing for the Relief, Support, Employment and Removal of the Poor," *Public Laws* (1798), 348.

32. Ruth Wallis Herndon, "Racialization and Feminization of Poverty in Early America: Indian Women as the Poor of the Town in Eighteenth-Century Rhode Island," in *Empire and Others: British Encounters with Indigenous Peoples, 1600–1850*, ed. Martin Daunton and Rick Halpern (Philadelphia: University of Pennsylvania Press, 1999), 186–203.

33. TCM 8 Mar. 1757, Providence TCR 4:152.

Chapter 1: Birth, Infancy, and Childhood

1. *Acts and Laws* (1767), 229; *Public Laws* (1767), 17–19.

2. "An Act regulating the Proceedings in Cases of Bastardy," *Acts and Laws* (1767), 17–19.

3. TCM 10 Mar. 1777, Coventry TCR (1775–89):38a.

4. Examination of Demas and Rufus Potter, TCM 11 Mar. 1790, Providence TCR 6:108.

5. TCM 5 Dec. 1785, Bristol TCR 2A:269; Joseph P. Hayward to Westerly TC, 25 Sept. 1801, TCM 28 Sept. 1801, Westerly TCR 6:51.

6. Hopkinton expenditures for poor relief in 1784 are recorded in town council and town meeting records for that year. See Hopkinton TMR, vol. 1 and Hopkinton TCT, vol. 2.

7. Ruth Wallis Herndon, "Indentured Servitude of Children as a Community Strategy in Early New England," paper presented at the annual meeting of the Omohundro Institute of Early American History and Culture, Austin, Texas, 13 June 1999.

Chapter 2: Family Life

1. TCM 29 Nov. 1757 and 4 Aug 1781, Providence TCR 4:164, 5:192, italics added for emphasis.

2. *Public Laws* (1798), 483.

Chapter 3: Work Life

1. TCM 8 Aug. 1794, Providence TCR 6:349–50.

2. TCM 30 July 1744, West Greenwich TCR 1:np; TCM 13 May 1751, Portsmouth TCR 4:56.

3. TCM 28 Dec. 1761, Westerly TCR 3:679–80.

4. Providence TCR 4:167–68, 4:356–59; 5:167–71; 5:350–55; 5:388–401; 7:66–71; 7:197–201; and PTP 2:38.

5. Bartlett, May 1788, 10:275. For a discussion of the fight to ratify the constitution in Rhode Island, see John P. Kaminski, "Rhode Island: Protecting State Interests," in *Ratifying the Constitution*, ed. Michael Allen Gillespie and Michael Lienesch (Lawrence: University Press of Kansas, 1989), 368–90.

6. Rhode Island town councils functioned as the lowest court in the colony's judicial system, responding to complaints from townspeople, taking depositions from witnesses, and issuing rulings on local matters. Bowdish was thus complaining about the council's action as a "ruling" from a lower court.

Chapter 5: Old Age and Death

1. Examination of John Horn, TCM 5 Nov. 1787, Providence TCR 6:26; Examination of Michael Field, TCM 26 Oct. 1799, Providence TCR 7:409.

2. *Newport Mercury*, Monday, 10 Aug. 1772, p. 3; TCM 23 Dec. 1793, Glocester TCR 2:102–3 (italics mine); TCM 7 Oct. 1758, East Greenwich TCR 3:45; TCM 5 Apr. 1790, Hopkinton TCR 2:315; TCM 14 May 1773, Warwick TCR 3:24.

3. TCM 24 Feb. 1759, East Greenwich TCR 3:50; TCM 1 Sept. 1783, Exeter TCR 4:123; TM 16 Apr. 1783, Warwick TMR 3:137–38; 26 Nov. 1787, Warwick TCR 3:284–85.

4. *Acts and Laws* (1767), 201; TCM 14 Oct. 1760, Exeter TCR 2:97; TCM 27 Aug. 1754, Jamestown TCR 1:76; TCM 31 Jan. 1756, Providence TCR 4:136.

5. TCM 20 Oct. 1788, 18 May 1789, and 21 June 1790, Middletown TCR 2:183, 2:194, 2:201–2; TCM 5 May 1783, Charlestown TCR 3:135.

6. A man named Daniel Collins enlisted in the Rhode Island Regiment in 1780 and again in 1782 ("Regimental Book, Rhode Island Regiment," 5, 32, 57, Rhode Island State Archives), but this cannot be the same person. Daniel Collins the soldier was 19 years old in 1780 (when Daniel Collins the cooper was about 35), came from Nova Scotia, and described himself first as a laborer and later as a blacksmith.

7. Evarts B. Greene and Virginia D. Harrington, *American Population Before the Federal Census of 1790* (Gloucester, Mass.: Peter Smith, 1966), 66.

Conclusion

1. Town and provincial records give three shillings as the standard day wage for unskilled male labor in Rhode Island; other historians have found the same true for Massachusetts and Connecticut. See Ruth Wallis Herndon, "Governing the Affairs of the Town: Continuity and Change in Rhode Island, 1750–1800" (PhD dissertation, American University, 1992), appendix C.

2. In the latter part of the eighteenth century, the Providence workhouse overseer received 6s. per day to provide room and board for an adult, 4s. 6d. for

an older child, and 3s. for a very young child (TCM 10 Apr. 1776, Providence TCR 5:41–42). The workhouse rates presumed the inmate would provide some labor to offset her or his maintenance, so these are very low estimates of the cost of food and lodging; clothing was an extra expense. An adult would need to work steadily six days a week at such unskilled labor just to support himself or herself and two children at this minimal level.

3. In 1788 the Providence councilmen granted 35 tavern licenses and warned 34 illegal operators to apply for licenses. In 1799 they granted 83 licenses and no longer could estimate the extent of illegal tavern operations; instead, they sent a constable to investigate, warn all illegal operators, and report their names to the council (TCM 6 Oct. 1788, 7–26 Oct. 1799, Providence TCR 6:62, 7:400–411). For examples of transients being reprimanded for allowing disorderly behavior in their taverns, see TCR 26 Nov. 1768 (Benjamin Austin), East Greenwich TCR 3:116–17; TCR 5 Apr. 1790 (Randall Briggs), Providence TCR 6:112.

4. "Rules and orders for employing the poor in the workhouse in the Town of Providence and regulating the same," 8 Oct 1773, PTP 2:82.

References

GENERAL

Becker, Marshall J. "Hannah Freeman: An Eighteenth-Century Lenape Living and Working Among Colonial Farmers." *Pennsylvania Magazine of History and Biography* 44, 2 (April 1990): 249–69.

Benton, Josiah Henry. *Warning Out in New England, 1656–1817*. Boston: W.B. Clarke, 1911; reprint Freeport, N.Y.: Books for Libraries Press, 1970.

Blake, Francis E. *Worcester County, Massachusetts Warnings, 1737–1788*. Worcester, Mass.: F.P. Rice, 1899; reprint Camden, Maine: Picton Press, 1992.

Burn, Richard. *The Justice of the Peace, and Parish Officer*. 12th ed. London: Strahan and Woodfall, 1772.

Chaplin, Anne Theopold. "Rindge Warnings Out." *New Hampshire Genealogical Record* 7 (October 1990): 145–53.

Cray, Robert E., Jr. *Paupers and Poor Relief in New York City and Its Rural Environs, 1700–1830*. Philadelphia: Temple University Press, 1988.

Creech, Margaret. *Three Centuries of Poor Law Administration: A Study of Legislation in Rhode Island*. Social Service Monograph 24. Chicago: University of Chicago Press, 1936.

Dayton, Cornelia and Sharon Salinger. "Mapping Migration into Pre-Revolutionary Boston: An Analysis of Robert Love's Warning Book." Paper presented at the McNeil Center for Early American Studies, University of Pennsylvania, 10 September 1999.

Greene, Evarts B. and Virginia D. Harrington. *American Population Before the Federal Census of 1790*. New York: Columbia University Press, 1932; reprint Gloucester, Mass.: Peter Smith, 1966.

Gross, Robert A. *The Minutemen and Their World*. New York: Hill and Wang, 1976.

Heads of Families at the First Census of the United States Taken in the Year 1790: Rhode Island. Washington, D.C.: U.S. Government Printing Office, 1908.

Hembry, Phyllis, ed. *Calendar of Bradford-on-Avon Settlement Examinations and Removal Orders, 1725–98*. Wiltshire Record Society 46. Trowbridge: Wiltshire Record Society, 1990.

Herndon, Ruth Wallis. "Governing the Affairs of the Town: Continuity and Change in Rhode Island, 1750–1800." Ph.D. dissertation, American University, 1992.

———. " Literacy Among New England's Transient Poor, 1750–1800." *Journal of Social History* 29, 4 (June 1996): 963–65.

——. "'She died an expence to this town': Poor Relief in Eighteenth-Century Rhode Island." In *Down and Out in Early America*, ed. Billy G. Smith. University Park: Penn State University Press, forthcoming.

——. "Women of 'no particular home': Town Leaders and Female Transients in Rhode Island, 1750–1800." In *Women and Freedom in Early America*, ed. Larry D. Eldridge. New York: New York University Press, 1997. 269–89.

Herndon, Ruth Wallis and Ella Wilcox Sekatau. "The Right to a Name: Narragansett People and Rhode Island Officials in the Revolutionary Era." *Ethnohistory* 44, 3 (Summer 1997): 433–62.

Hitchcock, Tim, Peter King, and Pamela Sharpe, eds. *Chronicling Poverty: The Voices and Strategies of the English Poor, 1640–1840*. Basingstoke: Macmillan, 1997.

Holbrook, Jay Mack. *Rhode Island 1782 Census*. Oxford, Mass.: Holbrook Research Institute, 1979.

Indentures of Poor Children Bound Out as Apprentices by the Overseers of the Poor of the Town of Boston, 1734–1805. Vol. 3. Boston: Boston Public Library.

Jones, Douglas Lamar. "The Strolling Poor: Transiency in Eighteenth-Century Massachusetts." *Journal of Social History* 8 (Spring 1975): 28–54.

——. *Village and Seaport: Migration and Society in Eighteenth-Century Massachusetts*. Hanover, N.H.: University Press of New England, 1981.

Kaminski, John P. "Rhode Island: Protecting State Interests." In *Ratifying the Constitution*, ed. Michael Allen Gillespie and Michael Lienesch. Lawrence: University Press of Kansas, 1989. 368–90.

Lainhart, Ann S. "Records of the Poor in Pre-Twentieth-Century New England." *National Genealogical Society Quarterly* 81 (December 1993): 257–69.

Leet, Glen. "Rhode Island Abolishes Settlement." *Social Service Review* 18, 3 (September 1944): 281–87.

Lockridge, Kenneth A. "Land, Population, and the Evolution of New England Society." *Past and Present* 39 (1968): 62–80.

Mackey, Howard. "The Operation of the English Old Poor Law in Colonial Virginia." *Virginia Magazine of History and Biography* 73 (January 1965): 29–40.

McCusker, John J. and Russell R. Menard. *The Economy of British America, 1607–1789*. Chapel Hill: University of North Carolina Press, 1985.

Melish, Joanne Pope. *Disowning Slavery: Gradual Emancipation and "Race" in New England, 1780–1860*. Ithaca, N.Y.: Cornell University Press, 1998.

Nash, Gary B. "Forging Freedom: The Emancipation Experience in Northern Seaport Cities, 1775–1820." In *Slavery and Freedom in the Age of the American Revolution*, ed. Ira Berlin and Ronald Hoffman. Urbana: University of Illinois Press, 1986.

——. *The Urban Crucible: Social Change, Political Consciousness, and the Origins of the American Revolution*. Cambridge, Mass.: Harvard University Press, 1979.

Rhode Island 1790 Census. See *Heads of Families at the First Census of the United States*.

Rollins, Alden M. *Vermont Warnings Out*. 2 vols. Camden, Maine: Picton Press, 1995–97.

Simister, Florence Parker. *The Fire's Center: Rhode Island in the Revolutionary Era, 1763–1790.* Providence: Rhode Island Bicentennial Foundation, 1979.

Taylor, Maureen Alice. *Runaways, Deserters, and Notorious Villains from Rhode Island Newspapers.* Vol. 1, *The Providence Gazette, 1762–1800.* Camden, Maine: Picton Press, 1994.

Trattner, Walter I. *From Poor Law to Welfare State: A History of Social Welfare in America.* 6th ed. New York: Free Press, 1999.

Ulmer, Barbara. "Benevolence in Colonial Charleston." *Proceedings of the South Carolina Historical Association* (1980): 1–12.

Withey, Lynne. *Urban Growth in Colonial Rhode Island: Newport and Providence in the Eighteenth Century.* Albany: State University of New York Press, 1984.

Wolf, Stephanie Grauman. *As Various as Their Land: The Everyday Lives of Eighteenth-Century Americans.* New York: HarperCollins, 1993.

CHAPTER 1: BIRTH, INFANCY, AND CHILDHOOD

Berkin, Carol. *First Generations: Women in Colonial America.* New York: Hill and Wang, 1996.

Gundersen, Joan R. *To Be Useful to the World: Women in Revolutionary America, 1740–1790.* New York: Twayne, 1996.

Herndon, Ruth Wallis. "Indentured Servitude of Children as a Community Strategy in Early New England." Paper presented at the annual meeting of the Omohundro Institute of Early American History and Culture, Austin, Texas, 13 June 1999.

Leavitt, Judith Walzer. *Brought to Bed: Childbearing in America, 1750–1950.* New York: Oxford University Press, 1986.

Levy, Barry. "Girls and Boys: Poor Children and the Labor Market in Colonial Massachusetts." *Pennsylvania History* 64 (1997): 287–307.

Rorabaugh, W. J. *The Craft Apprentice: From Franklin to the Machine Age in America.* New York: Oxford University Press, 1986.

Towner, Lawrence William. "The Indentures of Boston's Poor Apprentices, 1734–1805." Colonial Society of Massachusetts *Publications* 43 (1966): 417–33. Reprinted in *Past Imperfect: Essays on History, Libraries, and the Humanities,* ed. Robert W. Karrow, Jr. and Alfred F. Young. Chicago: University of Chicago Press, 1993. 36–55.

Ulrich, Laurel Thatcher. *A Midwife's Tale: The Life of Martha Ballard, Based on Her Diary, 1785–1812.* New York: Knopf, 1991.

Wolf, Stephanie Grauman. *As Various as Their Land: The Everyday Lives of Eighteenth-Century Americans.* New York: HarperCollins, 1993.

CHAPTER 2: FAMILY LIFE

Berkin, Carol. *First Generations: Women in Colonial America.* New York: Hill and Wang, 1996.

Cottrol, Robert J. *The Afro-Yankees: Providence's Black Community in the Antebellum Era.* Westport, Conn.: Greenwood Press, 1982.

Crane, Elaine Forman. *A Dependent People: Newport, Rhode Island, in the Revolutionary Era.* New York: Fordham University Press, 1985.

———. *Ebb Tide in New England: Women, Seaports, and Social Change, 1630–1800.* Boston: Northeastern University Press, 1998.

Flaherty, David H. *Privacy in Colonial New England.* Charlottesville: University Press of Virginia, 1972.

Greene, Lorenzo J. *The Negro in Colonial New England.* New York: Atheneum, 1969.

Gundersen, Joan R. *To Be Useful to the World: Women in Revolutionary America, 1740–1790.* New York: Twayne, 1996.

Herndon, Ruth Wallis. "Racialization and Feminization of Poverty in Early America: Indian Women as 'the poor of the town' in Eighteenth-Century Rhode Island." In *Empire and Others: British Encounters with Indigenous Peoples, 1600–1850,* ed. Martin Daunton and Rick Halpern. Philadelphia: University of Pennsylvania Press, 1999. 186–203.

———. "Women of 'no particular home': Town Leaders and Female Transients in Rhode Island, 1750–1800." In *Women and Freedom in Early America,* ed. Larry D. Eldridge. New York: New York University Press, 1997. 269–89.

Piersen, William D. *Black Yankees: The Development of an Afro-American Subculture in Eighteenth-Century New England.* Amherst: University of Massachusetts Press, 1988.

Plane, Ann Marie. *Colonial Intimacies: Indian Marriage in Early New England.* Ithaca, N.Y.: Cornell University Press, 2000.

Wilson, Lisa. *Ye Heart of a Man: The Domestic Life of Men in Colonial New England.* New Haven, Conn.: Yale University Press, 1999.

Wolf, Stephanie Grauman. *As Various as Their Land: The Everyday Lives of Eighteenth-Century Americans.* New York: HarperCollins, 1993.

CHAPTER 3: WORK LIFE

Anderson, Fred. *A People's Army: Massachusetts Soldiers and Society in the Seven Years' War Provincial Troops, 1754–1762.* Chapel Hill: University of North Carolina Press, 1984.

Applebaum, Herbert. *Colonial Americans at Work.* Lanham, Md: University Press of America, 1996.

Bolster, W. Jeffrey. *Black Jacks: African American Seamen in the Age of Sail.* Cambridge, Mass.: Harvard University Press, 1997.

Bridenbaugh, Carl. *Cities in Revolt: Urban Life in America, 1743–1776.* New York: Knopf, 1955.

———. *The Colonial Craftsman.* Chicago: University of Chicago Press, 1950.

Chapin, Howard M. *A List of Rhode Island Soldiers and Sailors in the Old French and Indian War, 1755–1762.* Rhode Island in the Colonial Wars Series. Providence: Rhode Island Historical Society, 1943.

Cottrol, Robert J. *The Afro-Yankees: Providence's Black Community in the Antebellum Era*. Westport, Conn.: Greenwood Press, 1982.

Crane, Elaine Forman. *A Dependent People: Newport, Rhode Island, in the Revolutionary Era*. New York: Fordham University Press, 1985.

——. *Ebb Tide in New England: Women, Seaports, and Social Change, 1630–1800*. Boston: Northeastern University Press, 1998.

Genealogical Abstracts of Revolutionary War Pension Files. Waynesboro, Tenn.: National Historical Publishing Co., 1990.

Greene, Lorenzo J. *The Negro in Colonial New England*. New York: Atheneum, 1969.

——. "Some Observations on the Black Regiment of Rhode Island in the American Revolution." *Journal of Negro History* 37 (April 1952): 142–72.

Gundersen, Joan R. *To Be Useful to the World: Women in Revolutionary America, 1740–1790*. New York: Twayne, 1996.

Herndon, Ruth Wallis. "The Domestic Cost of Seafaring: Town Leaders and Seamen's Families in Rhode Island, 1750–1800." In *Iron Men, Wooden Women: Gender and Seafaring in the Atlantic World, 1700–1920*, ed. Margaret S. Creighton and Lisa Norling. Baltimore: Johns Hopkins University Press, 1996. 55–69.

Innes, Stephen, ed. *Work and Labor in Early America*. Chapel Hill: University of North Carolina Press, 1988.

Jones, Jacqueline. *American Work: Four Centuries of Black and White Labor*. New York: W.W. Norton, 1998.

Lemisch, Jesse . "Jack Tar in the Streets: Merchant Seamen in the Politics of Revolutionary America." *William and Mary Quarterly* 3rd ser. 25 (July 1968): 371–407.

Massachusetts Soldiers and Sailors of the Revolutionary War: A Compilation from the Archives. 1896; reprint Salem, Mass.: Higginson Book Co., 2000.

Mayer, Holly A. *Belonging to the Army: Camp Followers and Community During the American Revolution*. Columbia: University of South Carolina Press, 1996.

Neagles, James C. *Summer Soldiers: A Survey and Index of Revolutionary War Courts-Martial*. Salt Lake City, Utah: Ancestry Inc., 1986.

Neimeyer, Charles Patrick. *America Goes to War: A Social History of the Continental Army*. New York: New York University Press, 1996.

Piersen, William D. *Black Yankees: The Development of an Afro-American Subculture in Eighteenth-Century New England*. Amherst: University of Massachusetts Press, 1988.

Puckrein, Gary Alexander. *The Black Regiment in the American Revolution*. Providence: Rhode Island Black Heritage Society, 1978.

Quarles, Benjamin. *The Negro in the American Revolution*. Chapel Hill: University of North Carolina Press, 1961.

Rhode Island 1777 Military Census. Transcr. Mildred M. Chamberlain. Baltimore: Genealogical Publishing Company, 1985.

Rider, Sidney S. *An Historical Enquiry Concerning the Attempt to Raise a Regiment of Slaves by Rhode Island During the War of the Revolution*. Rhode Island Historical Tracts 10. Providence: Sidney S. Rider, 1880.

Rorabaugh, W. J. *The Craft Apprentice: From Franklin to the Machine Age in America*. New York: Oxford University Press, 1986.

———. "'I Thought I Should Liberate Myself from the Thraldom of Others': Apprentices, Masters, and the Revolution." In *Beyond the American Revolution: Explorations in the History of American Radicalism*, ed. Alfred F. Young. DeKalb: Northern Illinois University Press, 1993. 185–217.

Russell, Howard S. *A Long, Deep Furrow: Three Centuries of Farming in New England*. Hanover, N.H.: University Press of New England, 1976.

Smith, Billy G. *The "Lower Sort": Philadelphia's Laboring People, 1750–1800*. Ithaca, N.Y.: Cornell University Press, 1990.

Snell, K. D. M. *Annals of the Labouring Poor: Social Change and Agrarian England, 1660–1900*. Cambridge: Cambridge University Press, 1985.

Towner, Lawrence William. *A Good Master Well Served: Masters and Servants in Colonial Massachusetts, 1620–1750*. New York: Garland Press, 1998.

Towner, Lawrence William. "The Indentures of Boston's Poor Apprentices, 1734–1805." Colonial Society of Massachusetts *Publications* 43 (1966): 417–33. Reprinted in *Past Imperfect: Essays on History, Libraries, and the Humanities*, ed. Robert W. Karrow, Jr. and Alfred F. Young. Chicago: University of Chicago Press, 1993). 36–55.

Vickers, Daniel. *Farmers and Fishermen: Two Centuries of Work in Essex County, Massachusetts, 1630–1850*. Chapel Hill: University of North Carolina Press, 1994.

Wolf, Stephanie Grauman. *As Various as Their Land: The Everyday Lives of Eighteenth-Century Americans*. New York: HarperCollins, 1993.

Young, Alfred F. "George Robert Twelve Hewes (1742–1840): A Boston Shoemaker and the Memory of the American Revolution." *William and Mary Quarterly* 3rd ser. 38 (October 1981): 561–623.

———. *The Shoemaker and the Tea Party: Memory and the American Revolution*. New York: Beacon Press, 1999.

CHAPTER 4: REVERSAL OF FORTUNE

Cronon, William. *Changes in the Land: Indians, Colonists, and the Ecology of New England*. New York: Hill and Wang, 1983.

Diamond, Jared. *Guns, Germs, and Steel: The Fates of Human Societies*. New York: W.W. Norton, 1998.

Duffy, John. *Epidemics in Colonial America*. Baton Rouge: Louisiana State University Press, 1953.

Estes, J. Worth and Billy G. Smith, eds. *A Melancholy Scene of Devastation: The Public Response to the 1793 Philadelphia Yellow Fever Epidemic*. Canton, Mass.: Science History Publications, 1997.

Riley, James C. *The Eighteenth-Century Campaign to Avoid Disease*. New York: St. Martin's Press, 1987.

Thomas, Keith. *Man and the Natural World: Changing Attitudes in England, 1500–1800*. New York: Oxford University Press, 1996.

CHAPTER 5: OLD AGE AND DEATH

Fischer, David Hackett. *Albion's Seed: Four British Folkways in America*. New York: Oxford University Press, 1989.

——. *Growing Old in America*. New York: Oxford University Press, 1977.

Laderman, Gary. *The Sacred Remains: American Attitudes Toward Death, 1799–1883*. New Haven, Conn.: Yale University Press, 1996.

Stannard, David E. *The Puritan Way of Death: A Study in Religion, Culture, and Social Change*. New York: Oxford University Press, 1977.

Wilson, Lisa. *Ye Heart of a Man: The Domestic Life of Men in Colonial New England*. New Haven, Conn.: Yale University Press, 1999.

Wolf, Stephanie Grauman. *As Various as Their Land: The Everyday Lives of Eighteenth-Century Americans*. New York: HarperCollins, 1993.

Index

GENERAL INDEX

(Includes cross-references to Personal Names)